THE NEW CLICK TO CALM

Solutions for All Dogs in a Challenging World

Emma Parsons

karen
pryor
CLICKER TRAINING

The New Click to Calm
Solutions for All Dogs in a Challenging World

Karen Pryor Clicker Training
Sunshine Books, Inc.
49 River Street, Suite 3
Waltham, MA 02453 USA
U. S. (Toll Free) 1-800-472-5425
781-398-0754
www.clickertraining.com

For information about special discounts for multiple-copy purchase, please contact
Karen Pryor Clicker Training sales:
U. S. (Toll Free) 1-800-472-5425 or 781-398-0754 or wholesale@clickertraining.com
© 2021 by Sunshine Books, Inc.

Editing: Nini Bloch
Copy Editing: Marie Clougher
Cover/book design: Lindsay Davisson
Cover photos: Alicia Kerr, Katerina Lyubomirova
All images by author unless otherwise noted.

First edition published 2021

Printed in the United States of America

ISBN-10: 1-890948-284
ISBN-13: 978-1-890948-283

Library of Congress Control Number: 2021933385

This book is dedicated to Lizzie-Taylor, my golden retriever who was always joyful in mind, body, and spirit.

October 21, 2007–November 5, 2020

Mystic Charmed Lizzie-Taylor, CD BN AX AXJ MXP2 MJP NFP CGC

Table of Contents

List of Behaviors

(in order of appearance)

Foreword

It's hard to believe that it has been more than 15 years since Emma Parsons first published her groundbreaking book, *Click to Calm: Healing the Aggressive Dog*. I clearly remember hearing Emma talk about the Click to Calm methodology at ClickerExpo, and looked forward to reading her first book with great anticipation. I loved the fact that Emma took a fresh approach to dealing with aggression. At the time, I was particularly focused on her protocol of clicking and reinforcing any minimal reduction in the unwanted behavior. The story of Ben, Emma's dog-reactive golden retriever, was a compelling case study that demonstrated how effective the Click to Calm methodology could be. Over the past 15 years, Emma has implemented the protocol extensively, incorporated feedback from working with clients, improved the protocol's techniques, and updated instructions and procedures. She has combined all of that knowledge and experience in *The New Click to Calm: Solutions for All Dogs in a Challenging World*.

There are several things worth noting about this new book. First, the word "aggression" doesn't even appear in the title; the scope of this work is much broader. I love that the book is about "solutions for all dogs in a challenging world." So many of the techniques a trainer might use to deal with aggression are useful in other difficult situations. If you have a dog that won't let you take away his toy without snapping at you or a dog that pulls with too much enthusiasm when he sees another dog in the distance, *The New Click to Calm* provides answers and plans that can help you find a solution.

Second, I appreciate that Emma takes you through each step of the training process, starting with foundation behaviors and basic skills that all dogs should know. Problem-solving protocols and books often share valuable information about steps and procedures for resolving a problem behavior, but they assume some level of previous training or knowledge. Emma doesn't make that assumption. In the first two sections of the book, she presents basic information designed to help all trainers and caregivers. Part I focuses on creating structure and building trust, key elements that must be in place before you can implement a plan to help your dog. In Part II, Emma lays the groundwork for problem-solving by sharing training plans and suggestions for setting up a good training session, training the basics, and teaching emergency behaviors.

Third, the book proceeds to identifying the problem behavior, recognizing the triggers, and devising a plan for addressing the challenge. *The New Click to Calm* is chock-full of training suggestions and strategies for resolving a wide variety of problems. Emma also discusses the many things that can go wrong, and how to prepare for and deal with those unexpected situations that, inevitably, arise. She broadens the problem-solving lens far wider than just a focus on aggression, which makes her new book a particularly useful resource.

What I find remarkable about this book is that it speaks effectively to both the professional trainer and the average dog parent. Emma has structured the book to lead the reader from beginning steps and prerequisites through problem-solving plans for many common challenges. *The New Click to Calm* should be a go-to resource for all trainers and for anyone who wants a road map to help navigate the challenges many dogs face living in our busy human world.

—Ken Ramirez

Introduction

My first book, *Click to Calm: Healing the Aggressive Dog,* published in 2005, was directed at caregivers who had dogs with aggression issues. That was 15 years ago! *Click to Calm* was a revolutionary and controversial book. The reason for all the attention was simple: I chronicled my success using marker-based, positive reinforcement training to change responses in dogs with aggressive behavior. These dogs react to "triggers" in the environment: something they perceive as arousing or threatening, like a toddler, a blaring fire truck, or a large black dog. The Click to Calm protocol gave the dog a specific, reinforceable behavior to perform in the face of a trigger and put him in the driver's seat so that he could keep himself safe.

Most of us envision being out and about with our dogs routinely and can't imagine missing a child's soccer game or a visit with friends, or taking a vacation without our dogs. But behavioral issues often eliminate opportunities for dogs and their caregivers to participate in socially reinforcing and mutually beneficial events and, instead, replace those wonderful experiences with feelings of isolation, loneliness, or embarrassment. From firsthand experiences with my dogs, I empathize with my clients when they tell me stories of how they have been shamed in public, how they have been kicked out of recreational classes, and how family members no longer come to their homes because their dogs are too loud and obnoxious. The financial and emotional cost of committing to a dog with significant behavioral issues is often high. These clients want to eliminate the physical and emotional stress in their dogs that accompanies these behaviors, and they want to end the fallout for themselves as caregivers as well. Because I have learned so much from my clients and their dogs since *Click to Calm* was published, I wrote *The New Click to Calm: Solutions for All Dogs in a Challenging World.*

What's New

For all—not just "aggressive"—dogs
A major theme of this book is that you can use the new Click to Calm protocol on almost any unwanted behavior. Click to Calm's methods have broad applicability because I focus on the

behavior I want to change, not the label that it's given. The protocol is not just for aggressive dogs. I wrote this new book for all of us who have dogs that bark and lunge at the end of a leash for whatever reason—not just "aggression." It is for dogs that seem to be fearful of people and other dogs. It is for young dogs that run up to and try to play with every dog they meet, and it is for older dogs that suddenly get quite "cranky" around other dogs. It is for caregivers and trainers who, unexpectedly, find themselves with a dog with a temperament that is utterly foreign to them. The new Click to Calm protocol is an effective strategy for all.

For our busy, challenging world

Adapting to the crowded, busy human world is challenging for dogs. If you are unprepared for these challenges, you may end up with behavior issues that no dog or caregiver deserves or wants. A single unfortunate incident can create a behavior issue in even the most well-adjusted dog. You can prepare for these challenges by teaching behaviors that can keep your dog out of harm's way. The right behaviors can save your dog's life, minimize the behavioral fallout from an incident, build resiliency in your dog, and save you heartache.

In *The New Click to Calm* you will find instructions for more than 35 critical behaviors that I believe caregivers and professionals should teach dogs to keep them safe in the world. In addition to preventing problems, these same behaviors form the nucleus of the detailed Click to Calm solutions described in this book. If you do nothing else, I hope you will use this book to teach your dog or your client's dog these critical behaviors!

For faster results

We long to have more manageable dogs—the sooner, the better. Many dogs have behavior issues that their owners correctly characterize as troublesome but not dangerous. Some dogs react to just a small number of environmental stimuli or triggers. With other dogs, sadly, the opposite is true. In all cases, dogs with behavior issues can't improve fast enough. The refinements I've made to the Click to Calm protocol can accelerate the changes you want to see in your dog's behavior.

For addressing specific problems

I take a series of deep dives into three common contexts where owners experience unwanted behavior: 1) helping dogs with people issues (Chapters 14 and 15), 2) helping dogs with dog issues (Chapters 16 and 17), and 3) managing the dynamics of a multi-dog household (Chapters 18 and 19). In each of these sections, you'll find detailed protocols for addressing the common manifestations of the presenting problem—everything from dogs that "guard" possessions or food to dogs that "freak out" in public settings to dogs that don't get along at home. These detailed training sequences will save you and your clients time, false starts, and anguish.

For a more effective protocol

If you are familiar with the original Click to Calm protocol, you'll notice three significant changes in the new Click to Calm.

1. **Keep moving.** If you and your dog keep moving whenever your dog is exposed to a trigger, your dog's (and your) body stays calmer. Exposing your dog to a trigger while you are in motion helps prevent "freezing," often a sign of an impending "explosion." It is especially important to avoid freezing in the early stages of the process, while your dog is learning to be calm in the presence of the trigger and learning to orient to you.

2. **Pay more for what you want more of.** A critical milestone in the Click to Calm process is when your dog learns to reorient to you after seeing the trigger. I now recommend differentially increasing the value of reinforcement your dog receives from you while he learns this behavior. I have found that dogs learn this critical step faster when we "pay" them better.

3. **"Click, *back up,* and feed."** The Click and Feed training loop has always been a critical part of Click to Calm. I've now added "back up" into that loop. You use the "back up" step to:

   a. Remove your dog from a stressful situation. This added step gives both you and your dog time to breathe and lower stress and anxiety. Moreover, it allows your dog to eat his treats peacefully, actually enjoying the taste, without the pressure of another dog or person staring at him.

   b. Reassess your working threshold. Was that last exposure easy or was it too difficult? In the next exposure, should you come in closer or should you work with your dog farther away?

   c. Set yourself up for the next repetition. You can start the next repetition smoothly since your dog is no longer face-to-face with the trigger.

How to Use This Book

My goal with this book is to convey what I believe every dog—and, more importantly, his caretaker—should know to create a rich and rewarding life together. Understanding the Click to Calm methodology is useful for any dog, from the bouncy teenage Great Dane that becomes airborne when guests arrive, to the abused rescue dachshund that, unpredictably, turns some encounters with other dogs into potentially dangerous mayhem. Since readers will read *The New Click to Calm* with different aims and perspectives, here are my suggestions for getting the most out of this book:

If you're new to dog training or haven't tried positive reinforcement training, then start at the beginning so that you learn the principles you can use to teach your dog, whether or not you find him "challenging." If you acquired a dog recently, pay special attention to Parts I and II. They're designed to set up you and your dog so that you can avoid reactivity, aggression, and other problems from becoming an issue. This is the "prevention" section of the book. The principles outlined in Part I, Chapter 3 provide the structure for your dog to learn how to learn and to operate in human society successfully. He'll understand that his behavior can earn him what he wants. Beyond training the Basic Behaviors, it's worth investing your time to teach some of the Emergency Behaviors in Part II, Chapter 7, so that you and your companion can be better prepared to cope with the unexpected. The "unexpected" can happen to any of us; it may be your dog reacting to something or, for example, another dog reacting to your dog's perfectly appropriate behavior.

If your dog arrives with "issues," or he starts to develop a behavior you don't know how to address, Part III offers a starting point for confronting the fallout, diagnosing the problem, and plotting a course for addressing the issue. For most dogs, that means using the Click to Calm methodology.

If you're already familiar with Click to Calm, read about the critical changes I've made in the methodology in Part IV. Parts V through VI expand on Click to Calm. Part V customizes the Click to Calm method to dogs with people issues first and offers specific solutions to common people–dog issues (Chapters 14 and 15). Chapters 16 and 17 customize the Click to Calm method to dogs with dog issues and offer specific solutions to common dog–dog problems. Both sections explain how to move beyond the basic Click to Calm methodology if you think your dog might tolerate greater levels of interaction with his former "triggers. Since many caregivers have more than one dog, Part VI addresses how to manage these busy households, especially when one of your dogs doesn't get along with the others.

Reaching Your Goals

I have always believed that dogs are here to make us better people and that we are here to give them better lives. Dogs are mentors, as I found out with Ben, my reactive golden retriever whose behavior spurred me to develop the Click to Calm protocol in the first place. For our dogs, teaching us traits like patience and perseverance is no easy task! It was hard for me to give up my dream of training and traveling with an obedience trial champion. Instead, I had to focus on how to help Ben feel better in his normal, everyday life. I had to put his needs before my own, eliminating any kind of expectations that I had for myself and, more importantly, for him. This was not a challenge I welcomed back then! Now, however, I feel extremely blessed by the lessons I learned from Ben and for all the wonderful people and dogs that, as a result, I have been able to help.

I wish for you the same success that I have had with Ben and with my students' dogs. I hope that this book will help you and your dog live a meaningful and enriching life together.

PART I
Creating Structure and Building Trust

When you bring a dog into your home, you are starting an experiment in cross-species communication and living. Canines and humans may both be highly social species, but they see, interact, and communicate with the world very differently. Successfully integrating those two worlds—forging a relationship between members of two species—can produce an extraordinary partnership. Any training depends on it, and it all starts with communication and trust.

1
Closing the Communication Gap

We all need structure in our lives. Every one of us needs to know which behaviors to demonstrate in certain situations. Dogs are no different. The biggest challenge for dogs is that they have to conform their behavior to human standards. We have brought them into our alien world. With humans and dogs, the issue is that what is required from one isn't necessarily required—or desired—from the other. Contrary to popular belief, most dogs don't just know how to be a "good" dog! Dogs are dogs. Each day, dogs are euthanized for doing "doggy" things like barking, biting, digging, and chewing. It is the caregiver's responsibility to give the dog the correct information so that he can be successful, but that can be challenging.

We are different species, and we communicate in different ways. Humans are a verbal species. We talk to dogs to make behavior change whereas dogs use body language to communicate. They vocalize as well, but the majority of canine communication comes from body language. It is no wonder there is a communication gap—and it's easy for us to misinterpret how our dogs perceive our interactions with them—and vice versa.

Most dogs crave attention! They love it when their caregivers talk to them, pet them, and include them in their daily activities. There is nothing better than positive interaction, but if our dogs can't get enough positive interaction, they will just as eagerly seek negative attention that can also reinforce behavior. Keep in mind that *any attention you pay to a behavior is reinforcing*.

Say you are walking your dog and a friend approaches and wants to greet him. Watching your friend advance, your dog jumps up, dancing on his hind legs with excitement. Embarrassed, you yell at your dog to "Sit!" three times, but he cannot contain himself and continues jumping gleefully as your friend pats him. Your friend says, "That's okay! I don't care if he jumps up. He's a small dog anyway."

You wanted your dog to sit or at least keep four feet on the ground while he was being petted. Instead, in your attempt to quiet your dog, your desperate verbal cues and your extended eye contact (that your dog interprets as attention) ended up reinforcing him for jumping. Your actions ensure that he will repeat this behavior. Worse yet, your friend petted and praised your dog anyway, despite his jumping, so he was doubly reinforced.

Unfortunately, we tend to interact with our dogs when they are doing something inappropriate, reacting to behavior that we don't like. But the dog doesn't know he's doing something "wrong." In his attempt to adapt to confusing human society, a dog seeks information by offering behaviors and noting the consequences. That's how a dog learns and how he creates the structure he needs in his life. Consider the case of Colby.

The Toy Thief

Colby is a two-year-old golden retriever just adopted by a family with two children, ages 10 and 14. Colby enters his new home and sniffs every room with the children in tow. He picks up a new baseball glove and parades around the house with it. One of the kids, fearing that Colby might damage his purchase, scolds Colby, chases him, and finally tackles him, trying to pull the glove out of the dog's mouth. Colby growls. The boy backs away as Colby begins to chew the glove.

The next evening, as the family gathers in the living room watching a movie, Colby goes over to his basket of new toys, grabs a stuffed animal, and happily prances around the room with his purple dinosaur. He looks at the family members, but no one seems to notice. Puzzled, Colby drops the toy, runs into the kitchen, snatches one of Dad's winter boots, and tosses it in the air. Dad hears the thud as the boot lands and comes to investigate. Colby picks up the boot, and Dad gives chase. Mom joins in. What a fun game! As Mom reaches down to wrestle the boot out of Colby's mouth, he growls. She backs away.

What is Colby learning? Which behavior gives the dog the attention that he wants? Which behavior causes the humans to respond in a way that fulfills Colby's desires? Where will this behavior pattern lead for Colby?

Colby is quickly learning that chewing on some objects gains him the attention that he craves and that growling allows him to continue chewing by making the people go away. When Colby behaves appropriately (by human standards), his family ignores him—and behavior that is ignored will eventually disappear. But when Colby creates a commotion of some kind—taking a child's toy, or chewing a shoe, or growling—he has total control over his environment. If Colby's family had focused instead on *catching him being good* and *always* reinforcing him for being good, Colby's story would be heading toward quite a different conclusion.

Reinforce What You Like

Animals tend to repeat behaviors that get reinforced. Think about the behavior that you want from your dog and, in daily life, notice and reinforce him with a treat, a pat, or soft praise when he is offering that behavior. Be sure that you interact with your dog at those moments you want him to remember; that way, he will repeat the behavior. Tell your dog how great he is when he brings you back the tennis ball and drops it at your feet. Or when your toddler is crawling around on the floor and your dog stands calmly and observes. These are coveted moments. Don't take them for granted!

If you want your dog to be calm in the house and settle quickly, be sure that you reinforce only that behavior in that context. For example, if your dog is pawing at you or barking at you to go outside to play, wait until your dog calms down. Once that goal is achieved, go to the cabinet and retrieve his ball. Teach your dog the direct correlation between his quieting and your invitation to play.

Eliminate Nuisance Behaviors

Your dog may practice behaviors that are guaranteed to get your attention: barking, whining, pawing, growling, and even biting, to name a few. Unfortunately, either yelling at the dog or cajoling him to stop doing whatever he is doing gives him attention and only reinforces the behavior and increases its occurrence. Instead, identify these nuisance behaviors when they occur and ignore them if you can.

Nuisance behavior may get worse before it gets better. Just as you might kick a vending machine that fails to deliver the bottle of water you just purchased, your dog will also get frustrated when he discovers that the behavior that worked well for him in the past doesn't produce the desired results anymore. Sometimes the behavior escalates before your dog gives up and the behavior dies out.

If you cannot ignore the behavior, you have the option of interrupting the behavior at a lower intensity. For example, if your dog barks relentlessly for 10 minutes, see if you can interrupt your dog when he takes a breath or if he starts barking more softly. At those moments you may be able to feed and then redirect your dog to another activity.

> ### CASE STUDY: Charlie, The Night Owl
> Evelyn's young American Eskimo dog, Charlie, was a very busy dog, as Eskies can be. He ran around the house making up games to play; a favorite was, repeatedly, retrieving the Kong after tossing it down the cellar stairs. Charlie liked to be up early to start his day—so early that Evelyn couldn't get a good night's sleep.

About 3:00 a.m., Charlie often started pawing at Evelyn and nuzzling her hand. In the beginning, she thought that he had to go outside, so she got up to let him relieve himself (he did, but then he wanted her to play). After a week, Evelyn realized that Charlie's early-morning awakenings were becoming a habit, and the habit wasn't confined to nighttime. When Evelyn consulted me, she was exhausted. Although she had tried to tell Charlie to go away in the middle of the night, he was relentless. She found herself getting up just in case he really had to potty. The thought of cleaning up urine in her lovely home upset her.

I explained to Evelyn that she was rewarding her dog's lively behavior by, eventually, giving in and playing with him. Why wouldn't he continue to pester her if he was getting what he wanted? She had to break the cycle. I advised Evelyn to ignore the behavior whenever it happened, including the next time Charlie started to paw her in the middle of the night. If she was in bed, she was to remain silent and turn over. In the daytime, she should pick up Charlie's tennis balls, put them in a closet, and engage with him only after he was calm and quiet. Evelyn needed to make it clear that tennis-ball play only happened on her terms and that quiet, calm behavior was the key to starting any games.

It took about a month, but the strategy worked. Not only did Charlie's behavior improve, but Evelyn realized that she hadn't spent enough time stimulating Charlie mentally. His nuisance behaviors had developed as a way to engage with her. She added some mentally challenging activities to Charlie's day—and they both slept well at night!

The way to create the structure you want in your dog's life is through training, both formally and informally. Training is simply channeling a dog's natural information-seeking behavior toward behavior you prefer to provide your dog the structure that he needs. Ignoring your dog being a nuisance takes away his opportunities to self-reward and to perfect his obnoxious behavior. Reinforcing your dog for the behavior you want is an investment in building trust and building a partnership. Both efforts, outlined in the next chapter, pay off.

2
Disrupting Old Patterns, Launching New Ones

To start improving your dog's behavior, in terms of reactivity, aggression, or any other issue, you must do your best to take away all opportunities for your dog to rehearse inappropriate behavior. The more your dog behaves obnoxiously, the better at it he will become, and the more he will demonstrate it in certain environments. As a result, both the intensity and frequency of the unwanted behaviors will increase. This is especially true of self-reinforcing behaviors that dogs engage in just because they are fun and feel good to the dog, from excessive mounting to counter-surfing to barking at the mail lady or the neighbor's dog if it results in chasing the "intruder" away.

The danger is this: the demonstration of reactive behavior quickly becomes a behavior chain. As in all behavior chains, there will be a cue—or trigger—that sets the chain in motion. Unfortunately, in everyday life the presentation of the triggering cue often is beyond your control. Consider, for example, a dog that is reactive to children. That fear might have started with the actions of a single child (who yelled at or kicked him). With repetition, the fear becomes generalized so that now it's triggered by every child in any environment. Now, every time that dog sees a child, he barks and lunges at the end of his leash. Regardless of the outcome, the cue that starts the behavior chain is the appearance of the child in the environment. In a public setting, you have no control over the type of people your dog sees, and that presents a challenge if you are trying to prevent your dog from rehearsing reactivity. You face the same dilemma with a dog that is sensitive to other dogs, adults, or any other kind of trigger.

Preventing Rehearsals
For most caregivers, minimizing opportunities to rehearse undesirable behaviors means that they have to make substantial, though often temporary, changes to the home environment. If the living room window offers the dog unlimited opportunities to "patrol" the neighborhood all day, then the caregiver will need to relocate her dog to another area of the house or somehow block his visual access. (Half shades or shutters are a great choice for blocking the lower portion of windows

while allowing the sunlight to come in.) If the dog runs the fence line when the neighbor's dog is out, then the caregiver will need to bring in her dog when the neighbor's dog is outside.

Some caregivers may find that management in such situations is more of a band-aid solution and that the dog never truly understands that the behavior is unacceptable or learns how to behave differently in the presence of the trigger. Remember, the first step in stopping the behavior is stopping the behavior! That means stopping it while a suitable replacement behavior is being developed.

In some cases, you cannot stop all rehearsals. There are caregivers who live in the middle of the city and have to take their dogs for walks daily. They may see 30 to 40 strange dogs during a walk—not to mention the ride in the elevator getting to the first floor. Caregivers can only do the best that they can. Following the Click to Calm methodology, these caregivers can see change in the behavior, but improvement might not occur as fast as they would like.

Maxing Out Your Dog-Training Bank Account

Think of your dog's behavior as a bank account and moments of trust as deposits to that account. Ideally, you want to make far more deposits than withdrawals. You may have to make an occasional withdrawal because of a huge or unexpected expense, but the amount of emotional damage from such a withdrawal is determined by how much money you have managed to save (or how much trust you've built up) long term. Reinforcement history for both desired and undesired dog behaviors functions in the same way.

Let's say, for example, that your dog is nervous with other dogs. You have worked a number of years to keep your dog's attention on you when you expose him to other dogs in a public setting. You take your dog for a walk in the park and a dog runs up to him off leash. Your dog is scared and reacts. Since you have been putting lots of deposits into your account over the years, chances are that the withdrawal will be minimal. The recovery should be quick. Now if encounters like this occur many times over a very short period, your dog's trust in you will begin to wane. The balance in your account will start to dwindle.

The more you expose your dog to his triggers successfully without offering your dog the opportunity to rehearse unwanted behaviors, the more deposits you make into your trust bank account, and the safer your dog will feel. On the other hand, the more your dog rehearses the reactive or unwanted behavior (the more large withdrawals you make), the worse the behavior will get. Are you making more deposits or withdrawals? Collect the data. If you do a little bit of both, then your balance will be zero, and you won't see much of an improvement in the behavior at all. If you are making lots of deposits, then you will definitely see an increase in your dog's ability to tolerate his triggers.

Why Physical Punishment Might Fail

Reactive or aggressive behavior is difficult to modify, in part because it usually evokes a huge emotional response in the handler. Though reactivity and aggression are perfectly normal behaviors for canines, they frighten and embarrass humans. Few people envision that a dog that appears aggressive on the street is actually a warm and loving companion to the people in his family 99% of the time.

It is no wonder, then, that we seek methods that seem to guarantee quick fixes. Physical punishment seems an obvious answer. If a dog "goes off," either hang him on a prong collar or zap him with an electronic collar. If the consequence is sufficiently severe, shouldn't it wipe the behavior out of the dog's brain? Not necessarily. First of all, consider that physical punishment can be abusive, and, to maintain the original threshold of the suppressed behavior, it may have to be administered in increasingly intense doses. Implementing punishments, as well as their disastrous side effects, can put a dog at risk of developing hyper-vigilance, irrational fear, hypersensitivity, heightened irritability, implosive/explosive behavior, hyperactivity, aggression evoked with minimal provocation, withdrawal and social avoidance, loss of sensitivity to pleasure and pain, and depressed mood. In the case of my dog-aggressive golden retriever Ben, the side effects of the punishment he received from a trainer were more difficult to deal with than the original behavior it was meant to cure. After a training expert hung him up on his prong collar, he soon reacted viciously to all dogs rather than growling at a few.

Punishment can damage the relationship that you have with your dog. You want your dog to feel safe with you, not threatened. Moreover, fear stops the learning process for both humans and dogs.

The most serious danger in using punishment is that it often can feel good to the punisher, which mistakenly leads us to believe that we have "fixed" the behavior. The next time, we might be tempted to punish harder and faster.

Not only is punishment risky, but it also fails to teach the dog the appropriate behavior. The dog does not learn what to do next time when faced with a similar situation. To adequately solve the problem, the caregiver must ask, "What do I *want* my dog to do when he sees another dog?" It is not enough to say, "I just don't want him to bark and lunge!"

Preventing rehearsals, avoiding punishment, and investing in trust-building training are essential to making your dog a happier, more confident member of your family. The next chapter outlines how the changes you seek start at home, offering simple coaching principles you can implement throughout the day with your dog.

3

Incorporating Home Management

The purpose of home management is to give you, the caregiver, a way to communicate with your dog that he understands. It has nothing to do with making your dog work for every type of reinforcement that he gets (as if he doesn't deserve any). Instead, it teaches your dog how to make reinforcement happen. He learns how to get what he wants through the behavior that he offers. It is your job to teach your dog which behaviors are acceptable. To be clear, training reinforcements do not include love and affection. You should be giving plenty of that on a daily basis—assuming your dog enjoys those activities.

When you live with a dog, every moment spent with him is a training opportunity. Training opportunities are not limited to time you spend training your dog in a formal setting. By following the protocol below, you will be "training" your dog throughout the day regardless of how busy you are. The protocol provides ample opportunities for your dog to learn.

Implement one or two of the following principles of home management every week or so, depending on your dog's progress. Be patient and persistent as you reshape the dynamics of your relationship with your dog. A byproduct of this training is that your dog learns to trust and respect you. By providing your dog an education and a safe place to learn, you will be preparing him to be confident and able to deal with life's changing circumstances.

To practice this protocol, you do not need any special training equipment. Dogs do just fine watching your body movement and listening to your voice. The key here is to make sure that you are reinforcing the behaviors that you want in the future.

Principle #1: Teach Your Dog to Say "Please"

Dogs can get very excited when you do fun things with them; going for a walk, preparing a meal, and playing ball are all high on the list. In anticipation of these activities, your dog might engage in nuisance behaviors that you may reinforce inadvertently. For example, if your dog loves to go for hikes in the woods, he may jump and bounce off your body from the moment you pick up his leash. If you try to maintain control by yelling at him to "Stop," instead of calming him down, you may amp up the excitement and encourage him to start barking at you as well! Left unchecked, these behaviors will only escalate.

It is critical to teach your dog one easy behavior that is incompatible with jumping, pawing, clawing, and charging (just to name a few obnoxious behaviors!). This is the equivalent of teaching a child to say "Please." Although there are several behaviors to choose from, a three-to-five second sit will do the trick. The advantage is that most dogs, even puppies, are already familiar with this behavior.

Let's say your dog has to go out to do his business. Simply give him the cue to sit at the door. Try not to repeat the cue more than once. As his hind end hits the floor, say "Yes!" and open the door. Opening the door is the reinforcement for that behavior. If you cue your dog and he doesn't respond, either because he doesn't know how or is too excited, help him to do so with a treat. Never walk away from your dog or withdraw eye contact. This is a teaching moment!

If you follow this first principle, pretty soon your dog will cue you that he wants something by offering a sit–stay. What a wonderful way to get your attention! Notice it, as this is behavior that you definitely want to reinforce! Give the dog whatever he wants (assuming that it is safe, of course) when he offers this behavior. This response is especially important for young and adolescent dogs that can be reactive.

Principle #2: Mentally Stimulate Your Dog Daily

Dogs need physical exercise each day, so we take our dogs on runs, hikes, and lots of walks. Dogs also love to figure things out. They love to use their minds, but how can we challenge them mentally? By asking them to make decisions? By allowing them to experiment with their behavior? By offering them puzzles to solve? Certainly. The evidence is clear that dogs benefit when they get to use their brains.

When dogs are not given opportunities to engage, boredom can set in. Bored dogs are the chewers, the barkers, and the biters. In their attempts to find something to do, dogs hone nuisance behaviors. Without the caregiver's awareness, many times these behaviors begin to spread into real-world scenarios. Meet Riley. To pass the time while her caregiver is at work, she sits in the bay window across the street from an elementary school. Riley loves to bark at the people, children, and dogs that pass by, especially at certain hours of the day.

Six months later, the caregiver takes Riley for a walk in the neighborhood. At the sight of another person and dog, Riley flies to the end of her leash, barking and lunging. Shocked, the caregiver tries to drag Riley away while apologizing profusely. What she doesn't know is how Riley spends her days. She just assumes that because nothing is destroyed at home while she is gone, everything else is fine. Not so! The behavior that Riley is demonstrating is exactly the same behavior that she practices at home. The only difference is that one happens behind a window while the other happens at the end of a leash.

Put yourself in your dog's position. You are left alone in the house nine to ten hours a day. You cannot turn on the television or the radio or read a book. You cannot pick up the phone. You cannot get a bite to eat. The only thing that you can do is sleep, walk around the house, sit on the sofa, and look out the window. Your owner has left you with a stuffed animal or squeaky toy, but soon it gets boring. What else can you do? Tear up the rug or chew on the pillows? Get into the garbage? This is what your dog does with 95% (or more) of his time. It's not surprising that when humans come home at the end of the day, our dogs will do just about anything to get our attention.

As caregivers, we need to be able to provide an environment rich in learning opportunities for our dogs. As dogs learn new behaviors and their minds expand and become more flexible, their reliance on inappropriate behavior to communicate and solve problems will decrease, and they will more easily make good decisions under stress.

Here are some suggestions to engage your dog's brain:

1. Start to feed your dog with food toys like a Kong at each meal. (Purchase a black Kong for the heavy chewers!) If you feed kibble, add something "sticky" like canned pumpkin or maybe a version of wet food that you are already feeding your dog. Peanut butter and plain yogurt also work well. (For more exciting recipes, see www. Kong.com.)

    a. Prepare several Kongs ahead of time and keep them in the refrigerator or freezer. If your dog is unfamiliar with this toy, pack it lightly at first so that the food falls out and then, over time, pack it more tightly. Dogs are different: some will work on a frozen Kong for hours while others will work on it for 30 minutes. For persistent eaters, a refrigerated Kong can keep them busier longer.

2. Sprinkle your dog's meal outside in the grass for a food hunt!

3. Instead of simply walking your dog each day, work on some basic behaviors such as sitting at curbs and heeling by your side. How about cueing a down–stay while you

are talking to a neighbor? Alternate these activities with opportunities for your dog to sniff and play.

4. Using your dog's meal to train him is also fun. For example, you can toss a piece of food in front of you (especially fun with a rolling piece of kibble) and, after your dog has eaten it, ask him to come and touch your outstretched hand. Reward with a treat, and then toss another treat. You can play this game with any behavior.

5. There are many different types of food puzzles that require dogs to turn over pieces of wood to reveal a treat, choose the box with the treat hidden inside, or paw an object until food falls out of the holes, among other examples.

Principle #3: Give Your Dog a Safe Space

Every dog needs a space to call his own. Whether that is a crate, X-pen, or a baby-gated laundry room, you should have a place where your dog can rest comfortably. Your dog needs to learn to trust that, no matter where you put him, this will be a safe environment to which he can retire. This is especially true for dogs that are sensitive to people.

Choose a space that your dog likes. If you are going to use a crate, see if your dog has a preference between one made of wire or one that is closed in on all sides with a few windows to peek through. (Remember that you can cover a wire crate with a blanket.) If you are unsure which type your dog might like better, see if you can borrow a crate from a friend and experiment. Instead of purchasing the correct size crate for your dog, buy the next size up. (You want your dog to have plenty of room to spread out and play with his toys.)

The easiest way to acclimate a dog to a crate is to feed him there. Place the food inside the crate gate, saying a cue like "Go Kennel" just as your dog is entering. Leave the door open as he eats. It is fine if half his body sticks outside the crate. With time, he will become more comfortable going all the way in. Only then should you consider actually closing the door, gradually building up the period your dog spends inside.

All wonderful things happen in the crate! Whenever you put your dog in the crate, give him some mentally stimulating, but safe, toys or treats. A frozen, stuffed Kong or a meaty bone can work well. Put your dog in the crate both when you are home and when you are leaving. Putting your dog in the crate only at bedtime and only when you leave the house can quickly destroy the positive cue of going into the crate. Think of the crate as your dog's bedroom.

Choose the site of your dog's safe space carefully. Don't put the crate in a super-busy area unless you find that your dog is more comfortable there. If you have a people-sensitive dog, put the crate in a location where your visitors cannot see the dog, and vice versa. Upstairs baby-gated bedrooms or home offices tend to work well. Crates near entryways can be traumatic for a people-sensitive dog since he has to cope with the spatial pressure of those well-meaning visitors who want to interact with him. Unless your dog really needs the seclusion, it is better not to isolate your dog from your family completely. Your goal is to help your dog settle down peacefully within an active environment.

If you are crate-training a puppy, set up a variety of crates (or X-pens) in the house. You can put one in your bedroom, one in the kitchen, and one in the living room. Switch your pup out accordingly.

The wonderful thing about crates is that you can travel with them; you can take your dog's safe space anywhere you go. For example, if your dog is nervous around children, you can crate him at your sister's house when her children are around.

Dogs should not be kenneled for more than three hours at a stretch. Eight to nine hours a day is simply too long! A doggy daycare or dog walker can be an excellent option if you must be away from home that long. To give your dog more space during extended periods of solitude, use a baby gate to block off a certain room in the house. Condition your dog to this room as you would condition your dog to a crate.

Principle #4: Choose the Right Toy for the Right Occasion

There are three categories of toys that entertain your dog: general, mentally stimulating, and interactive. It helps to understand how to classify toys and how to use them to your advantage.

General: These toys are the ones that your dog hangs out with from day to day. It is a good idea to put these toys in a basket or drawer and rotate them. Better yet, teach your dog to pick up his toys at the end of the day and return them to the basket. The next morning, hold out the basket and allow your dog to pick out a couple for the day. Dogs, like children, tire of a toy that they see repeatedly, regardless of whether or not they played with it. Rotating toys keeps your dog interested and saves you money since you won't need to buy a steady stream of new toys to keep his interest.

Mentally Stimulating: Use these toys when you need to keep your dog's mind occupied, if you're having a big party and don't want your visitors feeding your dog inappropriate food, for example. Instead, put your dog in his safe space and give him a mentally stimulating toy. This will keep him happy and content. Examples of mentally stimulating toys are Kongs, Busy Buddies, and any other food puzzle toys. Teach your dog how to use these toys beforehand. Check out sites like Pinterest and YouTube for more exciting ideas.

Interactive: These are the toys that involve you playing with your dog. Frisbees, tennis balls, and tugs are just a few. Keep all of these toys in a closet or drawer and only bring them out when you are ready to play with your dog. For example, keep a box of tennis balls waiting by the door to your fenced-in yard.

Principle #5: Teach Your Dog the Guidelines of Play

Playing with your dog is a fabulous way to build your relationship. Just as humans play into adulthood, so do dogs. A new study released by Bristol University has found that play is the key to dogs' well-being. The study of 4,000 dog owners showed that dogs that don't engage in a lot of play suffer from behavioral issues such as anxiety and aggression. Fewer playtimes also lead to an increase in whining, jumping up, and failing to come when called.

Choose constructive games to play with your dog, like hide-and-seek, soccer, or fetch. These games can add a lot of pleasure to both of your lives and become powerful reinforcers for your dog. Be sure that the timing of your game reinforces only desired behavior. Before you play, ask your dog to sit (or choose a different behavior) and let the game begin! End the game while your dog is still happy and enthusiastic. Give your dog lots of cookies for relinquishing the toy before putting it away for the next time (show your dog where you are storing it).

Playing with your dog not only cements your relationship, but it has been scientifically proven to help prevent behavioral issues such as anxiety and aggression. Aim for connection; toys aren't necessary.

If you are playing a retrieval game, teach your dog to retrieve first. Play a tennis ball game where you have two balls, one in each hand. Throw one and ask your dog to retrieve it. When he returns with the first ball, you can either ask him to deliver it to your hand or ask him to drop it by your foot. Throw the second ball. Again, ask him to bring it to you, then throw the other one. Continue this game while your dog is still having fun. Stop before your dog wants to.

For a variation on the ball retrieve, ask your dog to sit and stay beside you and then roll the ball. Be sure that his eyes track it as it rolls. Count to five and then point your hand in the direction of the ball. Release him to retrieve it. When he arrives back, give him a treat. This is a fine way to teach your dog how to mark an item that you would like for him to retrieve (a TV remote comes to mind!).

Tug is a wonderful game to relieve stress for your dog, especially for juvenile dogs. For this game to remain safe, however, your dog must learn to drop the toy prior to playing, and the game should begin—and end—on your verbal cue. Adults can play tug with the dog as long as the dog has never bitten them or another member of the family. Children should not play tug with the dog simply because it is a safety hazard. A child could fall back and bang his head on a piece of furniture, or the dog could jump forward, trying to get the toy, and knock over the child.

If you play tug with your dog, the game starts when you ask him for a behavior. For example, you can present the tug toy, ask him to sit, and, once he does so, cue him to grab the toy. Tug the toy horizontally between you. Maintain control. Do not allow your dog to take the toy away, shaking it from side to side by himself. This is a cooperative game! Once you have played enough, you end the game by telling him "Out" or "Drop" and stash the toy away. The easiest way to teach your dog to drop the toy is to give your verbal cue and then put a fabulous treat on his nose. After a few repetitions, he will be dropping the toy instantly.

Since there is a fine line between over-stimulation and aggression, avoid games where you are only roughhousing with your dog. Pulling skin and slapping your dog on his ribs can send the wrong message. Think about the behavior that you want your dog to demonstrate when he is meeting new people. If you always play roughly with your dog, then that is how he might try to interact with all people. How you and your dog play together will affect how your dog plays with the other people in his life, regardless of their age or size. Dogs find playtime with you enormously reinforcing, so consider carefully when and how you are playing.

Principle #6: Make Object Exchanges Fun for Your Dog

The quickest way to teach a dog to become possessive and defensive is to constantly take coveted items out of his mouth, but you can teach dogs to relinquish objects to you willingly.

Think about this: you have a $100 bill in your hand. A friend walks by and takes it away. You look at your friend questioningly, wondering if he is going to return it. He doesn't. The next day, you have a $50 bill in your hand. Your friend says hello, takes the $50 bill and leaves. Aaaaargh! The next day you have two $100 bills in your hand. You see your friend approaching. This time you don't wait until he swipes your money! You either run in the opposite direction or you tell him in no uncertain terms that, if he tries to take your money, he'll get into trouble. (This response is akin to a dog growling.)

Now think about this: you have a $100 bill in your hand. A friend walks by, takes it, and gives you two $100 bills. You look at your friend in joy and disbelief. The next day, you have a $50 bill in your hand. Your friend says hello and replaces the $50 bill with a $100 bill! We love this friend! The next day you have two $100 bills in your hand, and your friend asks if she can have one of the bills. You bet! You would gladly share what you have in anticipation of a greater payoff!

The same principle will work with your dog: he'll readily relinquish something if he perceives that what's on offer is even more desirable. You just have to calibrate the hierarchy of benefits correctly—and then you don't have to get into a tug of war or a dangerous confrontation with your dog over something he's got in his mouth. See page 55 for specific instructions.

Principle #7: Negotiate Doorways and Tight Spaces Safely

In general, dogs are sensitive to tight spaces. In your home, the doorways can become quite narrow if more than one family member, other dogs, or other pets move through them simultaneously. It is no surprise that aggressive interactions in doorways are common. Some dogs get testy if you try to move them off a bed or couch. To avoid this pitfall, you can easily teach your dog to relinquish space. The "Excuse Me!" game (p. 57) is super-easy and fun to teach.

Principle #8: Accustom Your Dog to Handling

Caregivers must be able to handle their dogs. When your dog has an ear infection, impacted anal glands, or a split paw pad, he needs to allow you to examine and medicate him. Often, we only pay special attention to our dogs' sensitive body parts at moments like these. Teaching our dogs to accept handling should be a part of any caregiver's training program. Not only do we need to have the ability to handle our dogs, but others—particularly veterinary technicians and groomers—do as well. It's simple to accustom your dog to your touching him all over with just some treats (see p. 58). Hint: It helps to start with a relaxed, sleepy dog. There will be times when you will need to medicate your dog, and it will not be a fun experience for either of you. If you train your dog to tolerate handling, the experience will be so much less traumatic.

Now that you've started creating a structure for you and your dog that promotes building trust and improving communication, you're ready to train more specific behaviors that can make him a welcome member of society. Clicker training, introduced in the next section, offers a successful way to do this by precisely reinforcing the behaviors you want to see in your dog.

PART II

Laying the Groundwork

Practicing the Home Management principles in Part I gave your dog a structure to operate in and a way of communicating with you based on mutual respect and trust. Your dog has figured out that his behavior can make good things happen. Now you're both in the perfect place to learn the basics of clicker training and to become fluent in the training process. You'll be teaching your dog the basics as well as emergency behaviors that will serve your partnership well.

4
Clicker Training:
The Universal Language

Clicker training is the term for a method of reinforcement-based training that uses a signal or marker to let the dog know that his behavior will earn him a reward. For instance, if a dog hears a click as he plants his butt on the ground, then he understands that sitting is being reinforced. "Clicker" refers to a device that makes a sharp, unique clicking noise when you press it; it is the tool that many trainers choose as their "marker." Clicker training offers a universal language that all species can "speak" and understand. The clicker provides a simple, clear form of communication between verbal humans and nonverbal animals. The sound of the click means the same thing every time and to every participant: when the learner hears the click, he knows that whatever he did at that point in time is why he is being reinforced.

Information is empowering to any animal and helps to shape the animal's attitude toward the environment in which it lives. Once the animal realizes that it is in control of its own environment and the consequences of its actions, confidence grows. With this success comes joy and confidence for both teacher and learner. This confidence-building is why clicker training produces dramatic results with animals in shelters, for example. Nothing in their environment smells or sounds familiar. Introducing shelter animals to the clicker opens up a reliable method of understanding and communication within their surroundings. Clicker training can provide security in the midst of confusion.

Clicker training puts the focus on what the learner is doing *right* instead of what the learner is doing *wrong*. The clicker trainer looks for and captures pieces of behavior that she wants the learner to recognize and repeat. It is within this framework that the relationship between teacher and learner is shaped and defined. It is a relationship built on trust. The trainer respects the animal's decision-making capabilities, and the animal trusts that the information it receives from the trainer will keep him safe. In this way, both teacher and learner depend on each other to navigate through life's many challenging circumstances.

The beauty of the clicker is that it is a convenient, quick, clear, and precise marker signal. It is void of emotion, and its meaning is not open to interpretation. The clicker gives you the ability to communicate directly with your dog regardless of the setting or circumstances. You can mark or capture a behavior that will be gone in an instant!

The clicker signifies clarity and confidence to the animal even if the handler might be hesitant or fearful, as is often the case with caregivers who are working with reactive or aggressive dogs. The clicker tells your dog that you are in control of the situation whether or not you feel that you are. The sense that everything is under control ensures a safe learning environment for your dog. In order for humans or animals to learn new behaviors, they have to feel safe. They need the ability to focus on the task at hand.

Using Clicker Training to Treat Reactivity and Aggression

One of the major benefits of using clicker training to treat reactivity and aggression is that it incorporates both classical and operant conditioning simultaneously. By clicking and feeding your dog in challenging environments, you not only change your dog's emotional association with that environment (classical conditioning), but you can also pinpoint every correct decision your dog makes while he "operates" in that environment (operant conditioning).

Reactive vs. Aggressive

Throughout this book, I use the terms "reactive" and "aggressive." Generally, I use the word "reactive" to describe a dog that has the tendency to become over-aroused easily without causing physical damage. I use the word "aggressive" to describe a dog that has injured a person or another dog (although I would not necessarily call a dog that nipped a child after she stepped on his tail aggressive). Dogs do not have to bite to cause an injury. Violently muzzle-punching people and other dogs, for example, falls into the "aggression" category. When I meet with my clients, I ask them to describe the behavior that they see. I am not interested in any label that they might apply to the behavior. However, in this book I must be more specific.

Another important benefit of clicker training is that the clicker can interrupt behavior. Say your dog is about to start barking and lunging at another dog. When he hears the sound of the click, however, he turns toward you and anticipates receiving a treat, giving you the opportunity to move away from the trigger and rethink how close you want to get to the other dog.

If you are trying to capture quick moments of silence (your dog taking a breath in between snarling and growling), the clicker is the only tool that can mark these momentary behaviors precisely (your voice certainly cannot!). Bob Bailey once stated that, "The clicker is best used as a scalpel when carving out certain behaviors."

Simply hearing a click calms your dog physiologically. In her article "Amygdala: the Neurophysiology of Clicker Training," Karen Pryor explained one possible reason why: "The power of the click may well be in the possible relationship between clicking and the amygdala, a structure in the limbic system, or oldest part of the brain. Research in neurophysiology has identified the kinds of stimuli—bright lights, sudden sharp sounds—that reach the amygdala first, before reaching the cortex, or thinking part of the brain. The click is that kind of stimulus."

Other research on conditioned fear responses in humans shows that these responses are also established via the amygdala and are characterized by a pattern of very rapid learning, long-term retention, and a big surge of concomitant emotions.

We clicker trainers see similar patterns of rapid learning, long retention, and emotional surges, albeit with positive emotions rather than with fear responses. It may be that the clicker is a conditioned "joy" stimulus that the same primitive pathways acquire and recognize, which would help explain why the click is so different in its effect than a word, for example.

Is it possible that the sound of the click is not only physiologically calming for your dog but for you as well? If you are the handler of a reactive or aggressive dog, you feel a great deal of tension yourself. If the process of clicking your dog reduces that tension, then you are clicking and calming yourself as well as your dog. The default behaviors of observing, clicking, and reinforcing your dog, rather than exhibiting your own tension and fear, are calming and beneficial for you. This is the gift of clicker training for handlers whose hands shake as we expose our dogs to situations that we both find challenging.

Selecting the Proper Equipment

Before you begin to teach your dog any of the behaviors described in this book, read the instructions for each behavior carefully and make sure you have the proper equipment at hand. Here's what I suggest:

The Clicker: Clickers come in many shapes, colors, and sizes. The box clicker tends to produce a louder sound while the ergonomic clicker (with the button) produces a softer sound. The ergonomic clicker is often better for clients who have limited use of their hands and for dogs that are sound sensitive.

Choose a clicker that produces the sound that you need in whatever environment you are working in. For example, the box clicker is the best choice for working outdoors on behaviors such as recalls, while the button clicker is better for working inside on behaviors such as stays. Especially when you are working with reactive or aggressive dogs, you need the sound of the click to cut through whatever background noise is present in the environment. Do not assume that shyer dogs prefer a softer click. Some of the most sensitive dogs benefit from hearing a loud click well above the distractions in the environment. Experiment with a few different types of clickers to see which one you and your dog prefer.

If your dog is afraid of the clicker, use a sound that your dog can tolerate, such as a mouth-click or the click of a pen. If your dog happens to be noise-phobic, use a verbal marker signal such as "Yes!" or "Good!" Be sure that your verbal signal is short so that you can pinpoint the behavior that you want.

The box clicker (left) is louder than the more ergonomic button clicker (right).

The Collar: Choose a collar that is comfortable for your dog to wear. A buckle or martingale collar usually works well depending on your dog's breed. A front clip harness is a nice choice for a dog that tends to pull a lot. A head collar can give the handler tremendous control as long as her dog is comfortable in it. Keep in mind, however, that if the dog constantly tries to get the head halter off of his face, it can cause severe throat, neck, and spinal injuries.

Do not use any type of correction-based equipment, such as a prong, choke, or electronic collar. We need to provide a safe environment in which dogs can learn. Using a correction-based collar introduces the possibility that, if the dog makes the wrong decision, he may experience pain and discomfort. Coercion fallout could result (see "Why Physical Punishment Might Fail," p. 14).

The Leash: Use a leash that is comfortable in your hands. A five-to-six-foot leather, web, or nylon leash should work well for most of the exercises in this book. No flexi-leads or chain leashes, please! Although the flexi-lead is well suited for walking in large areas, it is not comfortable to hold in your hand, especially if you have to juggle a clicker and treats. You also run the risk of the line extending unintentionally, which could result in physical injury to both you and your dog. Chain leashes are simply not comfortable to hold. Only use a chain leash if your dog bites through any other kind of leash material.

For safety reasons, when you are working with large or aggressive dogs, it is wisest to use the Two-Leash system. In this system, your dog will have two separate leashes, each attached to a separate collar, head halter, or harness. For example, your dog might have a harness with a leash attached and a buckle collar with a leash attached. These are two separate systems. You hold two leashes, which means that if a collar or harness breaks, you have a back-up means of controlling your dog.

For a large, powerful, or aggressive dog, use two leashes, each attached to a separate collar, harness, or head halter. If one breaks, you'll still be able to control your dog.

The Reinforcement: Use the reinforcement that your dog will work for. Choose your reinforcers carefully, plan how to use each, and bring a plentiful supply (more than you think you could possibly need).

Treats: Treats tend to be the most popular form of reinforcement. They are easy to carry and you can adjust the value depending on your dog's taste buds.

Use soft treats when you are working on behaviors where your dog needs to swallow quickly and easily. Use crunchy treats for behaviors where you need your dog's head to stay low for longer periods of time, for the "Find It" behavior, for example (see p. 54).

Experiment with a variety of treats. Rate the palatability of your treats from one to ten, ten being the highest in value, one being the lowest. The higher the perceived value of the treats, the harder your dog will work for them.

A food tube is also an excellent way to reinforce your dog in situations that can be extremely challenging for him. It acts as a pacifier for your dog. Consider, for example, the dog-reactive dog that has no apparent threshold when he is exposed to other dogs and keeps reacting regardless of how much distance you open up. Allowing him access to the food tube keeps his mouth busy. The more he licks, the calmer he will become. Purchase an empty tube and fill it with something scrumptious like liver paste or smelly, wet dog food. If you have never used this tool before, you will need to teach your dog how to eat out of it before taking it on the road. Squeezable cheese in tubes or cans, or the canned pastes from the Kong company are fine alternatives for reinforcing a dog that is wearing a muzzle.

Toys: If you are going to use a toy to reinforce your dog, use one that requires that your dog interact with you directly. For example, a tennis ball on a rope can be a great toy for a quick game of tug. If you are going to use an interactive form of reinforcement, be sure that you have already taught your dog to "Give" or "Drop" the toy on your verbal cue.

Treat pouches: Treat pouches allow you to carry a large number of treats on your person and maintain a high rate of reinforcement while you are moving. Pick a treat pouch that allows easy access so that you can get your hand in and out of the bag and feed your dog quickly. A cheap nail apron from the hardware store works really well. You can fill it up with smelly, yummy treats, dispense them quickly, and then, after the training session, toss the apron in the wash.

Muzzles: Although there are many different types of muzzles, the basket muzzle will give you and your dog flexibility. The muzzle should fit over your dog's nose and mouth so that he cannot open his mouth enough to inflict injury but can still eat treats. As with a head halter, you will need to desensitize your dog to the muzzle before having him wear it during a training session.

Getting Started with the Clicker

When you begin to train your dog with a clicker, you promise your dog that every time he hears the click, reinforcement is coming, whether it be treats, toys, or touch.

The directions are simple:

1. When you see a behavior that you like, click once.
2. Give your dog a treat (or a reinforcement of some kind).

Do not reach into your bait bag until *after* you click. Clicking and reinforcing should be two separate actions. People used to think that for training to be effective you had to give the treat to your dog in a matter of "mini micro-seconds." Now we know that, as long as you give the treat in a timely fashion (within approximately five seconds), your dog will understand why he is receiving a treat.

Pretend that the click of the clicker is the click of a camera. Which piece of that behavior do you want to take a picture of? It will be the goal behavior for that exercise. For example, if you are teaching your dog to sit, you want to click just as your dog's hind end hits the floor.

Once your dog is performing the behavior that you want reliably, then you can start to insert a cue right before the dog does the behavior. In the example above, you would tell your dog to "Sit" and, just as your dog's hind end hits the floor, you click and reinforce. Cues can be anything that the dog can perceive; verbal cues and hand gestures tend to be the most common.

For behaviors that are harder to catch, you can cue the behavior as it is happening and then slowly, with successful repetition, move giving the cue to before the behavior happens so that your dog is actually responding to the cue and performing the behavior. A good example of this progression is the "Bow" behavior. First, you need to form an association between the word and the behavior. As the dog stretches into the correct position, give your dog the cue, then click and reinforce the completion of that behavior. As your dog becomes more familiar with the behavior and can execute it faster and more reliably, you can gradually move up the cue ahead of the bow.

There are three ways that you can teach your dog with a clicker:

The first is by *capturing* your dog doing a behavior that you like. For example, if on a walk with your dog, another dog comes up to sniff your dog's hindquarters, and your dog does not react, you can click that behavior and gently praise your dog. That way your dog knows that you approve of his response. If it happens again, you could insert a verbal cue such as "Easy," reminding your dog that this dog is not dangerous, just forward.

The second way is to *shape* your dog's behavior by clicking and reinforcing small approximations of the final behavior. Using the Click to Calm methodology described in detail later in the book, you will be clicking and reinforcing your dog for anything he does that is appropriate while in the presence of another dog, for example. Eventually he will see a dog and, instead of reacting, he will look at you instead. With shaping, you add the cue after you have trained the behavior completely.

The third way is to *lure* your dog with a treat and then click for the correct behavior. Although luring has limited uses, it is a way to help your dog learn a behavior, especially if he is not accustomed to moving his body in a certain way. For example, consider teaching your dog to lie down from a stand. Previously you might have taught him to lie down from a sit, so asking him to fold back into a down might not be a familiar behavior. To teach this motion, it helps to put a treat in front of your dog's nose. Slowly move the treat into his chest to help him arch his back until he folds into the down position. This technique can help him build the muscle memory required for that movement. As your dog continues to repeat this behavior, you could insert a verbal or gestural cue right as his body starts to fold down. Click and reinforce for the completed behavior.

Use the clicker for new learning only. Once your dog learns a behavior, you can replace the click of the clicker with a verbal marker, such as "Yes."

5
Setting up a Productive Clicker Training Session

Be clear about what you are trying to train. Since there are many different ways to teach one behavior, choose the one that is the easiest for you and your dog. Always know which behavior you are trying to teach and have a plan. That way, if things go awry, you can stop the session, release your dog to a fun activity, and rethink your plan.

Make sure that you prepare well before bringing your dog into a training session. Select an environment that will be quiet with as few distractions as possible. Choose your reinforcers carefully, plan how to use each, and bring a plentiful supply (more than you think you could possibly need).

Training Tips

Productive clicker training is both an art and a science. It's also a mechanical skill. You will improve with practice. Before conducting a training session, review the principles below and be sure that you understand them:

- Choose your training space wisely. If you are teaching your dog a new behavior, use a distraction-free environment. As the behavior becomes more reliable, you can slowly increase the distraction level. For example, start inside your home and then, when your dog has the basics down, take the behavior outside to a quiet place in your yard.

- When you are teaching your dog a new behavior, use a high rate of reinforcement. Frequent reinforcement keeps your dog focused on you instead of the environment and keeps his adrenaline levels lower.

- Short sessions are key, especially when you are working on aggression and reactivity exposures. Three- to five-minute sessions should be adequate; in certain situations, they may be too long!

- Use treats equal to the level of distraction in which you are working. For example, bring delicious treats to places where it might be difficult for your dog to perform the desired behavior. Use a less reinforcing treat when you ask for easier behaviors in a setting where your dog is used to working, at home, for example.

- Break up behavior into small pieces. You should only be working on one piece of a behavior at a time. This is especially true when you are teaching concepts like distance, distraction, duration, and difficulty.

- When you are working on one criterion, temporarily relax the others. For example, if you are working on a sit–stay, work on distance and duration separately. If you're working on increasing distance from your dog, keep the stays short (relax duration).

- When you are training a behavior in a new environment, know that, initially, the behavior might fall apart. In each new setting, "go back to kindergarten" and reinforce smaller steps toward your training goal, just as when you first started training that behavior with your dog. The more environments that you work in, the faster your dog will acclimate and generalize, and the more consistent the behavior will become.

Go Back To Kindergarten!

When you are teaching your dog a behavior, you must accept that, whenever you change the environment, the behavior is likely to deteriorate. That's because a new environment presents distractions (and, possibly, stressors and triggers), which make it harder for your dog to attend to and respond to what you consider a "reliable" cue for a "simple" behavior. Moreover, particularly young dogs that don't yet have a lot of training are still "learning how to learn," and that means that they aren't terribly proficient about generalizing. They don't have enough life experience to know that coming when called when playing with buddies at the dog park is the same as coming when called in the living room—and works just as well (or even better) at producing desired reinforcements. Generalization is a goal of all trainers: The more you can get your dog to perform a given behavior reliably in many different environments, the easier it will become for your dog to do. Those of us who compete in dog sports know this all too well!

Let's take a sit for example. This is a behavior that your dog has learned at home. It seems easy enough. Your dog can sit in the house, out in your yard, and on a walk. But what about when you go to the veterinarian's office and you cue your dog to sit on the scale? It's a no-go!

A veterinarian's office is not a place you frequent, and it is a place your dog may not associate with fond memories. You're asking him to sit on a metal thing that probably smells of other dogs in a room full of other animals. It is natural for your dog to balk at sitting at all, never mind on an object that he rarely sees. Instead of getting frustrated, take your dog "back to kindergarten." Cue your dog to get up on the scale via a hand target (see p. 40). Click and feed him for that. Now ask him to sit. You will find that your dog will be much more cooperative in new or stressful situations when you break down the behavior in pieces that he can understand.

Bear in mind that "changing the environment" applies not only to the physical setting but to who or what else (other people, dogs) is in the picture, the level of activity and noise, and even your position. For example, if you suddenly sat down and turned your back on your dog and told him "Sit," would he do it? The more behaviors you take on the road, the more reliable your dog's behavior will become!

- During a training session, give 100% attention to your dog so that you can observe the smallest behaviors—or lack of behavior—and click and reward it. Do not get distracted by visitors or people who speak to you while training.

- Keep a training journal so that you can track your dog's training progress, especially when you are working on reactivity and aggression issues. See suggestions under "Data Collection: Keeping a Training Journal," p. 125.

- Once your dog is familiar with the training process, start to vary your reinforcers.

- You can try exercising your dog before a training session. Some dogs benefit from heavy exercise while others might grow tired and cranky.

- Read all of the steps in a training exercise so that you understand the goal and the associated steps before trying anything with your dog.

- When you are working on behaviors, try not to help your dog by telling him what to do. If you constantly give verbal cues, they become meaningless and may actually confuse your dog. A confused dog is a stressed dog, and a stressed dog will soon become one that does not want to work.

- A dog that offers you 50 behaviors when you pick up the clicker and treats shows that none of the behaviors you have taught him are actually on cue. Check the behaviors for reliability (Does he offer that behavior *only* on that cue and on no other cues?).

- Get your dog used to you walking around with a clicker and treats in your pockets. You don't want the presence of the clicker and treats to become contextual cues that indicate you are "working." If they become contextual cues and your dog doesn't see them, he may not be interested in listening and learning.

- Know what the "true learning" equation looks like: you give a cue, your dog completes the behavior, you mark that the behavior is correct, and you reinforce your dog.

- A rule of thumb: If you are working with your dog and he fails to perform the behavior twice, lower the criteria to a level that he will understand. Remember that, even though your dog has performed the behavior in the past, that does not mean that the behavior is reliable.

- Practice working on various behaviors with your dog both on-leash and off.

- Before you venture out in public, practice your clicker mechanics until the technique feels effortless. Figure out which hand will hold the leash, the clicker, and the treats. A favorite solution: hold the clicker against the leash in one hand while the other hand dispenses the treats.

- Be aware of what scares, shuts down, or arouses your dog. Accept that even with the most careful planning, you will not control every aspect of the environment. Expect the unexpected. A sparrow could fly into the training facility or someone could roll luggage down the street and trigger your dog.

CASE STUDY: Anticipating Environmental Changes

A sudden environmental change occurs when something in a setting changes quickly, such as when a person stands up suddenly to get a drink of water, a chair falls over, or a new dog enters a dog park. In most situations, dogs will react by barking and/or running over to see exactly what caused the disruption.

One of my students told me, "My dog Tigger was great with all of the visitors until Mabel got up to get a Diet Coke. Then all hell broke loose! I don't understand this because Tigger was socializing with Mabel all day long. All of a sudden he didn't recognize her?"

Indeed, if Tigger had been socializing all day long with a sitting Mabel, when she got up, he may have perceived her as something "other," and that may have startled or threatened him. If you have a dog that appears to "go off" for no good reason after a period of perfectly calm behavior, be aware of these kinds of shifts in the environment and the effect they can have on your dog. Try to anticipate environmental changes by clicking and feeding your dog for looking at, and coping with, the new situation. If you have a dog that is sensitive to people, for example, ask your visitors to let you know before they change their position in the room. This will help you be ready to reinforce when your dog keeps it together.

The Perfect Training Loop

You want your dog to learn as quickly as possible, especially when you are dealing with reactivity and aggression. To accomplish this, you must know the principles of learning theory so that you can recognize what a clean training loop is. The cleaner your training loops, the quicker your dog will learn. Patty Ruzzo, a longtime obedience competitor, used to say, "Perfect behavior comes from practicing perfectly."

When you are training your dog to perform a certain behavior, think of each repetition as a training loop. It starts when you give the cue, the dog does the behavior, you mark it with either the click or a verbal signal, and you give a reinforcer. That ends the loop. Your goal is to always practice the most perfect training loop possible. Otherwise, you can get frustrated and your dog can get confused.

Technically, you start the training loop when you give your dog the cue. Make sure that your dog is looking at you before giving the cue. If your dog has just ended a training loop, wait until he has finished eating and is ready to focus. (It can be very tempting to give your dog a cue before he has finished eating his treat from the last repetition.) Think of your dog's eyes on you as the "start button" behavior. Your dog focusing on you is the cue for you to cue him.

Here is an example: You want to start working with your dog-reactive dog. You drive to the field where you know that a bunch of dogs play off leash within a fenced-in area. You get out your dog and your training equipment. You start by walking too close to the other dogs and your dog goes off. Hurriedly, you run back to the car. That training loop was a bust! You try again. This time you stay about 30 feet back from where the dogs are playing. You start clicking and feeding your dog for looking at the other dogs calmly and then looking back at you. You practice this about five times and then you take your dog back to the car. Eureka! That was several perfect training loops! There were no glitches at all. You had the opportunity to reinforce several repetitions of perfect behavior—and you were in complete control of the situation.

Here is another example in a different context: You are training your young dog in agility. You are practicing a sequence of jump—tunnel—jump. You give your dog the cue to jump, you cue the tunnel, and, just as your pup flies out of the tunnel, he goes off to sniff a piece of fuzz on the floor. Instead of ending the loop there, you ask your dog to complete the jump. Now there is a huge glitch in your training loop (jump—tunnel—sniff fuzz—jump).

Go back and practice this short sequence again so that your pup does it flawlessly. Otherwise, you will be embedding the glitch (sniff fuzz) in the sequence of the behavior that you are creating.

If you repeat flawed training loops enough, they can translate into problems such as your dog visiting the ring crew, your dog searching the floor to find something interesting, and so on.

No matter which behavior you are building, be sure that the training loops are clean. Your dog will learn faster, and he will be much more enthusiastic about participating in the activities that you provide for him. Never forget that when you are training behavior you are also building an emotion that gets embedded into that behavior as well.

6
Teaching the Basics

In this chapter, you will learn how to teach your dog basic obedience behaviors. These cued behaviors are the building blocks for many other behaviors that you will find necessary down the road. A dog that can walk nicely down the street with his handler has less chance of becoming overstimulated by a child riding his bike close by. Although traditionally the term "obedience" has implied subservience, it makes more sense to interpret it as mutual compliance. It is the handler's responsibility to teach her dog behaviors that will help make both of their lives easier. The handler should never assume that her dog knows what she wants if she has not taught the behavior reliably, as most of us have experienced with calling our dogs to come to us.

An educated dog has a closer relationship with his handler and can accompany her almost everywhere. This dog is a joy to be around. He offers his handler attention voluntarily and is rarely frightened, even in new situations. He knows that his handler will take care of him and guide him safely through life's many challenging circumstances. He is a confident, happy dog.

The behaviors described below are mandatory or must-know behaviors for every dog, especially for dogs in busy environments like the city. If you have a fearful, reactive, or aggressive dog, however, it's critical that he learn as many reliable behaviors as possible, behaviors that he can perform anytime, anywhere, under any conditions. In a crisis, these so-called default behaviors will give the handler a variety of options from which to choose to avert disaster. I've highlighted several of the most useful default behaviors below, each with explanations of how you can use it in sticky situations.

Read through all of the training information before trying each exercise. The description will tell you what the behavior is, why you should teach it, how to use it in real-life situations, and the secrets to training it successfully. Your goal is to introduce each concept to your dog and produce the cleanest training loops possible.

NAME RECOGNITION

Objective: Anytime you call your dog's name, he turns and looks at you.

You need to be able to get your dog's attention by calling his name, regardless of the distraction level in the environment. Calling your dog's name can interrupt potentially problematic behavior. Your dog also learns to refocus his attention on you and "await further instructions" and/or return to your side.

Especially helpful when…

- Your dog is about to start barking and lunging at a person or another dog. Sensing the danger, you have the ability to interrupt that pivotal moment.

- You have multiple dogs and need to cue each separately.

- Your dog is running toward a visitor and you are not sure of your dog's intentions. Nervous, you can call your dog back to you promptly.

How to teach the behavior:

1. Toss a treat.

2. As your dog is eating, say his name.

3. When he turns to look at you, click, and toss another treat.

4. Repeat Steps 2–3.

5. Practice this behavior both on leash and off.

Secrets to success:

- Always reinforce your dog for looking at you regardless of whether or not you cued it.

- If you do not usually allow your dog to eat from the floor, give your dog verbal permission to get the treat.

- If you constantly say your dog's name when you are speaking, give your dog a specific name for those times when it's critical that you signal him. For example, if your dog's name is Lizzie and you call her "Liz" all of the time, when you want her full attention, say her full name.

- Never use your dog's name to punish or scold him.

EYE CONTACT

Objective: On cue or on his own, your dog offers you eye contact freely.

A dog that readily offers you attention, no matter the circumstance, is able to focus on your cues for appropriate behavior. Your dog should always feel comfortable looking into your eyes or up into your face. Steady eye contact with you gives your dog comfort and guidance when he needs it most. While many dogs offer this behavior freely, some do not. Some dogs are reluctant to look into anyone's face, including their guardians' faces. If your dog seems excessively shy about eye contact, consider using the luring method described below.

Although the Click to Calm methodology will teach your dog to look at you voluntarily, it is nice for handlers to have the ability to cue it when necessary, especially in an emergency situation.

Name recognition and eye contact are often closely intertwined. I usually advise my clients to start with name recognition and then notice all of the eye contact they are getting. The two behaviors happen together.

Especially helpful when…

- Your dog has been severely traumatized by his last caregiver. Every time he looked at the handler, he got punished in some way. Now that you have adopted him, you need to help him feel comfortable about offering this behavior.

- Eye contact is often the first indication that your dog has "heard" you. For example, if you call your dog to you, the first sign that he is about to come may be his re-orienting to your face. Therefore, you need to reinforce this behavior heavily.

How to teach the behavior:

1. Position your dog in front of you. Vary the body position that you are in.

2. Every time that your dog orients to your face, click and give your dog a treat.

3. If he has trouble looking up, lower a yummy, stinky treat to his nose and slowly bring the treat up to your eyes.

4. As he looks up, click and give your dog the treat.

5. Practice this exercise as many times as needed for your dog to look into your eyes happily.

6. You can put this behavior on a verbal cue, such as "Watch Me" or "Look."

Secrets to success:

- Always reinforce your dog for looking at you regardless of whether or not you cued it.

- Reinforce approximations of this behavior if your dog cannot look at you straight away.

- Never force your dog to look up into your face.

- If your dog is hesitant to give you eye contact, see if sitting instead of standing in front of him helps. You might also try sitting at your dog's side instead of facing him straight on.

- When offering eye contact becomes reliable, start testing the behavior by taking your dog with you on errands. Don't say anything! When your dog looks at you on his own, click and give him five treats! Remember to reinforce your dog for any part of the behavior he offers: a flick of the ear in your direction, a side turn toward you, or a head turn in your direction.

HAND TARGET

Objective: On cue, your dog follows your hand and touches it with his nose.

Hand targeting is one of the most important behaviors that you can teach your dog, so it makes sense to train it as a default behavior. It has so many applications; you can use it as a recall cue or as a cue for your dog to greet people courteously (see "Hand-Target Greeting," p. 66). If you teach your dog to follow your hand or finger, you can move him from place to place without actually touching him—a crucial skill to use with a dog that could bite if you try to pick him up or guide him by the collar. A hand target is also a godsend when you are training fearful dogs to walk upstairs or across a slippery floor. Teach the hand target with much joy and praise.

Joy is built right into the ability to cue your dog to chase (and touch) your hand. You can invite your dog to bounce up to touch your hand above his head or incorporate the hand target into lively chase games. In a stressful situation

Teaching your dog to target your hand is both fun and super-practical. You can use the cue as a precise recall, as a method to guide your dog, as a bouncy release, and as the start of sending your dog to touch an object.

where there is little room, you can engage your dog in a quick hand-target game, asking him to touch your hand in different positions. That gets both of you moving and dispels some of the tension. This behavior is so effective because it is easy for both the handler and the dog to master. Just like people, dogs love to do behaviors that they understand and do well. Hand targeting falls into this category beautifully. With knowledge comes confidence, and with confidence comes control over environmental circumstances.

Especially helpful when...

- Your dog is out in the yard smelling the leaves and you need to call him into the house before going to work. You hold up your hand and say "Wylie, touch!" Wylie comes running at top speed to touch your hand! Click and treat party!

- Your older dog is anxious about walking across the shiny floor in your veterinarian's office. You put out your hand and your dog follows your palm cautiously as you lead him slowly into the exam room.

- Your small dog is uncomfortable being picked up and may snap if you try. To get him up on the couch beside you, simply cue him with a hand target. If you need to ask him to move over, instead of physically pushing him you can pat the empty space beyond him.

How to teach the behavior:

1. Present your empty hand close to your dog's nose on one side of his face. He's likely to investigate.

2. Click just as he touches his nose to your palm and then feed your dog.

3. Present your hand on the other side of his face.

4. Click just as he touches his nose to your palm and then feed your dog.

5. Repeat until your dog will touch his nose to your palm no matter where you place it.

6. Insert a verbal cue like "Touch" right before his nose touches your palm.

7. Once this behavior is reliable, take one step and hold out your hand to see if your dog will follow it. Click and feed your dog for touching your palm. If your dog does not follow your hand, shorten the distance to make it easier.

8. Practice until your dog can follow the palm of your hand no matter where you lead. Make it fun! Can he follow your hand around a tree or under a chair?

Secrets to success:

- If the hand target looks too much like a "Give me your paw" cue, teach your dog to touch your fist or a few fingers instead.

- If you present your hand and your dog does not lean forward to touch it, this simply means that your dog is not ready to reach across that distance yet. Move your hand closer.

- Do your best to click just as the dog's nose touches your palm. If you click too late, you might be reinforcing your dog for moving his nose away from the palm of your hand.

- If you present your hand and your dog does nothing, remove your hand. Only hold your hand out for a couple of seconds at a time. Next time present it closer to your dog's nose.

- If you have a small dog, you can use a target stick such as the end of a ruler or spatula so you don't have to lean over.

SIT

Objective: Your dog will sit reliably on cue in any environment under any circumstances.

If you teach your dog just one default behavior, make it "Sit." If your dog is anxious or confused, it is much safer for everyone if your dog will sit rather than bark and lunge on leash. Your sit cue will distract him from potential stressors, and he will be too busy responding to your cue to lunge or bark at another dog or person. Coupled with eye contact and stay behaviors, using sit is a very effective strategy for defusing potentially dangerous situations.

Especially helpful when…

- Without your knowledge, your children called in a pizza delivery. When the pizza delivery person appears behind your glass door, your dog starts running toward the door, barking and growling. Panicking, you scream the word, "Sit!" In response, your dog sits and stares up at you. Whew! Disaster averted!

- Your 10-year-old child, who was supposed to put your dog in his safe space when she returned home from school, forgot. Now your dog is chasing her because she's trying to keep her toy away from him. Of course, your dog thinks this is a fun game! Anxious about how the chase is going to unfold, you call your dog's name and cue "Sit!" Your dog slides to a stop and sits! From here, you can put your dog on his leash and escort him into his safe space with a sigh of relief and a stuffed Kong.

How to teach the behavior:

1. Hold a treat just above your dog's nose.
2. As he sniffs the treat, slowly bring the treat up over his head.
3. Click as his hind end folds into a sit.
4. Give your dog the treat.
5. Practice this behavior until your dog can sit easily.

6. Next, put this behavior on a verbal cue by saying "Sit" right before your dog's hind end hits the floor.

7. End the exercise on a happy note!

8. Take this behavior on the road, practicing it anywhere and everywhere.

Secrets to success:

- Lure the behavior only a few times. You should be cueing your dog with an empty hand as soon as possible. In the future, this motion could serve as a hand cue as well.

- Capture any offered sit with a click and treat every time you see it.

- In this exercise, you are teaching your dog the body position only. A stay is not implied; that is a separate exercise.

- Get your dog used to sitting on many different types of surfaces and objects such as tile, grass, or the veterinary scale.

- Teach your dog to sit in front of you, beside you, or behind you.

- Never force your dog into a sitting position.

- When your dog knows to sit on cue, make this a game by tossing a treat (this gets him on his feet) and then asking your dog to sit. When your dog sits, click and toss another treat. Repeat this game several times. Stop before your dog gets tired.

DOWN

Objective: Your dog will lie down reliably on cue in any environment under any circumstances.

Assuming that your dog is comfortable in a given environment, lying down is a relaxing position for him to be in. This position is not for dogs that are nervous or timid in a social setting. Those dogs will not find lying down comforting in a threatening or stressful environment. If you have a dog like this, work the behavior at home first and then take it on the road. (Note that the stay behavior is taught separately.)

Especially helpful when…

- You are taking your people-sensitive dog for a walk. You stop to talk to your neighbor across the street. Fearing that a jogger might run by, you cue your dog to lie down and stay while you exchange pleasantries.

- You are on a hiking trail. A strange dog appears around the corner. You ask your dog to lie down and stay behind you as you try to signal the other handler.

How to teach the behavior:

1. Have your dog standing in front of you.
2. Take a treat and bring it into his chest.
3. As your dog's head bows to follow the treat, click and feed your dog.
4. Repeat this exercise, and as you bring the treat lower into his chest, see if more of his body will fold back into a bow with each repetition.
5. Click and feed your dog between his front feet as his body starts to bend.
6. Repeat, and wait until his butt touches the floor.
7. Click as he lies down and feed your dog accordingly.
8. When the down becomes one swift movement, insert the verbal cue "Down" right before it happens.
9. Take this behavior on the road, practicing it anywhere and everywhere.

Secrets to success:

- Capture the down with a click and treat every time your dog offers it.
- This exercise teaches the position only. We will work on extending duration (the stay) separately.
- You can teach your dog to lie down from a sitting position, but if you need to cue a down in an emergency, your dog needs to know how to fold from a stand to a down quickly (teach this separately). You can also teach a down from a stand from a distance.
- Feeding your dog between his front feet will help press him to the floor. If you feed his mouth up high, inadvertently you may be feeding him for raising his elbows up off the floor.

STAY

Objective: Your dog will remain in a sit or a down reliably on cue until cued to do otherwise, no matter the circumstances.

Paired with a stand, sit, or down, teaching stay is the process of adding duration to the desired position. A reliable stay helps not only with simple management and husbandry tasks but also gives you and your dog extra flexibility handling potentially uncomfortable situations.

Especially helpful when…

- You have arrived at a dog training class and you have to take off your coat, get your treats ready, and assemble your crate. Your dog will sit and wait for you quietly instead of getting distracted or focusing on potential stressors.

- You have just taken your dog for a walk on a snowy day and have to clean his paws. You ask him to stand–stay as you clean in between his paw pads.

How to teach the behavior:

1. With your dog either beside you or in front of you, cue your dog to sit or lie down.

2. When he is in position, give him your cue to stay.

3. If he started out beside you, walk out in front of him and turn to face him.

4. Count to 5 either out loud or to yourself.

5. If your dog remains in position, click and feed him.

    a. If he is in a down, feed him in between his front legs.

    b. If he moves out of position after the click, technically he is still correct. However, it is best to feed him in the original position that he stayed in, so re-cue and then treat.

6. If your dog moves out of position before you click, cue him into position again. Do not feed him for getting back into position. Proceed as above.

7. After the 5-second stay is complete and you've clicked and treated your dog, re-cue the behavior for another 5 seconds. Note that, after you click, the behavior has ended, so you need to re-cue.

8. Click and treat your dog for remaining in position.

9. To end the session, give your dog a release cue like "All Done" in a neutral tone of voice.

10. If you started with your dog beside you, you can return to that position.

Secrets to success:

- At first, do not ask your dog to stay in a challenging environment.

- After the click, feed your dog in the position that you asked him to stay in.

- Extend duration slowly and only with success.

- When you are extending duration, "ping-pong" between shorter and longer time lapses.

- Once you have a 2-minute stay, you can decide whether or not you want to have a separate cue for "Wait." "Stay" means that you will return back to your dog, while "Wait" means that you will call your dog out of the stay.

- When you are first working on the stay, return to your dog. Do not call him out of the duration position.

- Work on only one piece of criteria at a time. For example, work on duration, distraction, and distance separately.

- Be consistent! If you ask your dog to sit–stay and he sinks into a down, make sure that you help him get back into the sit. (Never pull him up by the collar or scruff! Lure him.)

- Separately, work on changing your position and activity (sitting, standing while rummaging for keys in purse, and so on) while your dog is in a stay.

- To build your dog's confidence, ask him to stay in a variety of situations. Initially, remember to "go back to kindergarten" in each new environment. For example, ask your dog to down–stay with his back turned toward some sort of activity like your obedience or agility class. Or ask him to sit–stay on a street corner while waiting to cross.

- Always click for completed behavior. Do not feed your dog haphazardly in the middle of a stay.

HEELING

Objective: Your dog will walk on a loose leash despite any distractions.

When you put a dog on a leash, he is not able to make decisions for himself. He is attached to his handler no matter what the circumstance. If he finds a situation dangerous, he cannot flee. Sometimes his only option is to lunge and bark (and possibly bite!). A dog that pulls on his leash can injure his handler, causing broken bones, blackened eyes, and other bodily harm. He can also drag his handler into a busy street. When the dog pulls on his leash, the handler's only option is to pull back. Now opposition reflex is at play, and many times nobody goes anywhere! Teaching your dog to walk nicely on a leash will make it easy for you to take your dog anywhere, but your ability to walk your dog on a loose leash is also a safety issue and a critical life skill for your dog.

Teaching your dog to walk with you is a necessary skill for every dog that lives with humans—for the dog's sake and for the human's sake. The training starts with keeping your dog in position for one step. Reward your dog for staying in position at your side, using the hand closest to him.

Especially helpful when...

- Your dog sees a squirrel on the other side of the street and he starts to pull. You cue your dog to "Heel" to remind him to stay with you.

- Your reactive dog is at the vet's reception area filled with other dogs. The technician calls your dog's name and asks you to enter the exam room. With confidence, you can walk past all of the other dogs with your dog's attention on you.

How to teach the behavior:

1. Put on your dog's collar and leash.

    a. If your dog is an intense puller, a front-clip harness might work best.

    b. A head halter like a Gentle Leader can be effective as long as the dog is already comfortable with the fabric on his face.

    c. Use a leash that is easy on your hands, like one made of leather or fabric.

2. Keep the treats in the hand nearest your dog. For example, if you heel your dog on the left, you'll feed him with your left hand. Your other hand will hold the bunched-up leash (across your body) with the clicker pressed up against it.

3. With your dog by your side, take a step forward.

4. If your dog steps with you, click and feed your dog by your side. Be sure that you feed your dog close to your body.

5. Take another step and repeat Step 4.

6. Slowly increase the number of steps so that you reinforce the correct body position.

7. Start reinforcing your dog for every two steps, three steps, and so on.

8. As the behavior becomes more reliable, practice walking with your dog at different speeds and, separately, introduce distractions by walking outside, near other people, and near other dogs.

9. If your dog pulls away from you, stop all forward motion and start walking backward slowly. As the leash becomes loose, click and feed your dog for remaining close to your body. Repeat several times until you can start moving forward again successfully.

10. When you walk your dog daily, alternate between teaching your dog to heel and releasing him to explore and sniff. This is a winning combination!

Secrets to success:

• Heeling is one of the hardest exercises to teach dogs, especially youngsters! It is natural for them to be more interested in the environment than excited about walking with you. Be patient!

• Use extremely tasty treats that are easy to swallow. Make sure to take lots of reinforcers on your walk.

• Feed your dog either slightly behind you or right by your side. Dogs will gravitate to where they get primary reinforcement.

• Sometimes a harness that hugs the body (or a ThunderShirt) can help calm your dog and reduce his impulse to pull forward.

• For avid pullers, physically exercise your dog before taking him for a loose-leash walk.

• If you can, take your dog for a hike, clicking and feeding him while he is sauntering along smelling the leaves.

RECALL

Objective: Your dog will come to you promptly whenever you call him no matter what the circumstances.

A solid recall is one of the most important behaviors that you will ever teach your dog. The recall removes your dog from potentially challenging, even dangerous, situations and brings him directly to you. In addition to building a solid recall, you need to be able to get your hands on your dog if the situation requires it. Therefore, part of this training is teaching your dog that you will stick your hand in his collar when he arrives. In this way, you avoid having a dog that does "drive-bys" and then takes off again or that comes to you but then darts just out of reach when you try to grab his collar.

Especially helpful when…

- You want to call your dog back to you when he is playing with another dog.

- You are walking on the beach and you see some children playing in the sand. Afraid that your dog will greet them too exuberantly, you call your dog back to your side.

- You let your dog run loose in your fenced yard every morning. You need to be able to call your dog into the house quickly so that you can get to work on time.

How to teach the behavior:

Flying Fronts

1. Hold your clicker and treats in your hand.

2. Show your dog a treat and toss it a few feet from you.

3. As your dog runs to eat the treat, give your recall cue, and take a few steps back.

4. Click as your dog comes happily to you.

5. Ask your dog to sit.

6. Hold your dog's collar as you give your dog the treat.

7. Play this game again, and when your dog's behavior becomes more reliable, toss the treat farther and farther away.

8. Change the training environment, gradually increasing the distractions.

Traditional Obedience Recall

1. Hold your clicker and treats in your hand.

2. Ask your dog to sit and stay.

3. Walk a few feet away.

4. Turn and face your dog.

5. Call your dog.

6. As he starts to move toward you, click.

7. On his arrival, ask your dog to sit.

8.   Hold his collar with one hand and feed him multiple treats with the other.

9.   As your dog's behavior grows more reliable, start to increase the distance.

10. Work in different environments, gradually increasing the distraction level.

Ping-Pong Recalls

1.   Arm two or three friends and/or family members with clickers and treats. Everyone should use the same treats.

2.   One by one, take turns calling your dog using your recall cue.

3.   When your dog comes to the person who called, that person clicks, asks him to sit, and then gives him multiple treats while s/he places her/his other hand in the dog's collar.

4.   As your dog's behavior becomes more reliable, start to increase the distance between each person.

5.   Start inside, and gradually move outside, adding more distractions as your dog's recall becomes stronger.

Secrets to success:

• Always reinforce your dog when he comes to you regardless of whether or not you called.

• Never call your dog to you to punish him or do something unpleasant, to trim nails or to clean his ears, for example.

• Pay generously every time that your dog comes to you when called!

• You can vary the reinforcers. Favorite toys, treats, and petting work well here.

• If your dog's behavior is not reliable, then your dog cannot be off leash. Instead, attach your dog's collar to a long line (50 to 100 feet) so that you can reel your dog in any time that you need to.

• If your dog is out in your yard or in a field, only call your dog once. If he does not respond, secure him via the long line. As you are guiding him into the house or into your car, be sure that your shoulders are pointing forward as you walk. Refrain from facing your dog and trying to drag him with you or else the opposition reflex will set in and neither of you will move.

• If your dog's attention is elsewhere, call your dog's name, give your recall cue, and run in the opposite direction. When your dog follows you, have a treat party!

FOUR ON THE FLOOR:

Objective: No matter how arousing the situation, your dog keeps all of his feet on the floor when he is greeting people.

Over-exuberant greetings are one of the most common dog behavior problems. Knocking over Grandma or body-slamming the neighbor's three-year-old are not acceptable behaviors, even if they are sincere expressions of doggie love. If your dog gets excited when you or other family members (or visitors) come through the door, the solution is to teach your dog to keep all of his feet on the ground, no matter what.

Especially helpful when…

- You return from grocery shopping with your arms full and one ripped bag. Your dog is dancing with excitement but doesn't jump on you. You manage to get your bags to the counter and gratefully reward your dog with a game of tug.

- You are going to the theater with your neighbors. To exercise your dog before you leave, you played ball with him in the muddy backyard. You hear the doorbell ring, but you can't get to the door before your dog does. You grab some treats and find him sitting politely with his muddy paws squarely on the ground instead of planted on your visitors. You toss treats all over the floor.

How to teach the behavior:

1. Have your clicker and treats ready in a pocket during the day.

2. In situations where your dog might get excited, keep your body still as you click and feed him for keeping his four feet on the floor. It doesn't matter what position he's in.

3. Toss the treat far away from you.

4. After eating, he will start to head toward you; click and feed again.

5. Repeat two or three times per session.

6. Practice this behavior both standing up and sitting down.

7. Follow the same procedure when visitors come. The only difference is that you will have your dog on a leash. (You cannot give your dog the opportunity to jump on the guests.)

8. When your dog keeps his feet on the floor, click and drop the treat quietly at your feet.

9. If your dog is overly excited but manages to stay grounded, click and toss small pieces of crunchy dog bones on the floor. Feeding crunchy food will keep your dog's head

busier for a longer period and, as a result, will slow down the entire training process. Slower behavior equals calmer behavior.

Secrets to success:

- The more excited your dog is, the longer it should take him to eat his treats (and the louder your clicker should be as long as your dog is not afraid of the sound). You can either use crunchy dog treats or increase the number of soft treats that you scatter.

- If your dog likes to carry toys, this is another fabulous way to stop him from jumping. As people enter, hand him a toy so that he can "trophy" it around. Your visitors can give him attention and can pet him as he prances around with the toy.

- In greeting situations, it is hard for dogs, especially adolescents, to sit still. Refrain from using behaviors like sitting for petting or lying down on mats at doors until the behavior has been tested for reliability at that intensity. Most times that's not the case. Many dogs learn that if they jump up on someone, their handler will tell them to sit, and they will earn a click and treat. Jump–sit–click–treat is not the pattern of behavior that you want to reinforce.

STATION

Objective: Your dog goes to an indicated spot and lies there calmly until released.

The difference between a safe space and a station is that you use the station to manage your dog temporarily while you are doing a task. For example, while you are cooking dinner or doing homework with the children, your dog can be stationed on his mat with a Kong. This keeps your dog occupied while you are trying to concentrate. Having a dog that stations reliably helps avoid potential conflict; it is worth teaching as a default behavior.

You will teach your dog this behavior in two parts: 1) go to the mat and 2) stay there. According to the laws of learning, work on only one of these skills at a time. After your dog has mastered each skill, you will combine the two.

Especially helpful when...

- You're concerned that your dog may become possessive about food that your toddler drops on the floor. Before you give your child a snack, send your dog to a station while your child is eating—and give him an awesome treat for waiting at his station.

How to teach the behavior:

Step 1: Go to the Mat (adding duration at the end)

1. Decide what you will use for your dog's station. A mat, dog bed, or padded platform works fine. Have your clicker and treats ready.

2. Put down the object (mat, for example) that you're using as the station.

3. Click and feed your dog for looking at the mat. Be ready! Don't lose that first "What is that?" look from your dog. When you feed, toss the treat away from the mat to set up for the next repetition.

4. Continue to click and feed your dog for interacting with the mat. Click for one paw on, two paws on, and so on until all four feet are on the mat.

5. As you work on this exercise, work on distance by tossing the treat farther and farther away from the mat.

6. Next, start to extend the duration that your dog is standing on the mat.

7. Once your dog is running to the mat eagerly, insert a verbal cue right before he does so. Click and feed, still tossing your treat away from the mat.

8. Continue until this behavior starts to become reliable.

9. If you want to shape a down on the mat, wait for a sign that your dog is about to lie down. This could be his head dropping down, elbows bending, and so on. Or, if your dog already knows how to lie down on a verbal cue, you can cue that behavior.

10. When you are working on the down, click and feed your dog's head closer to the mat. This will keep your dog on the mat, and the down position might come easier.

11. Once your dog starts lying on the mat, slowly start withholding the click to extend his duration on the mat.

12. Start timing how long your dog can stay on his mat. Record data and proceed accordingly.

13. If your dog gets up before the time is up, simply escort him back to the mat. Do not give him a treat for returning.

14. At the end, click and feed your dog in the down position on the mat, feeding him between his front feet.

15. Release him from the mat.

Step 2: Stay on the Mat

1. Bring your dog to the mat and give your dog the Down cue. If your dog is unfamiliar with this cue, teach this behavior separately (see p. 43).

2. To extend duration, you can either give your dog a favorite chew toy or you can feed your dog for staying on the mat longer. Use a clicker rarely here because you want to keep your dog as quiet and calm as possible while practicing this exercise. Simply stay nearby and feed your dog for staying on the mat. As your dog becomes more comfortable, start predicting how long your dog can lie there without getting up. Review the data and set realistic expectations for your dog. When you are done, don't forget to release your dog.

A common misconception is that if your dog can lie down on his mat for a certain period of time, he will be able to do so during the highest levels of distraction, when people enter your home, for example. As you will see in later chapters, there are more effective ways to deal with overexcited or problematic reactions to visitors than stationing your dog on his mat.

FIND IT

Objective: On cue, your dog will look for treats that you have scattered in the grass or on the floor.

This exercise works well as an interrupter and is a lifesaver as a default behavior. It keeps your dog's head busy! If your dog is about to jump on a visitor at the door, scattering treats and telling your dog to "Find It" will change his focus from excitement to concentrated seeking.

Especially helpful when...

- Your dog likes people but is uncomfortable with them touching him. You are out on a walk and your neighbor reaches forward to touch his head. Afraid that your dog will react, you scatter treats and tell him to "Find It" so that he can quickly escape the precarious situation.

- A dog is off leash in the park and is now making his way toward you and your dog. Fearing that your dog will have a reaction, you walk your dog behind a stone wall and scatter treats, cueing your dog to "Find It." Your hope is that your dog's head will be busy and he will not notice the other dog moving in your direction.

How to teach the behavior:

1. Ask your dog to sit.
2. Take a handful of treats, show them to your dog, and scatter them on the ground.

3.   As you scatter the treats, cue your dog to "Find It."

4.   Wait until your dog eats all of the treats.

5.   Once he is done, release him verbally so that he knows that all of the treats are gone.

Secrets to success:

- Use food that your dog really loves! Crunchy food will keep his head busy longer.

- You can either ask your dog to stay as you scatter the treats or cue your dog to "Find It" as you are in the process of scattering them.

- If you need your dog's head busy longer, toss your dog's treats in the grass.

OBJECT EXCHANGE

Objective: On cue, your dog willingly releases an object he has in his mouth for a treat or other item of value

If you practice mutually beneficial object exchanges with your dog, your dog will always give you items willingly. Teaching your dog to exchange an object will encourage him to bring the object back to you when cued, so if your dog steals an object, it will be easy for you to get it back. He will learn that giving the object back is much more fun and rewarding than hiding under the couch with it. For dogs with aggressive tendencies, the benefit of object exchanges is that the dog will not consider a human a threat to whatever he possesses. He will begin to love having humans take things away from him because giving up an item predicts great rewards. Basic object exchanges are simple to teach.

Please note: If your dog is showing aggressive tendencies around food or objects, or you know you have an unpredictable resource-guarder, it's critical to teach him to nose target different objects (see p. 64) before teaching object exchanges. If at any point during this training you fear a serious confrontation, walk away.

Especially helpful when…

- Your Lab puppy has grabbed a sock from the laundry and is chewing intently. Fearing he may swallow it, you grab his favorite treats, crouch by him calmly, and toss the treats on the floor. He abandons the sock as he scarfs up the goodies.

- Your children's friends are playing with Barbie dolls when your young dog grabs a doll and hides under the coffee table. One of the children's friends is about to crawl under the table, and you're unsure of how your dog will react. Instead of panicking, you can just call your dog to you and exchange the doll for a big, tasty treat.

How to teach the behavior:

Basic Exchanges (also good for puppies)

1. If your dog has an object that you need him to forfeit, approach him quietly or call him to you.

2. Once you are with your dog, click and toss your dog a handful of wonderful treats higher in reinforcement value than what he has in his mouth. (You can also toss the treats away from you and the object.)

3. As your dog eats the treats, see if you can pick up the object.

4. If you are successful, click again and say, "Thank you," tossing another handful of treats away from the object.

5. If you can, give the object back to your dog and repeat the exercise.

Formal Object Exchanges

1. Make sure your dog is hungry before starting an object-exchange training session. Give your dog a low-value item. If you are not sure whether you will be able to take it away, hold the other end of it.

2. Give a verbal cue like "Give" or "Thank You."

3. Take the item out of his mouth. If he is reluctant to release the object, try placing a treat on his nose, trading with another similar object (one tennis ball for another tennis ball), or showing him the treat first to see if he will relinquish the object then.

4. Click. For his compliance, give him a treat of higher value than the object you are practicing with.

5. Give the object back and repeat these steps a few times.

6. If at any time your dog drops the item himself, anticipating the treat, insert the word "Drop" as he does so, clicking and treating the action.

7. On the last exchange, after giving your dog the treat, alternate between walking away with the object (you can reduce any anxiety your dog may have by showing him where you are stashing it) and giving him the object and leaving (assuming that it is safe for your dog to keep it). Your dog learns that sometimes he gets to keep the object and sometimes he doesn't. Aim to leave the item with your dog for half the repetitions.

Secrets to success:

- Never chase your dog into a tight space (for example, under a piece of furniture) or grab him by the collar to get the object back. Doing so can greatly increase the risk of being bitten.

- Capture the behavior by clicking your dog when he drops an object. If you can do so repetitively, assign a verbal cue like "Drop" to the behavior.

- When you are working on this behavior, keep any other items that your dog would consider valuable off the floor.

- The treat that you are using has to be of greater value than the object you want him to give up.

- Work four to five days with one object before moving to one of higher value.

- Move to the next level only after your dog has mastered the previous level. If your dog shows any signs of aggression, it means that you went too far, too fast. Go back to the previous successful level.

- If you do not feel comfortable approaching your dog when he has an object, simply walk away and ignore your dog. Your safety is always paramount, regardless of what object your dog has. If you walk away from him, his ploy to get you to chase him to get the object back has failed.

EXCUSE ME!

Objective: Your dog readily yields space to someone approaching him.

If you can teach your dog to move (either responding to a verbal cue or to someone simply approaching him), you can avoid tripping over him, his blocking your way, or possible territorial encounters (such as your dog hogging the couch and growling if you try to drag him off).

Especially helpful when…

- Your 80-year-old mother is living with you after a long illness. Now she is well enough to get up to make herself something to eat. Your dog is in the doorway. Even without a verbal cue, your dog sees her coming and promptly gets out of her way.

How to teach the behavior:

1. You are in the kitchen about to get a drink of water. Your dog is lying in front of the sink.

2. Show your dog a treat and toss it in the direction opposite the sink. (Make sure that you use a treat that your dog can see against the color of the floor.)

3. As he starts to get up to eat the treat, click. (That treat can be the reinforcement for that click.)

4. After your dog is done eating the treat, click again, and toss a treat a little farther than the first. Now party! Good boy!

Secrets to success:

• Practice this game until your dog starts to move when he sees you (or others) coming.

• You can insert a verbal cue like "Excuse Me!" and toss lots of treats as your dog relinquishes space.

HANDLING

Objective: Your dog remains relaxed and comfortable whenever you handle any part of his body.

You do not need to use the clicker during the exercise below. If you have already conditioned your dog to station on his mat (see p. 52), then you can play this game there as well. It often helps to start this exercise when your dog is in a relaxed, even sleepy, state. Eventually work this exercise in various body positions: sit, down, and stand. There will be times when you will need to medicate your dog, and it will not be a fun experience for either of you. If you work on the exercise described above, however, the experience will be so much less traumatic!

Especially helpful when...

• On a walk, your dog starts limping. He lets you examine his front foot and you find a burr between his pads. Problem solved.

How to teach the behavior:

1. Starting with your dog in a down or a sit, touch an area of his body where he is least sensitive. For example, if he loves it when you touch his ears, start there.

2. Stroke the ear once.

3. Give him a treat.

4. Stroke again.

5. Give him a treat.

6. Flip his ear over.

7. Give him a treat.

8. Next, pretend that you are looking inside his ear.

9. Give him a treat.

10. Continue in this manner until you have explored all parts of that one ear.

11. End the session and play a favorite game with your dog. It should not take any longer than 1–2 minutes. Explore only one body part per session.

12. As your dog starts to understand this game, you can add verbal cues like, "Touching Ear" right before you actually touch. Say these words in a soft, gentle tone. As you continue, assign a verbal cue for all of his body parts. We want him to love it when you touch different body parts!

Secrets to success:

- When you get to body parts that your dog is uncomfortable with, only touch and feed your dog a few times.

- If your dog visibly shrinks when you reach out your hand, do not continue to touch your dog. Instead, hold out your hand near that area without touching and feed. Continue touching the air around him until he visibly relaxes. Once this happens, you can proceed as above.

The Pros and Cons of Eye Contact

You want mutual eye contact when you are teaching your dog. But what if you break eye contact when you are talking to a neighbor or looking at a scoreboard? If you look at your dog every time you work with him, your eye contact becomes one of the cues that holds the behavior together. This link between your eye contact and his performance can be problematic when you are working with a reactive dog.

Your reactive dog must know that, no matter what else you are doing, you are still connected. It is his job to maintain the cued behavior. For example, my student Molly had a dog, Bruno, that was super-sensitive to people in motion. She called me after Bruno grabbed the glove of a jogger when they were out for their daily walk. Luckily, Bruno didn't injure the jogger, but the incident scared Molly.

Molly and I worked on teaching Bruno the Click to Calm methodology: when you see a jogger look at your caregiver. Everything went well until a few months later. Molly emailed me to say that on their walk Bruno had lunged after another jogger. She couldn't understand why since everything had been going so well. On further questioning, Molly told me that while she was walking Bruno, a neighbor had pulled up in his truck and they had had a brief conversation. She cued Bruno to sit while they talked. A few minutes later, a jogger rounded the corner and Bruno started to lunge and bark. It was all she could do to hold him back on his leash.

I asked Molly where her eyes were when she was talking to her neighbor. Of course, they were on her neighbor. If Molly always watches Bruno as he sits, her eye contact is a cue just as much as the verbal cue for sit. When she turns her head away, Bruno interprets it as a cue that releases him from sitting. And, when Bruno is released, he is more apt to react to the jogger.

I asked Molly to do an experiment. Set up a distraction (in this case, a dancing bunny) and cue Bruno to sit. Keep your eyes on him. That went fine. Next, I asked Molly to set up the same distraction and ask Bruno to sit while Molly was looking at something else. Bruno sat for a few seconds but then started scanning the room, his eyes resting on the dancing bunny as he started to pull toward it. The only conclusion is that when Molly wasn't watching, that cue for the behavior was missing, and the behavior started to fall apart.

Every environment provides certain cues that get "roped into" the known cues we give our dogs. After I teach my dog a recall in my living room and he comes to sit in front of me beautifully every time, I may discover that, when I take the behavior elsewhere, he no longer sits straight in front of me. Confused, I go back to my living room and realize that, in my dog's mind, he is not sitting straight in front of me, he is lining up with the picture that is hanging behind my head. That picture is a "contextual" cue. It exists in that context and is, as far as I am concerned, completely irrelevant to my dog's performance. However, he thinks otherwise.

Similarly, the reason obedience dogs get "ring-wise" (and may underperform at a trial) is that they figure out that in the show-ring environment with its specific set of cues, they don't receive the reinforcement they might get at home or at their normal training class. What other cues are there? The judge, the trial crew, the ring gates, other people waiting around for their turns—and part of it could even be the handler's own nervousness. It pays to be aware of the cues that come with an activity or setting, cues that might affect your dog's performance.

EYE CONTACT NO MATTER WHAT

Objective: Your dog offers you eye contact as he responds to a cue even if you are distracted and looking elsewhere.

Although we tend to have one designated cue for each behavior, we are cueing our dogs inadvertently all the time with other cues: eye contact is one of them. As a caregiver, you have to be sure that your dog's behavior is reliable, even when you are not looking at him. What if you have a reactive dog and you are checking into a hotel? Or you are in a line at a pet store? Or any place where your attention is going to be focused elsewhere rather than on your dog? Without the reliability of having your dog's attention in a public setting, these situations could end badly. It's a worthwhile investment to teach your dog to be able to respond to cues without your full attention.

In the following exercise, all you care about is that:

1. Your dog is offering you eye contact regardless of whether you are paying attention to him.

2. Your dog does the cued behavior (indicating that he can respond to the cue even when you aren't looking at him).

How to teach the behavior:

1. Pick a behavior that is easy for your dog to do. Try a Sit.

2. Cue your dog to Sit.

3. Fix your eyes on an object in front of you, like a clock on the wall. Make sure that you can still see your dog's head in your peripheral vision. Adjust the height of your eyes accordingly.

4. As long as your dog keeps sitting, feed him 10 treats while you are looking at the object in front of you. Don't look down! (This is harder than it sounds!)

If your dog can maintain eye contact and perform a cued behavior even if you are distracted and not looking at him, that skill is a form of insurance that your dog will perform cued behaviors even in stressful situations.

5. Once you have fed 10 treats, look down and release your dog.

6. Cue your dog to sit again and repeat Steps 3–5.

Secrets to success:

• When your dog is responding to the cue, make sure that you can still see his head in soft focus.

- Start with simply feeding your dog (just so you can get used to feeding your dog without looking at him). Once you've got the feeding down, then move to clicking and feeding your dog for maintaining eye contact and the correct behavior.

- Work on this exercise for all of your dog's most common behaviors, including sits, downs, heeling, and recalls.

As your dog becomes more reliable about maintaining eye contact and responding to cues without you looking at him, take the exercise on the road, for example, by talking to people while your dog is maintaining a behavior.

If you have a reactive dog, whether he's a people-shy puppy, an overly exuberant adolescent, or a conflicted rescue dog, you need these basic behaviors before you move on with your training. You also need a set of maneuvers, practiced so well that you could do them in your sleep, that can help you and your dog get out of sticky or risky situations. These are what I call "Emergency Behaviors," detailed in the next chapter. Emergency behaviors should be as much a part of laying the groundwork for teaching your dog how to cope with life as the "Basics."

7
Teaching Emergency Behaviors

When you are training any dog, you must be able to control the environment as much as you can, particularly if you have a reactive, fearful, or aggressive dog. Dogs, as well as people, like predictability. We all like to know what to expect when we are dealing with a certain set of circumstances. But what about those times when circumstances change in an instant? What do you do? Where do you go? Are you, the handler, thinking clearly at that very moment? Or are you simply reacting in fear? What information will your dog learn from situations like this? Can he trust you? Probably not!

Consider Beth as an example. She is walking her dog-sensitive dog in the city square. So far, the walk has been pleasantly uneventful. Her dog has passed numerous dogs without so much as a growl in their direction. As they turn the corner, a woman with a Sheltie suddenly appears. Beth hurriedly pulls up on her leash as her dog starts to lunge and growl. The Sheltie reacts as well. The women are almost bumping into each other as they try desperately to move past each other.

What could Beth have done differently? If Beth had exposed her dog to numerous novel stimuli in her training sessions, maybe her dog wouldn't have reacted as strongly. Her dog would have been familiar with unexpected changes in the environment. That preparation would have been ideal. But maybe Beth is not that far along in training her dog to deal with sudden encounters with other dogs. If Beth had trained the "Let's Go" cue, she and her dog could have moved in the opposite direction, away from the reaction unfolding in front of them. Or maybe a well-trained "Get Behind" cue—Beth signaling her dog to move behind her—could have worked. Beth's dog could have hidden behind her, shielded by her body, until she released him. Whatever "emergency cue" Beth used would likely have improved the outcome of the unplanned encounter.

The behaviors described in this chapter are ones that you can rely on in emergency situations such as the one described above. I've grouped them according to their function. Read through this chapter and pick a few of these behaviors to teach your dog. Teach them slowly and thoroughly. These behaviors need to be solid and reliable for both of you in order for them to work in an emergency situation, because, just like you, your dog will tend to react emotionally rather than rationally. The more solid these behaviors are, the more relaxed and confident you'll be as you move through life with your dog, and your dog will pick up on your mood.

Bolstering Courage

GO TOUCH

Objective: On cue, your dog will move away from you to touch a designated object with his nose.

For dogs that are afraid of certain objects, it helps to teach them how to approach (and touch) those objects confidently. If necessary, first review training the Hand Target (see p. 40). Note that the "Go Touch" behavior differs from "Touch" in that the handler is sending the dog away from her to touch an object rather than simply cueing the dog to touch her hand.

Especially helpful when...

- A package arrives. Your dog sees it on the chair and starts barking at it. He wants to investigate but his curiosity fights with his fear: For each step forward he takes, he takes two steps back. You can cue him to "Go Touch" and accompany him as you've practiced. By giving him your hand cue, he can focus on touching the box with much more confidence. After he makes contact, he relaxes and resumes his earlier activities.

- You are walking in the neighborhood and your dog sees a garden flag flapping in the wind. On leash, he starts dragging you toward the object. To gain control, you tell him to "Go Touch," and he slows down to a cautious and curious pace as he investigates the flag.

How to teach the behavior:

1. Extend your index finger.
2. Click and feed your dog every time he touches it with his nose.
3. Insert a verbal cue like "Touch." (Although you used the same verbal cue for touching your palm, your dog should know by the body part presented what he is expected to touch.)
4. When this targeting behavior becomes reliable, place your finger on, or close to, an object such as a chair. Start with a neutral object.
5. Ask him to "Touch."

6.   Click him for any approximation of touching your finger or the object itself.

7.   Toss the treat in the opposite direction from the object. You are reinforcing the release of spatial pressure by teaching your dog to move away from the object after touching it. Tossing the treat away from the object builds the drive to want to approach it again.

8.   As your dog becomes more comfortable getting close to the object, start clicking him only for touching the object—not your finger—and then toss the treat away from the object.

9.   With success, start inserting a verbal cue like "Go Touch."

10. As this behavior becomes more reliable, send your dog to touch different objects, building up to those he is more concerned about.

You can transfer the Hand Target to an object and build up to sending your dog to an object to touch. This is a fine way to get a cautious dog to interact with objects he's not sure about so he'll feel more comfortable.

Secrets to success:

• Work this behavior in short sessions. Two to three minutes are plenty!

• Never force your dog to touch an object that he is desperately afraid of.

• Be sure to capture any approximation that your dog will volunteer even if it is only looking at the object from a distance.

• After the click, make sure to toss the treat away from the object.

• Work first with items that your dog is familiar with. After he understands the game, you can start using more challenging objects.

HAND-TARGET GREETING

Objective: When you cue "Go Say Hi," your dog touches the hand of a stranger in a courteous greeting.

When the Hand Target becomes reliable, you can start to teach your dog to touch the hands of family members and, eventually, use the target cue as a greeting cue when your dog meets strangers. If necessary, first review training the Hand Target (see p. 40).

Especially helpful when...

- You are walking in the park with your people-shy golden retriever and meet an admirer who would like to say Hi. You cue your dog to "Go Say Hi." This is your dog's cue to touch the hand of the stranger politely.

Once your dog's Hand Target is solid, you can ask him to touch other people's hands, including those of strangers. This is an excellent way for your dog to politely "greet" people he may be fearful of or that he might bowl over.

How to teach the behavior:

1. Ask a family member to hold out her hand and give your dog the cue to touch the hand that is presented to him.

2. Click as your dog touches that hand, back up, and give your dog his treats. If you have already practiced the "Back Up–Sit" behavior, your dog should turn to face you automatically. Backing up lets your dog release himself from the spatial pressure.

3. As you continue to practice this behavior, insert a verbal cue right before your dog touches the hand of the other person. "Go Say Hi!" works nicely.

4. Practice this behavior with family members first before cueing it with strangers.

Secret to success:

- You want your dog to return to you after each interaction. If you decide that it is safe for your dog to hang out with the other person, you can always release your dog to do so.

BACK UP FROM HANDLER

Objective: Cued by an outstretched hand, your dog backs up, from you or from anybody else.

If you have a people-sensitive dog, you can teach him that a hand reaching out for him is a cue to back away. For a fearful dog that might lunge, this cue can keep everyone safer. For a fearful dog that might flee, the hand cue "normalizes" a scary situation by giving him a clear way to respond that removes the pressure. As needed, you can add a recall or down–stay to the Back-Up cue. This exercise starts like Leave It, but here you are focused on getting your dog to back up rather than avoid something attractive.

Especially helpful when...

- You have visitors staying for the weekend. Although you have advised your company to ignore your dog, they decide to try and pet him while you are in the kitchen. Coming out with refreshments, you notice that your dog is lying down at the far end of the room. Observing your dog's behavior, you are quite sure that you know what happened. One of your visitors approached him with an outstretched hand, and he backed off to the other end of the room. Sigh.

- You are out walking your dog and a stranger reaches out to pet him. Instead of lunging forward, your dog backs up and waits for further instruction.

How to teach the behavior:

1. Place a treat in your hand and make a fist. Make sure that your dog sees the treat.
2. Allow your dog to lick and paw at your hand.
3. When your dog stops trying to get the treat, click and feed your dog by allowing him to eat it out of your hand.
4. Produce another treat and repeat the exercise above.
5. This time, instead of clicking your dog for simply stopping to nudge, wait until he starts moving away from your hand.
6. Click as your dog takes a step back.
7. Open your fist and let him come forward to eat the treat so that you can reset him for the next repetition.
8. Repeat the behavior above.

9. As you continue, gradually increase the number of steps your dog takes away from your fist. Now when you click, start tossing the treat behind your dog at a distance to reinforce him for backing off and to encourage him to move farther away. Vary the treat placement.

10. When you reach the desired distance, change the cue from presenting your fist to a verbal cue like "Back Up." Say the new cue "Back Up," pause, then present your fist. Click and feed your dog for backing up. Gradually fade the old cue.

11. Once the back-up behavior is on the verbal cue, you can also add the cue of an outstretched arm in a "scram" motion, arm straight in front, palm down, but flicking your hand up. Follow the same formula as above to add this nonverbal cue.

Secrets to success:

- Teach your dog this behavior and then practice it with family members and friends first before cueing it with strangers.

- Although changing the cue seems repetitive, it is easier to move from a verbal cue to an outstretched arm.

- If your dog already knows how to back up, simply change the verbal cue to a gestural cue.

- Make sure you click as your dog is taking a step back (not after he completes the movement!).

- Vary the distance your dog backs up before you click. He should be able to take a few steps back as well as back up across a room.

Tempering Exuberance

WALK–LIE DOWN

Objective: On cue, your dog reliably transitions between heeling and lying down and back to heeling.

If you want to slow down your dog's approach to a person or another dog, teach him the Walk–Lie Down exercise. This exercise offers options for controlling his pace and body posture as you walk and lets you halt if you need to. That means that you can stop forward movement at any point if something in the environment should suddenly change. If on a walk you have a dog that lies down and refuses to budge, this cue solves the problem. When you have both moving (heeling) and not moving (sitting, standing, lying down) on cue, sit-down "strikes" will become a thing of the past.

Especially helpful when...

- When he first meets a child, your adolescent dog loves to throw himself on top of the child. To slow down the initial approach, you cue him to walk with you slowly and either sit or lie down so he is calmer by the time he reaches your little niece.

- You have a Great Pyrenees that loves to go for walks. Occasionally, however, he lies down and refuses to get up (and it always seems to happen in the busiest of places!). Cueing him to "Heel" from a down position gives you a way to jump-start him without having to drag him.

How to teach the behavior:

1. Cue your dog to walk by your side. Although you should teach him to walk on either side of your body eventually, start with the side that you usually walk him on.

2. Take 5–10 steps.

3. Stop forward movement.

4. Cue your dog to Lie Down. Lure him into the down position if needed. Take your time.

5. Click as his elbows hit the ground.

6. Deliver the treat between his front paws.

7. Count to 5 or 10.

8. Now cue your dog to heel with you again.

9. Click your dog for moving with you and feed him close to your side.

10. Repeat the instructions above until your dog is lying down quickly and reliably and moving forward briskly when cued to do so.

Secrets to success:

- Be sure to feed your dog the treat between his two front feet. It will help anchor him in place in the down.

- If you want your dog to sit or stand instead, follow the same instructions as above, substituting the body position that you want instead of the down. (Use a body position that your dog already knows. If he does not know the behavior, teach it separately, and then insert it back into this training equation.) Reward in position.

For practice, ask your dog to Walk–Lie Down as you move toward a high-distraction item like a treat on a plate or a remote-controlled toy. If your dog can't manage these distractions, chances are he will not be able to do so with another dog or a person.

By teaching your dog to drop into a down from a walk and to readily resume walking again, you can both modulate an over-exuberant approach to a person or another dog or get a reluctant dog moving again. Here a dog approaches another dog, showing self-control in a down (at top), and keeps his focus on his handler as he nears the dog, quickly greets him, and turns away on recall (left).

RECALL–BACK UP

Objective: On cue, your dog will stop and back up as he is barreling toward you on a recall.

This two-cue behavior solves the problem if you have an adolescent dog that uses you as a springboard when he comes to you on recall. The Back Up cue acts as a brake as he comes barreling toward you. Once he's slowed, you can re-cue the recall at a more measured pace. Do not work on this exercise until your dog has the Sit–Stay, Recall, and Back Up behaviors (see pp. 44, 48, and 67) on verbal cues reliably. Work on one piece of the behavior at a time. Note that Option 1 teaches your dog to stop and back up; Option 2 only teaches your dog to stop. If your dog knocks you over on recalls, teach this behavior as a default.

Especially helpful when...

- You call your dog from a distance and he runs straight at you. Instead of getting bowled over, you cue your dog to "Back Up" right before he ploughs into you. Once he's backed off, you can call him in from a shorter distance for a beautiful, calmer sit in front.

How to teach the behavior (Option 1):

1. Ask your dog to sit and stay.

2. Take several steps away from your dog.

3. Call your dog to you.

4. As your dog is coming closer, cue your dog to "Back Up."

5. As your dog starts to slow, click and toss the treat behind him. As your dog remains in that same position, click and toss treats behind him a few more times to reinforce him maintaining that distance away from you.

6. Repeat Steps 1–5 but start to click your dog for actually stopping. Click and toss the treat behind your dog.

7. Repeat Steps 1–4, clicking and treating your dog if he stops and makes any attempt to back up.

8. Once your dog begins to stop and back up away from you, click, toss the treat behind him, and then call him to sit in front of you.

9. Hold his collar with one hand and feed him the treat with the other. You don't need to click.

10. Practice the completed behavior until it is reliable.

How to teach the behavior (Option 2):

1. Call your dog and, when he has come about halfway to you, click and toss a bunch of treats where you want him to stop.

2. When he is done eating, click and toss more treats at that critical distance. End the session there.

3. In your next session, repeat the instructions above but, after your dog finishes eating the treats, call him to you.

4. Put one hand in his collar and then feed him a treat for coming. As your dog's response becomes more reliable, insert a verbal cue (like "Easy") right before you toss the treats.

Secrets to success:

- The hardest part of this exercise is for the dog to stop and back up away from you. Practice this piece often. It will be the first to deteriorate. (Option 1)

- When you are reinforcing, be sure to toss the treat behind the dog. (Option 1)

If backing up is difficult, eliminate it. The most important part of this exercise is to stop the dog's forward motion before he reaches you.

Hiding Your Dog

GET BEHIND

Objective: On cue, your dog will move behind you and remain there until released.

If a situation challenges your dog, you can cue him to get behind you and wait for a cue to be released. You are using your body as a barrier to shield your dog and keep him safe from unwanted encounters, such as with loose dogs. The Get Behind cue also enables you to safely check what's on the other side of a door before crossing the threshold.

Especially helpful when...

- You are walking in the woods and see an off-leash dog whose handler is on his cell phone. Cueing your dog to get behind you, you signal to the other person to call his dog back. A potential confrontation averted!

- You are walking in the neighborhood and a five-year-old starts running toward your dog. Since your dog is scared of children, you cue your dog to get behind you. Now you can explain to the child, and her mother, why it is important to approach a dog calmly.

- An off-leash dog is running toward your dog. There is no caregiver in sight. You cue your dog to get behind you and then whip out a deterrent spray to ward off the other dog.

How to teach the behavior...

1. Stand up, move your dog behind your back, and feed him at the middle of your back. Work to make your dog happy about being behind your back before moving on to the next step.

    a. If you have a small dog, you can put him on a table and step in front, feeding him behind your back. Or you can feed him from the floor with a spatula or a target stick of some kind.

2. Once your dog likes being behind you, use a hand target to guide him into this position.

3. As your dog's behavior becomes more reliable, insert a verbal cue right before moving your dog.

You can use your body as a barrier between your dog and the world. To start, you first have to train a dog that is used to facing you to be comfortable behind your back.

4. Gradually extend the time that your dog stays behind you.

If you have a reactive dog, you can use your Get Behind cue at doorways to place him behind you as you peek out to see if there's a trigger on the other side of the doorway.

Secrets to success:

- Because your dog rarely gets reinforced behind you, first allow him to become comfortable being in this space. The easiest way to do this is to treat him behind your back. Dogs go where they are being fed!

- Your dog can assume the position of your choice once he is behind your back. Sits and stands are usually the most common positions.

- Work the stay behavior behind your back for just as long as any other duration behavior.

- Because of the difference in context, you cannot assume that your dog can stay behind you as long as he can in front of, or beside, you.

UP AGAINST THE WALL

Objective: In a social situation, your reactive dog is comfortable when you sandwich him between your back and another object to keep him safe and unreactive to what's happening in front of you.

Sometimes it is critically important to be able to run and hide your dog behind something like a car or a rock. For this tactic to work, however, you will need to train your dog to be comfortable right next to a variety of objects.

Especially helpful when...

- You are in an agility class and a dog gets the "zoomies." Fearing that your dog will react, you place your dog behind you up against a wall and feed him treats for staying in place while the runaway dog is caught. Everyone remains calm.

Similar to the Get Behind cue, the Up Against the Wall cue lets you barricade your dog to protect him from a trigger you are about to encounter. He will be sandwiched between you and something like a wall. The trick to training this behavior is slowly moving your dog closer to whatever object you choose.

How to teach the behavior:

1. Position your dog up against a wall or another barrier. Cue your dog to get into heel position and stand beside him, with him between you and the wall.

2. See how close you can get to the object without your dog becoming tense.

3. Before he tenses, click and feed your dog in heel position.

4. In the next session, see if you can get even closer to the object.

5. Repeat Step 3.

6. Continue until your dog feels comfortable being right up against the object.

7. Once your dog is secure, cue your dog to stay, then turn around and face the environment for one second.

8. Click.

9. Turn back to your dog and give him a treat.

   a. If your dog moves when you turn in the opposite direction, turn your body gradually until you can face away from him.

   b. Work on your body position and the duration of the stay separately.

10. Slowly extend the time that your dog can stay behind you while you watch the environment.

Secrets to success:

• Teach your dog to get close to as many different types of objects (trees, cars, desks) as possible.

• Your goal is to have your dog stay behind you while you offer to improve the situation. For example, if a dog is running off leash in a class, you can stabilize your dog against the wall or a barrier while you toss treats into the middle of the floor, hoping that they will catch the runaway dog.

• Work on each part of this behavior separately.

• If eye contact is a factor, refer to "The Pros and Cons of Eye Contact" (see p. 59).

Dealing with Unleashed Dogs

If you are out walking in public with your dog-sensitive dog, you never want an un-leashed dog to approach him. No matter how hard you try to prevent these encounters, however, they will still happen. Do the best that you can to protect your dog from an unwelcome advance, but, if it happens, take these steps:

1. Look for a barrier that you can place your dog behind. Lead your dog behind a tree, trash can, or a parked car—anything that will separate the two dogs.

2. If you have a handful of treats, try throwing them at the other dog's nose. You can hope that the other dog will be hungry and will start foraging for your treats on the ground while you and your dog slowly make your getaway.

3. If you know there are no barriers on your walk, bring one with you. For example, you can quickly deploy a push-button umbrella that you and your dog can hide behind as you quietly move away. Be sure to desensitize your dog to opening the umbrella before you use it.

Exiting Gracefully

EMERGENCY RECALL CUE

Objective: On cue, your dog comes to you no matter what the circumstance, even if he's highly aroused or mesmerized by some distraction.

This is a fail-safe recall cue that you can use when your normal recall cue fails because the distraction is too high.

Especially helpful when...

- Your dog sneaks out the front door and dashes off to say "Hi" to the men at the construction site as the bulldozer is backing up. You scream, "Pugsy, come!" but get no response. Starting to panic, you yell out your emergency recall cue, "Look!" Your dog turns on a dime and returns to you. Whew!

- Your dog is in the middle of an aggressive explosion. Not knowing what to do, you say "Look!" loudly, and your dog stops and turns to look at you. Click! You are able to redirect him with another cue.

How to teach the behavior:

1. Pick a word or audible signal that your dog has never heard before and that you will reserve only for this use.

2. Choose a high-value treat that your dog never receives unless he hears this word or sound.

3. Give your signal and feed your dog. You are not working on an actual recall. You are simply conditioning the signal by pairing it with the special treat.

4. Walk away.

5. Repeat 10 times a day.

6. After two weeks, test the cue when your dog is elsewhere in the house.

7. Note the response.

a. If he comes enthusiastically, have a treat party!

b. If he doesn't, continue creating the association.

8. Continue to condition this word until you are satisfied with the response.

9. For maintenance, feed quick responses to the signal 5–6 times per week. When your dog's behavior is reliable, you can vary the reinforcement, but always make it something special.

Secrets to success:

• Be sure that you give the signal only once and then feed.

• Use a treat that is incredibly reinforcing, like something stinky and yummy!

• First test the signal in a low-distraction area (like your home) and gradually build to higher distraction areas (like the park).

• Any time your dog is running to you, it is fine to capture the behavior by slipping in your cue. Just be sure to reinforce exuberantly!

LET'S GO

Objective: When you are walking your dog in a social setting, on cue he will abruptly turn with you and move in the opposite direction to avoid a potentially challenging situation.

You should always have the option of simply turning away from whatever frightens or riles up your dog. He should follow you calmly in the opposite direction whether you are walking slowly or bolting away from a potentially dangerous situation. If you notice something up ahead that you fear will arouse, scare, or otherwise trigger your dog, this exercise will train your dog to wheel around 180° with you and leave the situation calmly and safely. Having this option will make you feel more confident, and that will make your dog more relaxed. This exercise may become one of his favorite games. He'll learn to read your sudden decision to reverse course (a handler stress cue) as an invitation to play.

Especially helpful when…

• You are walking your dog on a city street. Up ahead you see a woman whose dog is dragging her in your direction. Anticipating a problem, you head off in the other direction.

• You are heading toward the agility ring and notice a nearby competitor playing a vigorous tug game with her dog. Knowing that your dog might react, you spin around and increase your distance until you enter the queue.

How to teach the behavior:

1. Cue your dog to walk by your side on leash.

2. Do an about face. Turn and walk in the opposite direction.

3. Feed your dog as you are making the turn. This piece is important because most dogs will swing wide as they make the turn. If you reinforce close to your body while making the turn, your dog will stay nice and close.

4. Feed your dog by your side as you move forward.

5. Repeat, gradually increasing both the speed of the turn and your pace as you move away.

6. Practice in different environments, making a game of it. Give your cue in a light and happy voice!

Secrets to success:

*   Feed your dog close by your side.

*   Heighten the distraction by turning away from a toy or a treat on a plate.

*   Use the verbal cue that you would typically use if you were on a walk with your dog. If your inclination is to say something like "Holy Moly!" then use that as your verbal cue.

*   Be sure that you move away with your dog only when it is safe to do so.

COME QUICK!

Objective: On cue, your dog will move with you quickly past another dog—before he reacts to the trigger.

Especially helpful when...

*   You are training your dog outdoors when suddenly you look up to find that there is another dog and handler walking directly toward you. Trying not to panic, you stick a treat on your dog's nose and tell him to "Come Quick!" as you run with him to the opposite side of the road. Knowing that this is a fun game that you've played with him in the past, your dog runs beside you exuberantly, ignoring the other dog completely.

How to teach the behavior:

1. Start with your dog sitting in heel position.

2. Take a treat and put it squarely on your dog's nose and keep it there. Use the hand that's closest to your dog (left hand if the dog is on your left).

3. Give the verbal cue "Come Quick!" as you run forward with your dog.

4. After running a few steps, give your dog the treat that you're still holding on his nose.

5. With practice, start extending the number of steps that you run forward with your dog.

6. Be sure to practice this behavior in a variety of locations.

Secrets to success:

- If your dog has trouble running forward or you have trouble keeping the treat on his nose, take a few slower steps and then break into a run or trot. Go at the speed that is comfortable for both of you.

- Make sure you keep the treat on or close to your dog's nose as you are moving.

- Practice this exercise with your dog both on your left and on your right side.

CLICK A TIGHT LEASH

Objective: Any tightening of the leash is a cue for your dog to turn toward you and come in closer to you.

Walking a dog on a tight leash is a sure way to increase a dog's reactivity. No matter how many times you are told to loosen the leash, it is hard to do with a reactive dog when you yourself are tense. If you find it impossible to relax your grip on the leash, teach your dog to move into your leash when you tighten it. He will read your tightening of the leash as a cue to look at you calmly and await further instructions rather than as a cue of an impending bad encounter of some sort.

Especially helpful when…

- You are walking your dog and you see someone with a dog walking toward you. Immediately, you panic and tighten your leash. In the past, your dog would also have tensed up, knowing full well that when the leash tightens, it means that another dog is coming. Instead of playing out this familiar scenario, however, your dog relaxes into the tight leash and moves closer to you. You relax, knowing that your dog is within your reach and not about to lunge.

How to teach the behavior:

1. Have your dog in his collar and on leash.

2. Allow your dog to go to the end of the leash.

3. Take a tiny step back so the leash goes taut.

4. Your dog will likely turn toward you. When he does, click as the leash loosens.

5. Feed your dog close to your body.

6. Gradually increase your tension on the leash.

7. Practice this behavior both stationary (standing still) and moving (stepping back).

8. When your dog turns toward you consistently when you pull up tightly on the leash, start training in a variety of distracting environments to build up your, and your dog's, confidence.

Secrets to success:

• Always click as your dog loosens the leash!

• Notice and reinforce tiny increments as your dog releases the pressure.

• If at any time your dog seems anxious, stop the exercise and go back to the previous level of success.

LEAVE IT

Objective: Your dog leaves some object you wish he wouldn't interact with.

Using this behavior, you can prevent your dog from taking something that he shouldn't have.

Especially helpful when...

• You are out walking with your dog and you spot a chicken bone. As you come closer, you tell your dog to "Leave It' and he is able to walk by it safely.

• You are taking your medication late at night. Fumbling, you open the child-proof cap and a few of the pills fall to the floor. Your dog, hoping to get an extra treat, comes running to see what he can scoop up. Frightened that he might eat one of the pills, you tell him to "Leave It!"

• Your possessive, aggressive dog has just spotted a new toy that you purchased for your daughter. To prevent a confrontation, you tell him to "Leave It" so that you can secure it.

How to teach the behavior:

1. Work with your dog in a quiet room without distractions.

2. Place an enticing treat in your hand and make a fist.

3. Present your fist for your dog to sniff.

4. Click and treat your dog for backing away from your hand. If your dog sniffs and nudges your hand, ignore the behavior. When he stops sniffing and moves his head away, click and open your hand so that your dog can eat the treat.

5. Repeat the previous steps several times until your dog no longer sniffs your hand and immediately backs away.

6. Once your dog performs Step 5 reliably, attach the verbal cue "Leave It" before he moves away.

7. Put a treat on the floor. Make sure your dog knows it's there.

8. Stand close to the treat, with your foot ready to cover it should your dog decide to take it on his own. Wait.

9. If your dog moves toward the treat, lightly cover it with your foot so that it is inaccessible.

10. If your dog moves away from the treat, click and allow your dog to eat it.

11. Repeat the previous steps until your dog is moving away from the exposed treat readily.

12. Once he is performing Step 11 reliably, attach the verbal cue "Leave It" as he moves away from the treat.

Secrets to success:

- As your dog learns this skill, slowly raise the distraction level of the treat that you are using.

- If your dog is having difficulty leaving the treat initially, use a treat of a lesser value such as a piece of kibble or a Cheerio. As your dog becomes more successful, increase the reinforcement value of the food or object.

- Generalize the behavior to other objects, such as toys, tennis balls, and sticks.

- Once your dog starts leaving a variety of different objects, begin to click and feed him for leaving other "things," such as dogs, fast-moving objects, cars, and so on. Practice just as you would with any other object.

- Work in different environments with different sets of distractions. Be creative! Make the game as challenging as it can be. Here is an example: Put treats on the floor and start heeling your dog around them. (Start with one and slowly graduate to two, three, and so on.) Do not let your dog eat any treats off of the floor. Click and feed your dog from your hand for compliance. Eventually you will be able to click and tell your dog to clean up the floor as a jackpot or heel your dog to each treat individually and, on your release cue, let him eat the treat that you are pointing to.

BACK UP–SIT

Objective: When your dog is ahead of you and you move backward, your dog spins and comes toward you.

Your movements forward and backward are huge cues to your dog. Teaching your dog to move toward you as you back away from him gives you another tool to remove him from problematic situations instantly. If your dog lunges out ahead of you, your body moving backward will cue your dog to turn and come back into you.

Especially helpful when...

- You are walking your dog in the park and up ahead you see several young children playing Hide and Seek in between the trees. Your dog notices them laughing and running back and forth. Fearing that this could become a dangerous situation, you start walking backward. Your dog spins around and comes to you so that you can move away safely.

- You are allowing your dog to meet a friend who has come for a visit. Once your visitor is seated, your dog comes over and says hello. Within a few seconds, he is up in the person's face, trying to grab her scarf. Nervous about the close interaction, you call your dog's name and start walking backward. Your dog happily turns toward you and bounces into heel position.

How to teach the behavior:

1. Have treats in both of your hands. Stand up straight. Your dog should be sitting in front of you, toe-to-toe.

2. Feed your dog a treat out of one hand, keeping your hands in the middle of your body. Pretend that your elbows are stuck to your torso; you want to feed your dog close to your body.

3. After your dog eats the treat, feed your dog a treat out of the other hand.

4. Alternate back and forth, standing still.

5. Once this pattern is going well and your dog's nose is glued to your fingertips, add movement by taking a small step back. Don't move back until your dog's nose is glued to your fingertips. There should be no space between you and the dog.

6. As you step back, feed your dog out of one hand, as you practiced above. It doesn't matter if your dog sits.

7. Now take another tiny step back, feeding your dog out of the opposite hand as he comes into you.

8. As this movement becomes fluent, vary the number of steps you take backward.

9. Once your dog is coming in close, add the sit.

Secrets to success:

- If you find that your dog does not want to come in close to your body, practice that part separately until your dog is comfortable.

- To match this behavior to the actual context, toss a treat forward to mimic your dog pulling forward when he sees the trigger. Allow your dog to eat the treat and then start backing up, following the instructions above.

Use the Back Up–Sit to get your dog to spin away from a trigger and glue himself to your hands as you move backward, treating him. Top row: The dog chases a tossed treat (to mimic pulling toward a trigger) and, on cue, spins and runs back to the handler. Bottom row: The dog sits with his nose touching the handler's hands and gets a treat. On the far right, the dog is reaching forward; you want your dog closer, as close as he can get.

- Feed your dog where you want him to be, not where he is.
- The eventual goal is for your dog to come into you and sit, but the location of your dog's head glued to your fingers is more important than the position of his body.

Escorting Your Dog

HOLD MY HAND

Objective: Your dog is comfortable with anyone holding his collar and leading him somewhere.

The ability to walk with your hand in your dog's collar without alarming your dog is a safety issue, for him, for you, and for others who might handle him. Many dogs, especially those that have been dragged around harshly by their collars, become fearful or aggressive when someone places a hand in their collar and tries to lead them somewhere. Desensitizing your dog to the collar grab and walking him with your hand in his collar is a good investment.

Especially helpful when...

- You are at an obedience trial and you need to get your anxious dog to the ring. Instead of heeling your dog, you loop your hand in your dog's decorative collar and escort him calmly. Once in, your dog sets up beautifully!
- Something in the environment scares your dog. Instead of dragging him out quickly with his leash, you gently guide him by his collar, and he remains calm.

How to teach the behavior:

1. Touch your dog's collar (use a buckle collar, never a choke).
2. Click.
3. Remove your hand. This is a crucial step for dogs that react adversely to someone putting a hand in their collar. You need to release the pressure so that they will relax.
4. Feed your dog.
5. Repeat several times until your dog is comfortable with you touching his collar.
6. Next, loop a few fingers under his collar and follow Steps 2 through 4.
7. Continue working until you are able to slip all of your fingers under his collar with him stationary.

8. Next see if you can take a step while holding your dog's collar: Place a few fingers under the collar and take a step.

9. Click.

10. Take your hand off of the collar and feed.

11. If this is successful, add another step.

12. Continue to add steps as your dog is successful.

Secrets to success:

- If your dog is collar-shy, go slowly.

- If you notice any aggressive cues, back up to the previous successful level.

- Use a collar that you can get your fingers under and out from easily.

- Never use a prong or choke collar for this exercise.

- Do not ever allow anyone to drag your dog by the collar.

- Gradually increase the pressure on the collar and the number of steps that you take guiding your dog.

CHIN REST

Objective: On cue, your dog rests his chin in your hand and allows you to lead him.

If you teach your dog to rest his head in your hand, you can lead him through crowded spaces that are filled with people and other dogs without guiding him with his leash or collar. You can calm an anxious dog by giving him something to do with his head that connects him to you.

Especially helpful when...

- Your dog is limping, and your veterinarian has to check his back leg. As she flexes the muscles, you cue your dog to rest his head in your hand until she finishes.

- You are trialing your dog in agility, and he is nervous in the crowded, noisy environment. Knowing your dog's sensitivities, you heel your dog to the start line with his head in your hand.

- Your dog has to have his blood drawn. You cue your dog to put his head in your hand. Once there, you lift his chin up to the ceiling so that the veterinary technician can take the blood from his carotid artery.

Teaching your dog to rest his chin in your hand (above) and then to walk while resting his chin in your hand helps in medical situations. It also gives you another option for guiding your dog instead of by a leash or a collar.

How to teach the behavior:

1. Put your hand under your dog's chin. Make sure your dog's chin is actually sitting in the palm of your hand.

2. Click. Keep your hand under his chin as you feed your dog.

3. Practice this behavior many times.

4. Next, place your hand about an inch under your dog's chin.

5. Your dog should look for your hand.

6. As your dog lowers his head into your hand, click. Even if your dog doesn't actually touch your hand, click for any lowering of the head. Have your hand meet his head.

7. Feed with your dog's chin in your hand.

8. When your dog places his chin in your hand, start inserting a verbal cue like "Chin" right before he does the behavior.

9. Once your dog is comfortable with this behavior, extend the amount of time that he rests his chin in your hand.

10. Now vary the location of your hand. You can also add movement to your hand, as for the blood draw explained above, so that your dog keeps his chin in your hand as it moves.

Secrets to success:

- Work on this behavior slowly.

- Click any approximation of your dog lowering his head into your hand. This movement can be difficult for some dogs.

- Another option is to use shaping to teach your dog to put his chin on an object, like a chair, and then transfer that behavior to your hand.

- Work duration and location separately.

Moving Your Dog Hands-free

SHIFT LOCATION

Objective: Responding to a simple hand target, your dog moves where you want him to be without you having to drag him by his collar or pick him up.

You can use the Hand Target cue to move your dog from one location to another without picking him up or touching him. First, however, he needs to know how to target your hand (see p. 40) and be proficient at targeting your hand from a distance.

Especially helpful when...

- You have a small dog that nips you when you try to pick him up. Instead, you can cue him to move from the floor to the couch without confrontation.

- You have a large, filthy dog you need to get into a tub, or you need to position an arthritic dog on the scale at a vet's office.

How to teach the behavior:

1. Point where you want your dog to go. (A verbal cue is unnecessary.) For example, show your dog your index finger and guide your dog to the couch.

2. Click as your dog jumps up on the couch to touch your finger(s).

3. Toss the treat on the couch.

4. Next, use your hand target to guide your dog to the floor.

5. Click as your dog jumps down.

6. Toss the treat on the floor.

7. Teach your dog to follow your finger to many different locations, always reinforcing at the destination point.

Secrets to success:

- After clicking, toss the treat where your dog went so that you are reinforcing him for going to the destination.
- If your dog stops following your finger, it means that you are moving too far, too fast. Back up and reduce the distance.

EMERGENCY RELOCATION CUE

Objective: On cue (doorbell or knock at the door), your dog will dash to a designated spot and stay there until released.

How many of us have struggled to get a dog out of the doorway when the doorbell rings or someone knocks so that we can avoid some uncontrolled encounter? You can turn the doorbell chime or a knock on the door from a trigger for obnoxious behavior to a cue for your dog to make himself scarce, to go to a designated area and stay there calmly until you release him. Life will be more civilized—and safer.

Especially helpful when...

- The UPS delivery person rings the doorbell. You give your emergency relocation cue, and, instead of flying at the door and knocking you down, your dog dashes into the pantry. You take the big box from the delivery person (takes two hands), calmly set it down on the kitchen counter, and return to sign the receipt. After the delivery person leaves, you grab your dog's favorite toy and have a tug party in the pantry.

How to teach the behavior:

1. Pick a word.
2. Pick a place close by to use as a secure temporary holding space that your dog can run to safely and quickly.
3. Choose a special treat that your dog only receives when he is doing this work.
4. Say the word.
5. Run to the temporary holding space. In the beginning, you may have to get your dog excited to come with you.
6. Once he's arrived, give him the treats. Have a party! Stay with him as you give him the treats.
7. Practice several times a day.

8. As you continue, you should notice a switch. Once you give the cue, instead of enticing your dog to come to the space, you will be trailing your dog as he dashes to "his" space.

    a. Once your dog is taking the lead, you can start giving him the treat while you stay outside of the space. Imagine feeding over a baby gate or barrier of some kind.

9. Say your verbal cue as your dog is running to the special spot.

10. When your dog is responding reliably to your verbal cue, change the cue from a verbal cue to a sound like the ringing of the doorbell: new cue (doorbell), pause, backed by the old cue (verbal). The training session should look something like this:

    a. Ring the doorbell.

    b. Pause.

    c. Give your verbal cue as you run with your dog to the space.

    d. On arrival, give him lots of wonderful treats, one by one.

    e. Keep your dog in the space for 1–2 minutes.

    f. Release him with lots of praise.

Secrets to success:

- When transferring the old cue to the new one, present the new cue first, insert a one-second pause, and then give the old cue.

- Work this behavior at different times of the day and in different situations.

- When you are presenting the new cue initially, be prepared to entice your dog to follow you to the holding place using fabulous treats and great excitement.

- If you want your dog to be quiet in the holding space, work on that piece separately.

- Remember that this behavior is for emergency relocation and should only be used for a period of 5–10 minutes. If you have people coming over for an extended visit, your dog should be in his safe space if needed (see p. 18).

BACK UP–DOWN

Objective: On cue, your dog backs up and lies down until released.

There are times when it is convenient, and safer, to have a dog that knows how to get out of the way and stay put in a designated spot until released. These are the steps to add the down-stay to the back up from handler behavior (see p. 67).

Especially helpful when...

- You've just finished painting the guest room and need to get your exuberant dog out from underfoot as you remove the rollers and paint brushes from the room. You cue him verbally to back up and lie down in a corner of the kitchen so that you can clean up.

- Your senior dog has found something unspeakable to roll in and investigates. You cue him to back off and settle under the oak tree while you deal with the mess.

How to teach the behavior:

1. Give your dog the verbal or gestural cue to back up.

2. As your dog takes a few steps back, cue your dog to lie down. Give your dog a stay cue if needed.

3. Click and feed your dog between his front paws while he remains in the down position. Vary the duration of the stay.

4. Release your dog.

Secrets to success:

- Be sure that your dog can move from a stand to a down instantly.

- When you are working the Down–Stay, remember that, technically, the click signals the end of the behavior. If your dog moves out of position after the click, simply ask him to lie down again to receive his treat.

DROP ON RECALL

Objective: On cue, your dog will lie down at a distance.

You can use the Drop on Recall cue to signal your dog to remain stationary at a distance if some form of danger should develop. You may need to be able to go to and collect him, or you may need him to wait before it is safe for you to call him to you.

Especially helpful when...

- You are out on a trail with your dog and you see a family coming up the path with several young children. Knowing that your dog is uncomfortable with children, you cue your dog to lie down and stay where he is until the newcomers have passed.

- You unexpectedly have a visitor at the door. Before your dog has the chance to run to the door, you can give your dog a hand signal to cue him to lie down immediately.

How to teach the behavior:

1. Get a prop to use as a boundary. A broomstick or leash will do.

2. Decide what you want to use as a hand signal. Choose one that can be seen from a distance. I like to use my right hand raised above my head.

3. Put the prop between yourself and your dog.

4. Using your hand signal, cue your dog to lie down from a standing position. (See Down on p. 43.)

5. Click as his butt hits the floor and feed him a treat between his front feet.

6. Repeat this behavior until it is reliable.

7. Take a step back from your prop and repeat Steps 4–5.

8. Continue to take steps back until you can cue your dog from a distance.

    a. If at any distance you cue your dog and he doesn't lie down, go back to where you were successful.

9. After you have a down from a distance, position your dog a few feet behind the prop.

10. With you on the other side, call your dog and just before he makes contact with the prop, give your cue to lie down.

11. If he does so, click and go to your dog to feed him.

12. Continue to repeat Steps 9–11 until your dog is coming from a substantial distance.

13. Once this happens, remove the prop, call your dog, and just as he starts to come, give your hand signal. Does he drop? If so, continue to practice this behavior. If not, re-introduce the prop and switch off to a smaller and smaller prop until you don't need one anymore.

Secrets of success:

- Use a hand signal that your dog can see from a distance.

- Use props that lie flat on the floor.

- As the behavior becomes more fluent, introduce different types of props and place several in between you and your dog. For example, if I have three props, can my dog lie down when I give my cue at the first prop (the greatest distance from me)? This will help to solidify the behavior.

- If at any time your dog gets confused, go back to the previous step.

Dog training is not a linear endeavor, and things do not go as expected even with the best-laid plans. You may encounter some bumps along the road or see behavior emerging in your dog that startles or scares you and that you feel ill-equipped to handle. In the next section I discuss when there's trouble and what you can do about it. Keep in mind that you have worked hard to establish a solid foundation with your dog, and you can build on that.

PART III

When There's Trouble

Even if you've been scrupulous about implementing home management principles with your dog and trained Basic and Emergency Behaviors, he may have already developed behaviors you can't easily live with. Here are some thoughts on diagnosing and finding solutions to these challenges.

8
A Spectrum of Problems

Dogs are meant to enrich human lives. Whether you have adopted a dog or purchased a puppy from a breeder, you hope to share many joyful years with that dog. You want to live with this dog in peace, not in fear or frustration. That certainly was my intention with my Golden Retriever, Ben. I'm recounting his story here because it may reflect some of the struggles you are having with your own canine companion and give you hope that you can successfully integrate your dog into your life.

Ben, the Catalyst for Click to Calm

Without my golden retriever, Ben, I would never have developed Click to Calm. I purchased Ben as a puppy to turn him into an obedience trial champion. Years before, I had swooned watching competition dogs heel with their handlers. They pranced merrily along beside their handlers with beautiful eye contact and tails swishing in the air. What perfection! That's what I wanted, no matter what the cost!

I thought I had done everything right: researched the breeder, socialized Ben well, and hired a wonderful positive reinforcement trainer, Patty Ruzzo, to help me attain my dream. All was well until Ben was about six months old. I was leaving a training room, and as we walked down the narrow corridor to leave, a Welsh Corgi that was hiding under a chair snapped at Ben as we walked by. Much to my surprise, Ben snapped back. I gasped! At that point, I did not have a long history of owning dogs; I had no idea what a "reactive" dog was. I had had dogs as a child, but none were ever trained. My Mom's version of dealing with a dog that bit the mail carrier was to tell the mail carrier not to stick his hands into the mail slot. If he did, he deserved to be bitten.

So, seeing Ben respond in kind made me fear him and what the future might hold. I decided to sit back and watch. After about two to three months of watching Ben's reactivity grow (barking and lunging at the end of his leash) when he saw other dogs, I consulted an aggression expert and arranged to take an obedience class he was teaching for problem dogs. I knew that I might have to use punishment in some way, but I didn't care. This behavior had to stop. It had no place in the repertoire of an obedience-trial-champion-to-be!

On the day of the class, my husband Greg dropped off Ben and me so that he could find a parking space and we wouldn't be late for class. By chance I ran into the expert as he was making his way to the field where the obedience class was to take place. As we were walking, Ben laid eyes on the expert's German Shepherd. Within seconds, Ben started to lunge and growl at his dog. Not wanting to pass up a training opportunity, the expert hurried over and told me to hand him my leash while he placed his dog in the down position. He took the leash out of my hand and first gave Ben a correction, hanging him on his prong collar. Ben bared his teeth at this stranger who then gave him an even harder correction. At this point, Ben's body went limp. After seeing that Ben had surrendered, the trainer handed me back my leash with the words, "If he barks and lunges again, this is what you have to do to make that problem go away." It was at this moment that I realized that I could never do that to my dog: I didn't have the physical strength, and it was highly abusive to cause so much pain and suffering to any animal.

Unbeknownst to me, Greg had witnessed what was unfolding from across the parking lot. He was livid! "How could you let someone treat our dog like that?" he scolded. I just looked at him and said that I didn't know. I, too, was numb inside. I knew that I needed to use punishment, but I had never seen a punishment so severe. Sure, we corrected our dogs in obedience class, but we never strung them up like that.

We took the obedience class as planned that day. Ben did fine in class—if you call "fine" ignoring all of the dogs with a glassy-eyed look. I was skeptical. Although I knew nothing about aggression back then, I had the feeling that somehow this was going to blow up in my face! And that it did!

A week later I decided to take Ben to an obedience class to see what effect the expert's correction had had. I couldn't have imagined the reaction I got when Ben saw another dog exiting a vehicle. Instantly he flew into a rage. Growling and screaming with teeth bared, he lunged violently at the end of his leash, saliva pouring out of his mouth as the explosion raged on. There was no end to this: seconds turned into minutes as I painfully dragged him back to my van. Once inside, he started to calm down. And I cried all the way home.

After this, life with Ben was different. Not only did Ben react aggressively to other dogs close to him, but he also reacted to dogs about a hundred feet away. He even tried to attack dogs on

TV and reacted to dogs on signs or in photos. When the Taco Bell Chihuahua came on, I had to hold him back so that he wouldn't redirect onto our other dogs or fly at the large-screen TV. I also had to be careful about noises like jingling car keys. One time as I walked into the house, Ben greeted me at the door and then, seemingly out of the blue, started attacking my American Eskimo dog. On reflection, I realized I had come into the house and started petting Ben with the car keys rubbing together in my hand. I can only assume that those car keys sounded like the tags on a dog's collar rubbing together.

The house was no longer one of peace. Greg and I had to watch Ben constantly to be sure that he did not redirect onto one of our smaller dogs. Although Ben never bit another dog, he still caused injury: a punctured cheek and soft tissue injuries, just to name a few. Remember: a dog does not have to bite another dog to cause injuries. Our dog Nicholas's cheek got punctured because he happened to be standing next to Ben as Ben caught a glimpse of another dog walking by our house. Frenzied, Ben spun so quickly with an open mouth that a tooth cut into Nicky's muzzle. Soft tissue injuries resulted when Ben "attacked" my American Eskimo by throwing him on the floor and "muzzle-punching" him from above. Ben stopped playing with his tennis balls and woke up screaming at night, only quieting when I massaged him back to sleep. I explained to friends that I believed that Ben had Post Traumatic Stress Disorder, but many said that I was being anthropomorphic. I was convinced that if Ben could speak to me in my own language, he would say that he was sure that he was going to die when in the company of another dog. After much denial, it was here that my learning began.

The Road to Recovery
After fully acknowledging to myself and Ben that I had allowed a tremendously damaging incident to occur, I had to start looking for information. I read every book and attended every seminar that I could find on the subject of canine aggression. The suggestions were many: ask a group of friends to command their dogs to sit in a line facing Ben. Then ask Ben to lie down in front of them until he "submitted." If Ben didn't want to lie down, force him to do it anyway. Or, have a group of friends line up with you and let their dogs run up over a hill. Then let Ben loose. Once Ben was running, ask your friends to recall their dogs. Ben would realize that he was outnumbered by the oncoming horde and that he should "submit" to them then. The problem was that, first, I didn't have a bunch of friends to do this with, and second, I'm not terribly sure what "submitting" actually meant. Was Ben to grovel in front of them? Not attack them? Turn and run in the opposite direction? Crawl along the floor? What did "submit" physically look like? And would such a single incident teach him anything?

Back then, many dog-training techniques involved the supposed "integrity of the owner/dog relationship." In one seminar I witnessed a woman being told that if she could not verbally get her young German Shepherd to focus on her instead of barking and lunging at another dog, their relationship was meaningless. The dog didn't love her enough to give her his attention. The woman left in tears. I've always wondered what happened to her and her dog.

It was in the throes of this chaos that I met my friend and mentor, Karen Pryor, a pioneer in the field of animal behavior and training. She was the one who first introduced me to clicker training and to the idea that one could shape a dog's emotions, which was a far better way of dealing with fear and aggression than punitive alternatives. I remember Karen said to me: "We're going to train Ben like he is an aggressive walrus." I had no idea what she meant back then.

In the beginning, when I was so scared and desperate about rehabilitating Ben, I shall always remember one incident in Karen Pryor's clicker training class. I was standing with Ben on a leash in front of the gym's entry doors, listening to Karen teach. All of a sudden, two women entered the room with their Australian Shepherds. Ben flipped out, lunging and barking at the dogs while I struggled to hold on. Mortified, the women hurriedly left the room, apologizing. I was shaking and trying to get Ben back under control as Karen approached. Holding back tears, I remember her placing her hand on my arm and saying quietly to me: "Emma, it's OK. It's only behavior."

"Only behavior?" I screamed internally! How can this be "only behavior?" This so-called "behavior" has turned my life upside-down! Throughout Ben's training, I had struggled to put my own fears aside to start exposing him to other dogs. Because of this "behavior," not only had my obedience-competition dreams been flushed down the toilet, but I'd also been shunned, threatened, and banished publicly from all of the activities that I used to enjoy with my friends with more social dogs. So for Karen to quietly say, "It's only behavior" seemed a grave understatement.

But Karen was right. Her gentle reminder that Ben's issues were behavioral meant that they were subject to the scientific laws that govern behavior. Over the coming months and years, as I learned those laws and how to apply them to help Ben, we both made our way through the world with ever greater ease. He became my first and most important student and my best teacher. That was the beginning of Click to Calm.

I hope you do not have a dog that is as violently reactive as Ben was at first, but perhaps the following scenarios sound familiar:

- All you wanted to do was save a dog and give him a much better life than he had in the past, so it is absolutely heartbreaking when that adopted dog with a traumatic past starts to threaten your other dog. Although you have adopted many dogs successfully, this dog presents a far greater challenge.

- You purchased an agility prospect, a puppy that was growing up perfectly until, at about a year old, he suddenly starts growling at your 11-year-old son. Your heart sinks as you start to think about rehoming your dog.

- Your beloved but shy 10-year-old mixed breed suddenly starts barking violently and lunging at strangers he passes on walks.

- Your teenage puppy is so exuberant that he knocks over Grandma when she comes to visit. You can't play with him anymore without him getting so aroused that he starts biting your hands, and he recently pinned the neighbor's cocker spaniel "in play."

As a result, maybe you, too, are screaming "only behavior??!" These dogs exhibit a continuum of emotional responses: They are fearful, excitable, reactive, or aggressive. They are all difficult or dangerous to live with. The good news is that they all can benefit from training that uses the Click to Calm methodology as a starting point. With proper coaching, many dogs can move beyond their obnoxious, fearful, or threatening behavior. You cannot "cure" every dog, but you can make a dog more manageable and safer and less frustrating to be around.

Behavior and Emotions

Karen Pryor taught me that emotion and behavior are tightly linked and are largely governed by the same laws. Slowly, the scientific community is coming around to the view, long-shared by Karen, that we have the power to change emotions by shaping observable emotional responses (what we call "behavior").

Emotions are complicated because scientists can't agree on what they are. What's inarguable is that emotions can involve both behavioral and biological components, but the relationship between what we observe and what we label as a given emotion is not a neat and tidy association. An added complexity is that we can't ask canines about their feelings, so we give observed responses (behaviors) names, and those names (or labels) become shorthand for what we can see. But dogs can express different emotions through the same behavior (is that dog snarling out of fear, rage, or pain?). That's why any behavior specialist in canine aggression will inquire about the animal's physical health. Many species in pain can act aggressively.

The labels we apply don't have any impact on a dog's behavior. There are contexts, however, where the labels we use actually do harm. When we apply emotional labels to a dog, such labels can cloud our thinking about solutions. Once someone has labeled a dog as "aggressive," it marks the animal's very nature, and that, to many people, seems immutable to change.

You need to keep your focus on changing behavior. The emotions, as best we can tell, come along for the ride. My job, our job together, is to create the behavioral and biological response we want to see. That's the problem-solving lens of Click to Calm. Click to Calm is a protocol for shaping behavioral (and accompanying biological) responses from the undesirable to the desirable.

Before training, however, you need to diagnose the problem, make the decision to keep the dog and address the problem, and formulate a plan.

What's the Problem?

The first step in dealing with your dog's behavior is determining what sets it off. Every dog—just like every human—is different. The contexts in which these behaviors occur are just as varied as the events of each passing day.

Determine if there are medical issues causing the behavior

If your dog has an underlying medical issue that's causing his inappropriate behavior, one that can be addressed with medication, your problem may be solved. Checking with your vet is especially important if your dog has become aggressive. The day that you witness your dog's first aggressive response is the day that you should set up a veterinary visit, especially when you have an older dog that has just started biting unexpectedly. There are many medical issues that can cause aggression: pain, diminished senses, and plummeting thyroid levels, just to name a few. Ask your vet for a full veterinary workup: a manual exam, a complete blood count, a blood profile checking kidney and liver levels, urinalysis, a thyroid panel, and any other tests that your veterinarian thinks are necessary.

Consult a veterinary behaviorist

If your dog has severe aggression or fear issues with either people or dogs, or any other type of obsessive/compulsive behaviors, make an appointment with a veterinary behaviorist as soon as possible. It is really important to see a specialist as opposed to your primary veterinarian. Most veterinarians do not have a solid background in behavior. When they are asked which medication they might use for behavior issues like aggression, Prozac is usually their first choice. That drug may or may not be effective. A veterinary behaviorist will not only know which medication(s) to prescribe but also which training protocol to recommend.

Whether a dog needs to be on medication is sometimes a hard question to answer. When we think about dogs on medication, we think about dogs that bite or dogs with severe separation anxiety, but what about the over-exuberant youngster? Young dogs should not be on medication, right? Wrong! There are some cases where a caretaker's lack of training can make even the youngest dog fearful and anxious. Remember that dogs that are deprived of structure in their lives have only themselves to rely on and, at such a young age, their decisions are far from perfect. We do not want young dogs to learn that using their mouths gives them the information that they are craving.

Play detective

If you look hard enough, in many cases you can accurately predict when your dog will respond inappropriately. To assess your dog's behavior, ask yourself three questions:

1.   What is the behavior that you are trying to change?

2.   What happens before the behavior?

3.   What is the consequence?

For example: Your dog sits and looks out your bay window for several hours a day. When the mail carrier comes, he barks and charges at the window with teeth bared! You are frightened that at some point he will break the window and hurt himself or attack the mail carrier.

1.   *What is the behavior that you are trying to change?* The barking and charging at the window.

2.   *What happens before the behavior?* Your dog spots the mail carrier.

3.   *What is the consequence?* The mail carrier delivers the mail and then walks away and your dog settles down, his "protection detail" successfully completed.

When you are investigating your dog's trigger(s), be conscious of your body posture. Staring at a dog, extending a hand, and leaning forward are all human gestural cues that can be intimidating to a dog—he may view you as invading his personal space or his "bubble."

Although you can follow this detective-like model to evaluate your dog's behavior issue, it is best to work with an experienced professional trainer. Be sure to make an appointment with a veterinary behaviorist if you think medication might be beneficial.

Special Considerations for Dogs That Bite

Dogs that bite, for whatever reason, cause us the most heartache. It is important to talk in more detail about the special considerations and decisions you need to make when you are dealing with a dog that bites. We are not talking about the enthusiastic greeter who knocks you over and may nip your nose in his efforts to lick your face. He is a bundle of unbridled enthusiasm, full of joy and good intentions. He just doesn't know what to do with his mouth. Granted, it may be disconcerting and frustrating to live with such a dog, but there's no particular emotional trauma involved. He just needs to develop the manners that the Click to Calm methodology can teach him. We are talking about the dog that bites defensively (out of fear, to create distance) or offensively (out of rage, to discipline). These are the dogs, usually traumatized themselves, that often cause their owners psychological trauma.

Dogs that are aggressive toward their caregivers, other people, other dogs, or other pets present the most serious canine behavioral issue. Living with a dog that can potentially harm a person, especially a child, is risky. Caregivers who house a dog that can severely injure someone can be viewed as irresponsible. The difficulty lies in the fact that many people-aggressive dogs are fine 99% of the time with their families. It is when a relative comes to visit or when the caregiver tries to take her dog for a walk out in public that poses the most danger.

The world works against us! People love dogs and want to be friends with them. I have seen situations where a dog is snarling at a person and the person still asks the caregiver if it is OK to pet the dog. "I am a *dog* person!" the individual says, almost expecting his mere presence to calm the dog.

Even a caregiver's careful plans to manage a potentially dangerous dog may fail—as when a caregiver puts her dog away in his safe space while people visit, but the dog gets loose. If the dog bites someone, the liability risk could be high (not to mention the emotional toll it will take on the visitor and the caregiver's family).

What do you do? How do you deal with these scenarios emotionally? When you have a dog that is threatening you or family members, do you walk on eggshells in your own home, taking care not to anger your dog? How long do you wait for behavior change to happen? What improvement are you looking for? Is it OK for your dog to growl at the mail carrier but not OK to bite? Is it OK to snap but not OK to make contact with human skin? Do you feel comfortable bringing this dog back to the shelter or to the breeder? Do you feel as if it would be sending the wrong message to your children if you give him up? Could you adopt the dog out to a friend with no children with confidence? If the behavior doesn't improve (and gets worse), will you be able to take responsibility and re-home or possibly euthanize the dog? These are some of the questions that bombard your mind daily. Beyond identifying the dog's triggers, there are a host of other considerations you will want to consider.

Making the Decision

The decision of whether or not to rehabilitate a dog is a personal one based on many factors: cause of the bite, severity of injury, size of the dog, the dog's previous reinforcement history, what the dog's triggers are, family compliance, financial commitment, and time commitment. When I have clients in this difficult situation, I usually advise them to discuss the issue as a family and to come up with an agreed-upon timeframe in which to assess the dog's behavior. Six months to a year is a common time span. This list of questions should help with the decision-making process. It is best to discuss these questions with a qualified veterinary behaviorist or trainer.

1. **Cause:** Do we know why the dog is aggressive? Has there been some physical trauma that the dog has endured for years in a past life, or has this dog been exhibiting this behavior since he was a puppy? Although we all have a soft spot for the dog that has been abused by humans, can you keep this dog safely? Are you willing to do what it takes, even if it means leaving the dog at home when you attend a social event where everyone else will be bringing their dogs? Are you willing to leave your dog in his safe space when relatives come to visit? These are vital questions that you and your family need to answer.

2. **Severity of injury:** Did this dog growl at a child or did this dog bite one in the face? Did the bite require stitches? Surgery? Although one might say that the growling dog is less of a risk, I might argue that if the dog learns that growling works for him and the caregiver unknowingly reinforces the growling, then this dog could become just as dangerous over time as the one that bites without growling. The more serious the bite, the greater the chance that the dog might be unable to live with humans safely.

3. **Size of the dog:** Size matters! Is this an aggressive Chihuahua or a Great Dane? Although I have seen some pretty severe bites inflicted by small dogs, the fact is that bites from big dogs tend to do more damage.

4. **Reinforcement history:** How long has this behavior been happening? Five years or five months? How has the family reacted when the dog has shown aggressive tendencies? How many times has the dog been aggressive? To whom? No matter how long the dog has been demonstrating this behavior, you can always make progress in reducing the behavior. The brain is fluid and is always building new neural pathways. But the question remains: even if the behavior improves, will the family take delight in the dog? Will this be a dog that will brighten their lives? For how long? Although rehabilitating Ben was a ton of work, every day with him

was a blessing! If I had not had that commitment to him, I would not have had the stamina to work with him as I did.

5. **Triggers:** Do we know what triggers the dog's behavior? It is always harder to work with a dog when its triggers seem invisible. Does the aggression only happen at a certain time of day? Only when visitors come over? Or is it so intense that your dog barks and lunges whenever he sees a stranger in any location? It is much easier to work with a dog that has fewer known triggers than one that is in constant turmoil. (See p. 112 for more information on triggers.)

6. **Family compliance:** Do all members of your family want to help the dog? Are they aware of the sacrifices that they will have to make, both in the home and in social settings, to help the dog feel more secure? Are they willing to stop interacting with the dog in ways that they enjoy in order to improve the dog's behavior? When strangers want to pet their dog, are they emotionally strong enough to decline politely? Although not all family members have to train the dog, all still have to agree that they will do their part to avoid sabotaging the effort.

7. **Time and money:** Do you have the time to put into training? Do you have the funds to work with a certified trainer and/or to take your dog to a veterinary behaviorist? Can you continue the training for at least six months to a year? Consistency is key! Though clicker training can give you instant results, your dog must repeat the behavior enough that it becomes a habit. It takes at least eight weeks of perfect practice (please note the word "perfect") for behavior to become habitual.

8. **Convenience:** It is not going to be convenient to change your own behavior. Are you willing to put your behavior under the microscope? Will you be patient with other family members as they struggle to do this as well?

As you can see, the list of questions is extensive. Each situation is different, and every dog is different. Each caregiver has a certain list of expectations and specific objectives. In treating cases of dogs that are aggressive toward people and/or other animals, the goal is not to cure the dog but to lessen the risk that the dog will ever bite again.

In cases where dogs bite people or other dogs severely and frequently, the decision, though tough and incredibly heartbreaking, is agonizingly simple, especially if the caregivers have been working with a veterinary behaviorist or a certified trainer: safety first, always. The decision is painfully difficult when the dog that you love has bitten a few people for seemingly good reasons or when you have a dog that bites only 5% of the time and is cuddly and loving the rest of the time.

Here's how I view it: A dog that is truly aggressive toward people or other dogs has a mental illness. These dogs can no longer control their impulses to inflict harm. Or they have learned that biting has worked in the past to deflect humans. Although caretakers can make tremendous improvements in these dogs' responses, they will always have to manage and properly supervise these dogs throughout their lives, including using muzzles in certain settings. Is the caregiver up for that challenge? Will she knowingly assume the liability?

I have had some clients who have been severely bitten by their dogs but who would rather keep their dogs alive than go through the pain of losing them. As one of my clients told me, "The pain of putting my dog to sleep would be far worse than the pain inflicted on me when he bit off half of my ear." With proper medication, home management, and behavioral modification, this dog never bit the caregiver severely again, but that is not the outcome in all cases.

How to Know When to Give Up

When I see a client, I must remember that the behavior that I want from my dogs is likely going to be different from the behavior that she wants from her dog. I never tell a new client whether or not she should keep, rehome, or euthanize her dog. Instead, I give my client options. I explain what is needed for her dog to lead a happy and healthy life. After we have this discussion, most of my clients start working with their dogs, and, in one way or another, the behavior improves. Some of my clients don't want to train so they manage their dogs better, while others hate to manage but do a lot of clicker training. Whichever way they approach the issues, most are happy with the results.

If the dog has not yet bitten but there is a danger that he might do so, I think of this as a triage situation (especially if there are small children involved). I need to get the dog out of the house as quickly as I can. If he starts biting, then he no longer has the option of being rehomed because of the liability issue. Sadly, in these situations the dog pays the ultimate price.

For your dog to succeed, you need the time and money to manage and train your dog. This might mean going to a veterinary behaviorist and hiring a trainer. If you are unable to take these steps, you must make other arrangements to save your dog's life. I am not being dramatic here. Dogs lose their lives every day simply for being dogs.

There are many reasons why you might not have the resources to get a dog the help that he needs. If you are in this position, one of the greatest gifts that you can give your dog is to find him another home. Do not think of this as the lazy man's way out. When my clients tell me that they have decided to rehome their dogs, I praise their courage and strength for making a decision that will hurt them all deeply. They will tell me that they feel guilty.

Guilt is for those who knew that they were making the wrong decision getting a dog with severe behavioral issues but decided to do it anyway. It is not for people who really wanted a dog, but, unbeknownst to them, the dog had severe fear or aggression issues. Had they been aware of the dog's problems, they would never have taken him home. They simply didn't have the experience to deal with those problems, especially if there were small children in the home. I tell my clients that the only reason I would feel guilty is if I knew that I could not provide what the dog needed but kept him anyway. For example, if I kept the dog with the knowledge that if he bit one of my children I would not be able to keep him but would have no way to rehome him.

Each household is different and the expectations for dogs are different. My hope is that if you have a challenging dog you can find what you need in this book to make an honest decision about whether or not you can provide your dog with the mental and emotional support that he needs. If you decide that it is not an option and your dog has not bitten a person or another dog, work with a professional organization (breed rescue, shelter, return your dog to the breeder, etc.) to ensure that your dog is rehomed safely.

9
Work for Change

If you have decided to keep and work with your dog, wherever he is on the continuum of "obnoxious" behavior, here are the first remedial steps to take. Once you have determined your dog's triggers, you can plan to manage his inappropriate responses and train the behaviors or responses you want. As you work with your dog, keep the following guidelines from Part I in mind. Be sure to review the Home Management principles starting on p. 15. Only if you first stop your dog from rehearsing the target, unwanted behavior (see p. 12) can you work on changing his behavior, and/or your own.

With every dog it is important to build a communication system where both parties respect and learn from each other cooperatively. If you and your dog are going to be on the same page, you must build a mutual vocabulary. Teaching dogs which behaviors are appropriate gives fearful dogs a way to control their own destinies. For confident dogs, it is a win/win. You can teach them the behaviors you desire and, in turn, they will say, "Wow! Look what I can make them do! Now pay me!"

Training sessions do not have to be long and arduous. Five to ten minutes, twice a day, will do. A series of quick, two-minute sessions throughout the day, whenever you see an opportunity to train your dog, will work just as well. Capture behavior that you like when your dog offers it. For example, if you approach your dog and he doesn't growl, click and toss him a treat. Clicker training is ideal for this kind of coaching because it allows you to mark the correct behavior without having to put your hands on your dog. This option could be critical when you are teaching a dog that has shown aggression to you, a family member, or another pet. The clicker is also a precise tool. You can indicate the second your dog does the correct behavior so that he knows exactly why he is getting paid.

Teach Your Dog Default Behaviors

As a safety precaution and to build your confidence in your dog, it makes sense to train a number of behaviors that your dog can execute reliably anywhere under any conditions. These "default behaviors," are the ones that your dog not only will offer on cue but will offer uncued after enough reinforced repetitions because, in the past, they have worked so well to get him what he wants (like sitting instead of jumping up to get you to throw the ball). If he learns to control his behavior—even in stressful situations—you're that much ahead of the game. I especially recommend teaching your dog the following behaviors:

Default Sit (see p. 42): If you can verbally cue a sit at any time, from any body position and from any distance, then you can stop a threatening situation from getting worse.

Hand Target (see p. 40): Teaching your dog to follow your hand or finger enables you to move him without actually touching him, a crucial skill if he could bite if you try to pick him up or guide him by the collar.

Stationing (staying in a particular place, see p. 52): If you've trained your dog to go from any distance to a station (a mat, platform, small dog bed, for instance) and stay there, you can keep him—and others—out of harm's way...

Recall with back up (see p. 71): This default behavior is a must for adolescent dogs that, on a recall, run full speed at you and then bounce off of you. The verbal cue to "Back Up" slows him down so that he can reverse direction, and you can call him to you gently for a sit.

Down from a distance (see p. 90): This default behavior ensures that you can reliably "drop" your dog where and when necessary to keep him safe.

"Find It" (see p. 54): The "Find It" cue is a quick way to get your dog interested in something other than what he is focusing on, so it is a godsend if a known trigger suddenly appears out of nowhere, and you don't have time to react any other way.

Implement Additional Management Strategies for the Aggressive Dog

If you are working with an aggressive dog, safety is your first concern. The goal is to give your dog the information that he needs to acquire resources (food, water, control, attention) without any threat of confrontation with you or other family members. As the caretaker, you want to be as clear as you can be with your dog without taking away the joyful activities that he loves. You never want your dog to think about biting again. Please review the Home Management Principles (see p. 15). Teaching your dog to say "please" and ensuring that all play with your dog is gentle are paramount. In addition to Home Management Principles, the following management principles will help you and your family stay safe as you work on teaching your dog better ways to cope.

Feed Your Dog By Hand: If you have a dog that has bitten you, another family member, or another animal, there is no better way to start healing the relationship than by feeding your dog by hand (assuming that it is safe to do so). Instead of simply putting your dog's food in a bowl and walking away, personalize food offerings by feeding him for interacting with you in a kind and gentle manner. For example, feed him for working on specific behaviors such as sits, hand targets, and so on. Or feed him for looking at you, for playing gently with you, or for relaxing comfortably on his mat beside you. Vary the quantity of food that you give him each time. If you are feeding kibble, give him a few handfuls for a quick, reliable response to a down cue or, if you are feeding a raw food, deliver these morsels with a spatula or spoon.

If you have a dog that you cannot hand-feed, leave pieces of food in the spaces that you have occupied. Don't cue any behavior at this point. Let him simply get used to your presence. Some sensitive dogs cannot deal with the spatial pressure when a person leans forward to feed them. If you have such a dog, leave food in piles at your feet and walk away. Chances are your dog will watch from a distance and then, when you have left the area, will approach and eat the food.

Praise and pet for shorter periods: Some caregivers want to pet their dogs (especially "lap dogs") for long periods of time. These dogs often growl, snap, or bite their caregivers to make the handling stop. If your dog snaps or bites when you pet him, pet him only when he seems interested in interacting with you. If he is not comfortable on your lap, have him lie down beside you instead. Pet your dog consciously. When you are interacting with him, don't get so engrossed in a movie that you lose track of time.

Double the amount of physical exercise your dog gets—if that helps him: Some dogs relax with more physical exercise while others can grow more agitated. Which type of dog do you have? Make sure your dog gets adequate physical and mental exercise each day. Instead of leaving your dog alone all day, see if you can bring him to a doggy daycare a few times a week if he enjoys the company of other dogs or have a pet sitter visit him in the middle of the day. Be sure to let all personnel know if your dog has a behavioral issue.

Eliminate eye contact: If you are worried that your dog might get anxious and bite, watch your dog out of the corner of your eye. Do not stare at him directly. Doing so might unintentionally confront or challenge him. Take the necessary precautions. (See "Keep a long line attached to your dog's collar," below.)

Keep a long line attached to your dog's collar: If you need to escort your dog from one place to another, instead of guiding him by the collar, use a long line. That way, if there is an emergency, you can physically hold your dog away from your body or a family member can pull your dog away from you. You can purchase a long line at a pet store or make one yourself. On one end, fasten a clip to attach to your dog's collar. Leave the other end free (no loop) to prevent your dog from getting snagged on anything in the house or outside. When you attach the long line, be sure to give your dog treats for his cooperation. If your dog is sensitive to your body pressure, do not bend over your dog. Instead, bend at the knees, keep your body straight, and attach the line from there.

Keep your dog out of your bed: If your dog has slept with you peacefully for years, then there is no reason to remove your dog from your bed, as long as the context in which your dog has bitten is not related. If your dog's behavior has grown unpredictable, however, then it is best to get your dog out of your room. The difficulty is that while you are sleeping, you have no idea what your dog is doing. I have had clients who have woken up to their dogs physically attacking them in the middle of the night. Be safe! You can crate your dog by your bed, set up a dog bed nearby with an X-pen around it, or create a baby-gated space outside of your doorway. Safety is paramount.

Living and working with a challenging dog is no easy task, but if you've implemented the strategies I've suggested here, you've already accomplished much in nurturing and healing the relationship you have with your dog. Now you're in a good place to actually tackle the triggers that set off those behaviors you wish would just disappear.

PART IV
Implementing Click to Calm

With the diagnosis and management measures in Part III, you've now got a handle on what sets off your dog. Teaching the Basic and Emergency Behaviors in Part II gives you options for moving your dog to a safe place and calming his arousal. Now you're ready to intentionally expose your dog to his triggers. The Click to Calm process lets you do so in as positive, measured, and controlled fashion as possible. The trust your dog has in you will help teach him how he can keep himself safe in situations that had set him off previously.

10

The Process of Clicking with a Reactive Dog

A reactive dog focuses on a "trigger" (another dog, a baby carriage, a tall man, or a garbage truck) because he doesn't feel safe. He locks on to it so he can keep track of it, watch what it does, and prepare for his defense if it becomes more threatening.

Social Distance

For a dog to feel comfortable, he must trust and respect his caregiver and understand and manage appropriate "social distance" successfully. Both humans and canines need to maintain a certain amount of space around them to feel comfortable. In my consults, I often refer to this space as a "bubble." In a healthy human–dog relationship, I like to think that, ideally, you and your dog are in a *single* bubble together and that together in your bubble you navigate happily through the many circumstances of your lives. But, if your dog is fearful of other dogs, for example, you and he are no longer in one happy bubble. Instead, the seemingly huge bubbles of other dogs are pushing on either side of you, applying so much pressure that your dog can't think straight or even hear your voice.

When a human or an animal feels that his bubble has been invaded, he does one of two things: withdraws or confronts (this is the "fight or flight" syndrome). The ways in which humans and dogs withdraw or confront are as varied as the stars in the sky. Dogs can either run away from the source of their stress or challenge it in ways that are natural for them. Barking, growling, and snapping top the list of challenges. Dogs in conflict (feeling both fearful and feisty) might exhibit a combination of flight and challenge. These are the dogs that move forward to confront a challenge and, when the challenge moves toward them, run in the opposite direction.

Teach Your Dog to Keep Himself Safe

Many trainers promote the idea that, when your dog faces a trigger, you *first* need to get your dog's attention (turn him away from a trigger) and *then* deal with the distraction or trigger.

These training methods teach the handler of a reactive dog to cue her dog to "Watch Me!" or "God forbid, don't look at that other dog. Focus on me instead!" This path produces a dog that stares at his handler, as if transfixed, and begs her to work in the presence of other dogs. Sadly, this dog never gets the chance to learn that having other dogs (or whatever triggers him) in the environment is not a threat and that he can learn to keep himself safe by voluntarily checking in with his handler instead of merely responding to her cue. You can see the stress in his tense body and dilated eyes. When your dog is reacting, there is nothing that you can do or say to relieve his anxiety. Your only option in these circumstances is to leave the situation.

By contrast, Click to Calm targets the root of the dog's behavior—his stress from being around a trigger. If used properly, Click to Calm can help you teach your dog that the presence of the trigger is *the cue to look at you* for instruction—instead of you having to fight the environment and beg him for his attention. Once you have your dog's attention, you can cue your dog to perform another behavior that you have taught reliably and that is incompatible with reactive behavior. This pattern changes your dog's emotional reaction, and his behavior in response, to the trigger. Essentially, the Click to Calm protocol is a *familiarization* program: it gets your dog so comfortable with the trigger that he's able to turn away from it and, instead, focus on you and respond to your cues.

The biggest benefit of this training methodology is that your dog learns to *keep himself safe* when he encounters a trigger. The result is a dog that is calm, confident in the presence of a trigger—whether that trigger is a stranger, a child, a trash can, a black dog, or anything else that your dog is concerned about. Your dog feels more empowered and in control of the situation, and so do you.

Imagine that you are walking down the street and your dog sees a jogger running toward you. Before training Click to Calm, you had to stop, get your dog's attention, and ask him to sit so that he wouldn't lunge at the runner as she passed. Using the Click to Calm methodology in this same situation, your dog sees the runner coming toward you and gives you automatic eye contact. You can cue him to keep walking or to sit and stay. Whichever behavior you cue, your dog is focused on you voluntarily, not on the jogger running by. This protocol not only lowers the risk of your dog lunging and biting the jogger, but the training also reduces your dog's stress. The encounter isn't an "event." He can relax on this walk. Lower-stress encounters like these build his confidence.

How It Works

There are three stages of Click to Calm (from your dog's perspective, not yours):

1. Stage One: Recognize
2. Stage Two: Redirect
3. Stage Three: Replace

First (Stage One), your dog begins to learn that the trigger is no longer relevant. He soon *recognizes* that the sight and sound of the trigger predicts lots of clicks and cookies, or play or massage or a sniff fest!

Second (Stage Two), your dog learns to voluntarily *redirect* his attention from the trigger to you. When this happens, it feels like a miracle—for both of you. For you, it's the relief of having a dog that's calm and focused on you; for your dog, it's enjoying a bonanza of reinforcement and a sense of relief.

Third (Stage Three), now that your dog is focused on you, he can perform any reliable behavior that you have taught him. You *replace* your dog's reactivity with an incompatible or an alternative behavior and, hence, create a calmer dog in the presence of the trigger.

Essential Skills

Before you start working on the Click to Calm methodology with your dog, there are certain skills that you want to practice by yourself before exposing your dog to his triggers.

1. Perfecting skillful handling
2. Understanding the changing ratio of reinforcement
3. Learning patterns of movement

By the time you take your dog out into the world to work on exposures, your body should already know what to do in those stressful moments when you yourself are reacting. If you can manage your reactions, you can focus your full attention on handling and training your dog.

Perfecting skillful handling

Before you conduct a training session, you must figure out how to hold your leash and how to click and feed your dog rapidly and in succession.

If your dog heels on your left: Fold up the leash and hold it in your right hand. Your arm should be bent at the elbow and loosely positioned by your waist. Position your clicker against the bunched-up leash. Your treat pouch should be positioned behind your left hip. Dispense the treats with your left hand. Feed your dog close to your left leg.

If your dog heels on your right: Fold up the leash and hold it in your left hand. Position your clicker against the bunched-up leash. Your treat pouch should be positioned behind your right hip. Dispense the treats with your right hand. Feed your dog close to your right leg.

Understanding the changing ratio of reinforcement

No matter what type of reinforcement you are using, it fits into the Click to Calm methodology beautifully. Treats are the easiest form of reinforcement to work with because you can adjust the value of your treats to the level of challenge the environment presents. Toys and touch can also work well, depending on your dog, and sending your dog to sniff is often an excellent calming activity. Your goal is to reinforce your dog heavily for connecting with you voluntarily; therefore, you will be rewarding Stage Two far more than either Stage One or Stage Three.

As the "Threshold" section explains (see p. 122), when you click, you will always be moving away from the trigger to give your reinforcement. If you are using play or touch, it will be best to go behind a barrier of some kind to reinforce your dog.

Treats: In Stage One (training your dog to recognize and accept the presence of a trigger), you will click, move away, and give your dog one treat after each exposure, either delivering it directly to your dog or tossing it on the floor. Practice this pattern in rapid succession.

Deliver your treats in the easiest way possible. For example, some dogs like you to feed treats directly to their mouths while others prefer that you drop each treat on the floor. Tossing treats on the floor or in the grass can be very helpful if your dog is in a highly aroused state. Sniffing out food is a calming and absorbing activity for most dogs. If you use crunchy dog bones that your dog really likes, he will spend lots of time with his head down, sniffing and scarfing up all of the crumbs.

In Stage Two (teaching your dog to voluntarily look away from the trigger and focus on you), you will click, move away, and give your dog five treats (or more), counting them out one by one and taking a deep breath in between each one.

The reason you are increasing the amount of reinforcement in Stage Two is because when your dog turns to look at you instead of the trigger, it is an amazing moment. He is showing you that he trusts you to keep him safe in the situation, enough that he dares to look away from the trigger and at you! Since you want to encourage more of this behavior, you want your dog to understand that his glance at you will earn him a huge paycheck. When I took Dr. Susan Friedman's online learning theory course, I started wondering why I hadn't been paying dogs more initially when they made the critical switch from looking at the trigger to reorienting to the handler. When I started increasing the reinforcement for looking back at the handler, the results were immediate! This emphasis on heavy reinforcement is a game-changer for handlers working with their reactive dogs as well as for teachers of reactive-dog classes. Dogs now learn this step faster.

In the beginning, you might not feel relaxed with this reinforcement pattern, but as you continue to train you will be able to take deeper and deeper breaths. Incorporate these calming breaths directly into your training. Counting out loud helps you focus on each word that you are saying before you give the treat. Not only does counting give you focus, but it also pairs your voice with tasty treats. The result is that your voice will become much more meaningful to your dog during these exposures.

Stage Two treat delivery will look like this:

1. Click your dog.

2. Back away from the trigger.

3. Say "One."

4. Take a deep breath.

5. Feed your dog.

6. Say "Two."

7. Take a deep breath.

8. Feed your dog.

9. Say "Three."

10. Take a deep breath.

11. Feed your dog.

12. Continue until you have delivered five (or more) treats.

Practice this treat-delivery skill separately. You may not be used to giving your dog so many treats at one time, so it may not feel natural to you or to your dog. Humans can be stingy with treats because traditional training methods often have taught us that dogs should perform behaviors to please us, not themselves. If you have a one-click/one-treat dog, you may be startled at his reaction to this sudden bonanza and thrilled at his enthusiasm for the next training opportunity. There is no magic to the number five—the aim is simply to give many more treats at this stage than at any other. "More than one" is not enough!

In Stage Three you return to the one-exposure/one-treat pattern.

Toys: If you are using a toy to reinforce your dog, in Stages One and Three one click will equal five seconds of play. Be sure that you have the exposure to the toy on perfect stimulus control so that at the end of five seconds you can ask your dog to "Give" or "Drop," and he will do so willingly.

In Stage Two, one click will equal three bouts of five seconds of play. Practice this pattern ahead of time so that your dog becomes familiar with it. Be sure that you take a deliberate breath in between each play session.

Touch: If you are using massage to reinforce your dog, in Stages One and Three one click will equal five seconds of massage. Stroke gently and in a certain rhythm. Pretend that your dog's fur is a piece of velvet and that you are brushing the grain lightly. Refrain from hard slaps and pounding on your dog's body. You want this moment to be as calming as possible.

In Stage Two, one click will equal three repetitions of five seconds of massage. Again, count these strokes out loud to your dog, taking deep breaths in between. You might even decide to take your dog's mat with you during exposures so that you can click and bring your dog to his mat for added comfort.

Sniffing: If you are reinforcing your dog by sending him to sniff, in Stages One and Three, one click will equal about 20 seconds of sniffing. In Stage Two, one click will equal three bouts of sniffing (watch for your dog's body language to relax and adjust the sniff period accordingly).

Guidelines for Reinforcement				
After each click...	Treats	Toys	Touch	Sniff Fest
Stage One	1 treat	5 seconds of play	5 seconds of massage	about 20 seconds of sniffing
Stage Two	5 treats**	3 bouts of 5 seconds of play	3 bouts of 5 seconds of massage	3 bouts of 20 seconds of sniffing
Stage Three	1 treat	5 seconds of play	5 seconds of massage	about 20 seconds of sniffing

**Remember to count out each treat one by one and take a deep breath in between each one.

Learning patterns of movement
When you are exposing your dog to a trigger, it is important to try to keep his body moving (and yours as well). If your dog keeps moving, there is less of a chance that his body will freeze and stiffen, which means he is less likely to tense up and explode.

The Benefits of Moving

Years ago, I held a seminar at one of the world's oldest veterinary colleges in France that bounded a public garden. When it came time to do live demonstrations in the garden, there were no barriers to hide behind in an emergency or to give the dogs a break after an exposure. It was here that I discovered the beauty of movement and increasing distance between dogs and their triggers.

As each dog/handler team began to work, as long as the handler kept her dog moving, we had success. Some of the handlers moved back and forth away from the trigger while others traced a big oval with the apex of the oval nearest to the trigger. In either case, handlers reinforced their dogs when they had moved away from the trigger. Tossing the treats in the grass also made a huge difference, giving the dogs a calming and absorbing activity (sniffing out the food) to do. As a result of this success, I now recommend these two movement patterns to my clients.

Practice the movements below without your dog. See which movement feels more natural to you. Then pick one and practice it until you feel as if you could do it with your eyes closed. It's a dance you will do with your dog. You might also try testing its reliability by adding music when you practice. One possible benefit to adding music is that if you're feeling unsure of yourself during a real exposure, humming that tune might help calm you and keep you in "thinking" mode so that you can manage your dog and the situation better.

When you are certain that you have the dance, add your dog. Be sure to put your dog on his leash and collar so that you will match the context of the environment you will be working in. Whichever pattern of movement you choose, when you turn away from the trigger don't cue or talk to your dog. Talking will affect your timing, and your dog will come to depend on it. Instead, rely on your body language to give your dog a clean and clear signal.

BACK AND FORTH MOVEMENT

1. Take a step forward.

2. Click.

3. Turn your shoulders 180° and take at least 5 steps forward in the opposite direction.

4. Toss the treat on the floor (or feed your dog's mouth).

5. Repeat the steps above until the pattern feels natural to your body.

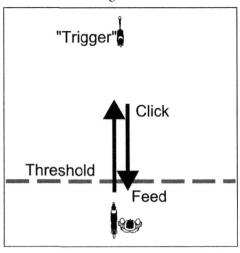

ARC MOVEMENT

1. Take one step forward.

2. Click.

3. Turn to your left or right (whichever is easier) and trace half an oval.

4. When you reach the opposite end of the oval, toss the treat on the floor.

5. Continue along the arc of the oval.

6. When you reach the apex, click and repeat Steps 3 and 4.

7. Continue this movement until it feels smooth.

In either case, after turning away from the trigger, don't forget to count out the treats and breathe.

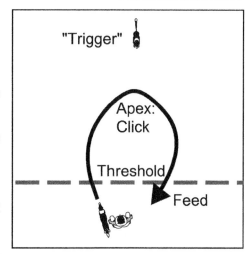

In practicing this oval-shaped movement, the key is to click your dog when you're closest to the trigger and to reward him at the other end of the oval, when you're farthest away from the trigger (and he feels less pressure.)

11
Setting Up a Training Session

How you set up your training session will likely determine how your exposures will go. Remember that when you are out in the real world, you have no solid control over the environment. You might think that no one walks a dog in this chosen spot at certain times of the day, but, lo and behold, look what's coming your way!

Before exposing your dog, be sure that you have taught your dog at least a few strong default behaviors (see p. 37). They do not have to be complex: Sit and heel will do. It helps you both if he also knows a few Emergency Behaviors (see p. 63). Being organized and prepared makes you more confident and successful—and your dog will pick up on that.

Think about what you will say if a well-meaning person comes over and tries to interact with your dog. To behave as a courteous member of society, state nicely that you are training your dog. Avoid stating that your dog is aggressive and that's why you are keeping him away from people. Telling people often enough that your dog is aggressive can become a self-fulfilling prophecy.

Location

Before you start training your dog, you will need to pick out a space to work. Find a place where you and your dog are safe from your dog's triggers. For example, if your dog is unstable with other dogs, you would not want to work him on an off-leash hiking trail. Every time that you expose your dog to a trigger accidentally, you signal to him that you are not protecting him properly.

If you are working outside, be sure that the space is private and will not be frequented by unwelcome guests, such as curious, talkative people or unleashed dogs. Make sure that you can increase your distance from a trigger substantially if necessary. Figure out where you will run if there is an emergency. Look for natural barriers such as trees, bushes, or parked cars. Can you run behind your car? Can you duck into the neighbor's driveway? You need to have a plan.

If you are working inside a training facility, be sure that the room is large enough to allow safe exposure to the trigger with a barrier of some sort for you to hide behind. A barrier can be anything from an X-pen with blankets thrown over it to a piece of agility equipment, like a tire, covered with a sheet. Whatever the set-up, be sure that you can enter and exit the room safely at any time.

Training Equipment

Before you start working with your dog, decide what training equipment you are going to use. If you have a very large dog or a dog that has bitten, for safety reasons it is best to use the Two-Leash system (see p. 27). As an extra precaution, consider working with a helper to keep things safe by using the Doggy Sandwich.

Doggy Sandwich

The Doggy Sandwich is an important safety procedure for crisis situations. The reactive dog walks in between a primary and a secondary handler, each of whom is holding a leash attached to a separate collar, head halter, or harness. The primary handler is the one clicking and feeding the dog for desirable behavior while the secondary handler is there to provide a body block if needed. The secondary handler can also assist by carrying extra treats or by handling the dog if the primary handler is unable to, for some reason. In addition, the secondary handler can give the primary handler emotional support if necessary. Both handlers can use their body weight to stabilize a large dog that is having a reaction.

If you are working with a powerful or reactive dog, you may want back-up help: another handler on a second leash. You'll keep the dog sandwiched between you, with you taking the lead in training. Your helper can provide both physical and emotional support.

Establishing the Threshold: The Invisible Line

When you begin exposing your dog to the trigger, you need to work at the level where your dog is curious but not over-aroused. Whatever might set off your dog needs to be at a distance that your dog can tolerate without triggering a reaction. Only gradually, as your dog feels more comfortable in the trigger's presence, will you be able to decrease that distance.

Think of the threshold as the invisible line that you draw across the spot where your dog would be his calmest when exposed to the trigger. That is where you want to start your exposure. Keep your dog behind that line. It could be 10 feet for some dogs and 100 feet for others. If your dog is constantly over-aroused, his brain does not have the capacity to learn.

Finding the threshold takes a bit of practice, and you will discover that the distance you need to be from a trigger will vary with the trigger and with where you and your dog are in the training process. The following exercise uses inanimate objects in your home and is good preparation for real-world exposures with riskier live subjects.

FINDING THE THRESHOLD

Objective: When your dog hears you click, he is able to turn toward you to receive reinforcement (or, later, turn away from the trigger toward you for a click).

This exercise offers an excellent way to practice adjusting your dog's threshold distance to the trigger before venturing out into the real world. It is an exercise as much for you as for your dog, since you need to know the signs when your dog is over threshold, at his threshold, or under threshold. You will take an object that your dog is very interested in—a trigger (maybe a treat on a lid or a remote-controlled toy)—and determine how far away you need to be from it to be able to click and feed your dog for looking at it calmly and then, eventually, for looking away from the object toward you. This technique will work the same when the triggers are people or other dogs, but this version offers less risk. You will be practicing your chosen movement pattern with your dog as well, to perfect the dance before you encounter real triggers.

How to teach the behavior:

1. Decide which room you are going to practice in and put your trigger on the floor. Turn it on if it is battery-operated.

2. Put your dog on his leash and collar and walk into the room.

3. Be ready for your dog's quick pull toward the object. Try to click before he starts dragging you toward the object. (If he is pulling you, he is over threshold.)

4. Start clicking your dog for looking at the trigger, move away, and then give your dog a treat.

5. Repeat until your dog is no longer pulling toward the trigger. Remember each time to move away, and then treat. Now your dog is under threshold, and you are practicing Stage One of the Click to Calm process!

6. Once your dog practices the correct behavior reliably, withhold your click and see if he turns his face toward you. If so, click, move away, and give your dog five treats individually. Give the treats slowly, counting out loud as you give each one. Take a breath in between. You are practicing Stage Two of the Click to Calm process.

7. If your dog's head does not swivel back to you, chances are that he has "Sticky Head" (see below). This means that he is right at his threshold and his head is "frozen." Take a step back and see how quickly he re-orients to you. When he does, click and feed five treats as described above.

Let's review:

- If your dog is pulling you toward the trigger, often barking as well, he is over threshold.

- If your dog is silent but cannot turn his head away from the trigger, he's still over threshold because he's sitting at his threshold distance. Moving him away from the trigger will help loosen his head. The Back Up–Sit works nicely here.

- If your dog can look at the trigger and then look at you, he is below threshold. This is always the goal behavior. Your dog is absorbing information at this point. Bravo!

This Dalmatian is clearly over-threshold, dragging her caregiver toward the enticing robo-dog. To determine her dog's threshold, the caregiver must move her dog back to the point where the dog can watch the toy calmly. That distance could be many feet away.

Secrets to success:

- Do your best to find your dog's optimal threshold and work from there. Avoid any temptation to close the gap to the trigger quickly regardless of how well your dog is doing.

- Be sure that you back up or move away after each click. Backing away from the trigger will give your dog time to take a breath and eat before venturing toward the trigger again. This also gives you a chance to reassess your next exposure level.

"Sticky Head"
When your dog is right at his threshold—the invisible line—you may see what I call "sticky head." Your dog is at the precise point where he's barely relaxed enough to

watch the trigger but too worried or mesmerized to do anything but stare at it. He's frozen. Transfixed, he can possibly even hear your click, but he has a hard time turning his head away from the trigger. His head is stuck and cannot be budged until you take a step back. That loosens his head immediately, so he can get his treats. Anytime you see that your dog has a "sticky head," take a few steps back and work accordingly.

If your dog seems so frozen or mesmerized by a trigger that he can't turn his head and look at you when you click, then he has a "Sticky Head" (above, left). He's too close to the trigger and, although he's not barking at or dragging you toward it, he can't function. You need to back off and create more distance to the trigger before he can turn toward you. Here, the handler called her dog and he turned his head reluctantly (above), but it took longer for him to make eye contact (left). Instead, if she had backed her dog off his threshold, he could have responded to the click and turned on his own.

As you will read in the remainder of this chapter, each time that you click your dog, you should move away from the trigger, and your threshold line, before reinforcing him. (This is hard to remember since we have all grown up with the term "click/treat!" and think we need to reinforce right away at that spot.) Remember that every time you expose your dog to a trigger, it can be stressful. Backing away from the trigger is a way of relieving that stress. I think of the trigger as pressure. I want to tell my dog (via the click) that he did the right thing at the right time by looking at the trigger and, later, at me. I want to reduce the pressure on my dog and let him enjoy his reinforcement in peace. When we are both ready, we again will face the trigger and then I will reduce the pressure. I think of this dance with a dog as "pressure on/pressure off." Although learning any skill is challenging, you want to work in such small increments that your dog will find this learning exercise a positive experience.

Data Collection: Keeping a Training Journal

Maintaining a training journal is a critical step in modifying your dog's behavior. Whatever your training goal, a journal will help you plan your training sessions and track your dog's progress. Remember that setbacks are part of the training process and provide valuable information that you can use to improve the structure of future training sessions. Be as kind to yourself as you are to your dog and avoid getting discouraged; just as your dog is growing in his skills, you are still developing yours as well.

Ask yourself questions like these:

1. How long was the session?

2. How close were you to the trigger?

3. Was your dog calm, over-stimulated, over-aroused, or over-threshold?

4. If your dog reacted, ask yourself,

    a. Did any specific behavior or action by the trigger stimulate the response? (For example, the trigger dog started tugging with a toy or lunged on the leash.)

    b. How did you respond? How well did your intervention work?

    c. After going over his threshold, how long did it take your dog to calm down to a level where he could start learning again?

    d. Was there more than one trigger present?

The Value of Records

When you are working on behavioral issues like reactivity and aggression, it is easy to get carried away with emotions. Your dog could have been non-reactive for several years, and then one day you turn the corner and the unexpected happens: your dog explodes in rage as another dog jumps out in front of him. At that moment, you are disheartened wondering if you should have ever embarked on this journey. How could this happen *again?* You can refer to your training journal to see just how much progress you have made. It always feels worse than it is!

Tracking trends in your training using a notebook, spreadsheet, calendar, or other record-keeping format with which you are comfortable will expedite your training. Draw a smiley face on the calendar for each successful session and note days on which you feel less successful with a pawprint. A paw print reminds us that our dogs are not "bad" dogs; they are simply being dogs. Reactivity and aggression are actually normal behaviors for all canines. These behaviors are only problematic when they spiral out of control or create dangerous situations for humans, dogs, or other animals. Once you have worked your dog through his reactivity, a journal is a great reminder of just how far you have come as a team.

12
Putting it All Together

The dog's learning process with Click to Calm reminds me of my own experience as a veterinary assistant at a practice that saw exotic animals, including snakes. I remember the first time one came in. The technician walked into the exam room with a wriggling pillowcase. I thought, "No. Don't even tell me…!" Although I couldn't take my eyes off the bundle, I backed out of the room and pretended to be busy doing something else. There was no way that I was ever going to be able to treat a snake medically. I watched in horror as they unrolled this animal across the treatment room to put ointment on its skin.

After a discussion with my boss, I knew that I had to overcome my fear and learn to master this skill. Each time a snake came in, I watched the technicians handle it lovingly. Gradually, I moved closer until finally one of the technicians said, "It's okay. Just touch his skin here (in the middle of his body). See how soft it is." It took me five months to acclimate, but after I felt comfortable being in a snake's presence and touching its skin, I was able to treat snakes just as I would any other animal.

Here, then, is the process that can help your dog overcome his feelings around his triggers and learn to function, and even enjoy, life around them.

STAGE ONE: RECOGNIZE

Objective: Your dog calmly looks at the trigger and then moves away from it with you.

This is the stage where you teach your dog to look at and listen to the trigger so that your dog can start to feel comfortable in the presence of the trigger. During this stage of training, you are not teaching your dog to ignore the other dogs (or some other trigger) in the environment, but rather to recognize and co-exist with them peacefully.

When you first start training Stage One, you are looking to develop a seamless rhythm: look—click—move back—reinforce—move forward— look—click—move back—reinforce. Once you and your dog feel confident with this process, you can start closing the gap between you and the trigger. Later on in training you may make the trigger more "triggery" (for example, by asking a person to wave his arms instead of standing still), but when you're just starting out with the Click to Calm protocol, it's easier to simply deal with the other variable in this process: distance to the target.

Playing with distance to the target helps you to both learn how to read your dog's body language as he encounters triggers and to gauge how close you can get to the trigger. Always remember that distance is your friend; maintaining proper distance keeps everyone safe. As you become more proficient at closing the gap between your dog and his triggers successfully, you'll be able to calibrate how much movement and noise your dog can tolerate from the trigger, but start off with a still, silent trigger. Slowly add movement or noise (not both at once) and increase your dog's distance from the trigger accordingly. It's a balancing act: either close the gap to the trigger or make the trigger livelier, but don't do both at once.

Clients often tell me, "I want my dog to like other dogs." My response is, "This training will be your best shot. First your dog has to learn to accept the presence of other dogs in his environment. Only then can you see where it leads. Maybe your dog will be curious. Maybe not. That's up to your dog to decide."

It's easiest to start with a motionless trigger (top) and graduate to a dog that's moving more (bottom). You can increase the trigger's noise or motion level or close the gap between your dog and the trigger, but don't change more than one variable at a time.

How to teach the behavior:

1. Put your dog on his leash and collar following the directions listed in "Perfecting skillful handling," p. 114. Keep your dog close to your body and start with him behind his threshold line.

2. Employ your chosen pattern of movement. Click and feed your dog at a high rate of reinforcement for seeing and hearing the trigger. Do not say anything. Instead, focus on the timing of the click and the placement of the reinforcement.

The Dalmatian looks calmly at the trigger dog (left). The handler clicks, moves her dog back, and reinforces her dog (right).

3. Ratio: 1 click = 1 treat; or 1 click = 5 seconds of play; or 1 click = 5 seconds of massage; or 1 click = about 20 seconds of sniffing

   a. If you are using the back-and-forth pattern, your first step will be toward the trigger (but behind the invisible threshold line).

      i. Click your dog for looking at the trigger. Then turn your shoulders 180° and walk in the opposite direction.

      ii. Take deep breaths as you move away from the trigger.

      iii. Feed your dog. (This allows your dog to eat in peace!) Assuming your dog already knows this pattern, his body will continue to move fluently with yours. Then repeat the pattern.

b. If you are using the circle pattern, your first step will be toward the trigger (but behind the invisible line).

    i. Click your dog for looking at the trigger. Then turn and start walking in a huge circle away from the trigger.

    ii. As you turn away from the trigger, take a deep breath.

    iii. Feed your dog when you arrive at the farthest point from the trigger. Then repeat the pattern.

4. Practice several repetitions of Stage One until your dog is performing this sequence smoothly. Then try slowly moving closer to the trigger, always mindful of your dog's body language.

Secrets to success:

- Be sure that you begin by clicking your dog as he looks at the trigger. Watch for fake head turns! Do not reinforce those!

- If your dog becomes over-stimulated, back away from the trigger immediately. Record the data.

- Dropping the treat on the ground can help to calm your dog faster.

- Remember to click, move away, and then treat! If you are using touch or a toy, go behind a barrier of some type first.

- It is better to work far away from the trigger and then close up distance instead of working too close to the trigger, having a reaction, and then trying to salvage the training session.

- If your dog needs a really high rate of reinforcement, try a food tube. Teach your dog how to eat from it before using it in a training session.

- If you must work your dog in a stationary position, do so for only three to five clicks at a time, and then take your dog behind a barrier to rest. This is hard work! If you are not going to move away from the trigger physically, then you need to create the time needed for both you and your dog to take deep breaths.

- If your dog has a hard time with the exposure regardless of the increased distance, place your dog behind a barrier and allow him to peek around the corner. Click, move your dog back behind the barrier, then feed. (The Back Up–Sit on p. 82 is perfect in this situation.) With success, gradually allow your dog to look a bit longer before clicking.

- If your dog reacts, it means you went too far too fast.

- Ignore the temptation to over-expose your dog when he's being successful. You should only practice a few exposures at a time.

- If you are concerned about treat quantity, deduct the amount of food that you feed your dog during the training session from his daily rations.

- If you find it beneficial, exercise your dog before a training session. Some dogs get mellow; others get cranky.

One of your main goals is to not get stuck in Stage One. If your dog gets so comfortable with Stage One "looking" that he starts whipping around to get his treat before you even click, move on to Stage Two. Your dog is already offering Stage Two behavior (reorienting from the trigger to you) on his own! He's ready.

STAGE TWO: REDIRECT

Objective: Your dog calmly looks at the trigger, voluntarily checks in with you, and then moves away from the trigger with you.

The goal at this stage is to teach your dog that the presence of the trigger in the environment *is the cue to turn and re-orient to you for further assistance.* This is the stage where the magic takes place! I can still remember, when I was exposing Ben to another dog, the moment he turned to look at me instead of barking and lunging. It was miraculous! The fact that he made that decision on his own was truly life-changing. Many students have told me that they also remember the exact moment when their dogs first looked at them instead of at another dog or other trigger. It is the direct confirmation that your dog trusts you enough to dare turn away from the scary thing and focus on you.

In Stage One, you were clicking and feeding your dog for looking at the trigger. Click, move him away, and then reinforce. In Stage Two, you will be exposing your dog just as you did in Stage One, but you will wait for your dog's head to reorient to you first before clicking. And, after moving away, you will reinforce your dog five-fold! By paying the dog much more for reorienting to the handler instead of to the trigger, the reinforcement history is now on your side.

How to teach the behavior:

1. Put your dog on his leash and collar following the directions listed in the "Perfecting skillful handling" section. Keep your dog close to your body and start behind his threshold line.

In Stage Two, your dog looks at the trigger (left) and then looks back at you (center). You click, move back, and feed your dog (right).

2.   Initially, click and feed your dog at a high rate of reinforcement for seeing and hearing the trigger. Do not say anything. Instead, focus on the timing of the click and how your body is moving. Be sure that you are breathing regularly. This will help to calm your dog. You are aiming to establish a rhythm.

3.   Once your dog's eyes are bouncing from you (after feeding) to the trigger, withhold the click for a second or two.

4.   When your dog turns voluntarily and looks at you as if to say, "Hey, I'm looking at the trigger! Where is my treat?" this is where you click, move away, and feed your dog five treats. Take your time!

   a.   Count out loud as you are dispensing each treat, taking a deep breath in between. Allowing your dog to eat the treat off of the ground can have more of a calming effect.

   b.   Although this stage is a subtle change, it is the piece that will teach your dog to look at you when he sees the trigger.

   c.   If you are using toys or massage, one click will earn your dog three rounds of five seconds of play or massage. If you are using sniffing, one click will earn your dog three rounds each of about 20 seconds of sniffing. Breathe in between.

5.   Practice this stage as much as possible. Remember that you will still need to reinforce Stage One many times when you are working toward and on Stage Two.

6.   As you continue to work, you have the choice of either working your dog closer to the trigger or making the trigger more noticeable in the environment while maintaining your original distance. For example, if the trigger is another dog, you can either start

closing the gap between your dog and the other dog or you can stay at the original distance and have the other dog become more animated—move, jump, or bark. Remember to work on only one variable at a time!

Secrets to success:

- The key to this methodology is to allow your dog to volunteer behaviors freely. You are never trying to persuade your dog to look at you. (If you cajole this behavior from your dog, you will be doing so for the rest of his life.)

- Keep sessions short and successful. Sometimes a session might last for one to three minutes or for five clicks. If you keep up with the data, your dog will tell you how long he can work without a reactive episode.

- If you are working in a confined space that makes it impossible to move away from the trigger, make up for the lack of distance by increasing time away from the trigger. Work for five to ten clicks and then take a break behind a barrier.

- When you are taking a break, allow your dog to participate in an activity that he loves: playing ball, sniffing, running, and so on.

STAGE THREE: REPLACE

Objective: Your dog calmly looks at a trigger, readily reorients to you, and responds to a cue in the presence of the trigger.

Now that your dog is choosing to work with you, you can cue a behavior that is incompatible with barking or lunging. Choose a favorite behavior that your dog knows reliably and that fits well into the learning environment. The ability to connect with your dog in this way ensures that you and your dog will meet life's challenges with confidence and joy instead of desperation and fear.

How to teach the behavior:

1. Put your dog on his leash and collar following the directions above. Start behind his threshold.

2. Review Stage One: Start by clicking and feeding your dog at a high rate of reinforcement for seeing and hearing the trigger.

3. Review Stage Two: Once your dog's eyes are bouncing from you (after feeding) to the trigger, withhold the click for a second or two. When your dog turns voluntarily and

looks at you, click, move away, and feed your dog five treats individually (or reinforce accordingly with play, massage, or sniffing). Take your time! Repeat this behavior three to four times.

4. The next time your dog glances at the trigger and looks back at you, click and reinforce, and then cue a reliable behavior for him to perform. "Sit" or "Heel" works fine here. "Get Behind" also works well if the distractions are super high!

5. Click and feed your dog for performing the intended behavior. If your dog defaults to a reliable behavior on his own, be sure to reinforce it as long as it is appropriate.

Secrets to success:

• Your "replacement" behavior should be one that is easy for your dog to do.

• Teach your dog a variety of reliable (default) behaviors so that you have several to choose from once you get your dog's attention.

• Ask for the default behavior only after you have clicked and fed your dog for looking at you voluntarily.

• If your dog looks at you but then goes right back to staring at the trigger, he is not ready to give you his full attention. If this is the case, go back to practicing Stages One and Two.

CASE STUDY: Harnessing Joie de Vivre

Click to Calm works extremely well for dogs that react aggressively to a selection of triggers, but it is also perfect for the exuberant adolescent dog!

Molly came to see me because her Labrador retriever, Rufus, loved other dogs so much that when they were in a classroom setting she had absolutely no control over him. Rufus dragged her into the facility, happily pulling her toward the other dogs, hoping to play. Although the other dog owners reprimanded Molly fiercely, all of her attempts to refocus Rufus failed. That was... until she tried Click to Calm.

Before class started the next week, Molly came into the facility early and started clicking and feeding Rufus each time another dog-and-handler team entered. He was totally focused on her the entire time. Once all the dogs were in the building, Molly waited a few more seconds to see if Rufus would focus on her. Yup! Five cookies please!

Now that she had her dog's attention, they could work on the class exercises alongside the other dogs. The same people that reprimanded Molly earlier in the month complimented her on how wonderful Rufus's temperament had become. A win for all involved!

Once you and your dog have mastered the basic Click to Calm protocol, your bouncy teenage dog may be ready for life's normal excitement. If you have a more challenging dog (for example, one that's reactive or aggressive to people or other dogs or is fearful of children or flapping flags), your work on Click to Calm is the starting point for equipping your dog with the skills for coping with life. For example, you can learn how to move your dog comfortably beyond merely sitting in the presence of other dogs to possibly interacting with them. Or you may learn how to guide your shy dog toward meeting and bonding with people. The key to progress is a solid foundation in the mechanics of Click to Calm.

Part of moving forward, however, is the inevitable stumbles that you will encounter. Since they can be emotionally devastating, it's best to be prepared. The next chapter details how you can plan ahead so you'll be ready to act when you can't think straight (use those Emergency Behaviors!). Your goals are to keep everyone safe, mend any rifts in your relationship with your dog, deal with your feelings, and adjust your training.

13

When it All Goes Wrong

You have worked hard teaching your dog the Click to Calm methodology. Now, every time he sees another dog, instead of lunging and barking, he turns and looks at you. Excellent! You also have enough foundation behaviors to cue when you need them. For example, you can cue your dog to keep heeling with you or stand beside you on a walking trail while another dog and handler pass by. Or, if another dog threatens your dog, he comes and finds you. Everything is going great until…

"There Was Nothing I Could Do!"

No matter how careful and thorough you are with your training, something is bound to go wrong. That's life. There will be times when someone leaves a door open or you will misjudge a training challenge. You will be walking in an environment that you have deemed safe when suddenly an off-leash dog appears out of nowhere, and you know your dog is not ready! Accept that you will make mistakes.

Sometimes the mistake is one that you have made willingly, assuming incorrectly that your dog is "all better." For example, many years ago I took Ben to a private obedience lesson. After the lesson, the instructor asked me if Ben could meet one of her senior dogs, Daisy. I should have declined immediately since there was no real reason why Ben should interact, but I didn't. I said "Well, let's see…"

I took off Ben's leash and allowed him to advance toward Daisy at his own pace. I was surprised by what happened. I thought he would walk around the room and slowly come up to Daisy, since that was what he had been doing with some of my friend's obedience dogs. Instead, he stayed by my side.

Thinking that Ben didn't understand what was happening, I gave him another cue, asking "Do you want to meet this dog?" in my sing-song voice. (This is a terrible cue! Way too long!)

Asking Ben the question allowed me to believe that Ben would be the one making the decision. As long as I respected his decision, there would be no trouble.. Up until that point, he had only said "No" twice in meeting about 80 dogs.

After I gave the cue, Ben took a few steps forward then turned to look at me. I should have stopped there, but I felt an overwhelming desire to see what he would do next. I cued him again. He took a few more steps toward Daisy and looked back at me again. Finally, I said in a sharp tone, "Ben, go meet that dog." And he did! He took a few steps forward, jumped on Daisy, and started muzzle-punching her violently. I ran in and pulled him off. As I did so, I noticed that there was blood running down his face. Daisy, trying to protect herself, nipped him above his left eye.

I felt horrible! I knew that it was the wrong thing to do, but why did I move forward? I moved forward because I thought that, with all of the good training and successful exposures, Ben was a different dog. That part of him was gone. At least I liked to think so, since I hadn't seen him react that way in years. But that part of him was still there, now tempered by all he had learned. It was a wake-up call for me.

It took something that dramatic to make me realize that my dog was actually making his own decisions. I had mistakenly thought that as long as I kept reinforcing Ben for what I wanted that he would be hard pressed to want to do anything else.

After that incident, it took about two full days for Ben to interact with me again. Hugging him close, I swore that no matter what happened in the future, I would never sell him out for a cheap boost to my self-esteem as a dog trainer.

Sometimes the mistake is one that takes you by surprise! There is no way that you can see it coming. My friend, Denise, had a basset hound named Mason that was reactive to people. Although he had never broken skin, he had growled and snapped at strangers as an adolescent dog. Fearing that he would get worse, Denise had immediately started working with him. Now that Mason was five, she could take him anywhere: family parties, social gatherings, and basset hound picnics. But Mason never really liked it when strangers touched him. Denise managed those situations by cueing Mason to hand target the visitor and turn back to her for treats. After a few of these repetitions, Mason visibly relaxed and then allowed the visitor to interact with him briefly.

At one point, Denise took Mason with her to Martha's Vineyard. On the boat, there was an older woman who came up to her, expressing her love of the breed. After a brief conversation, the woman asked if she could pet Mason. As Denise started to explain the protocol, the woman reached down to stroke Mason on the top of his head. Blindsided, Mason whipped his head around and as he opened his mouth to snap, one of his teeth grazed her skin, leaving a visible scratch. The woman was absolutely furious. Although Denise tried to explain Mason's wariness, the woman started yelling at her to "put her dog to sleep." Several onlookers started whispering and moving away from the pair. Luckily, the woman never contacted Denise after the incident, but Denise couldn't forget it.

Denise started to wonder if she should have even worked on the Click to Calm protocol with Mason. If Mason's first reaction was still to lash out at people, maybe Mason should be put to sleep or, at best, kept away from people that he didn't know. Why risk it? What Denise forgot was the wonderful reinforcement history that she had built with Mason prior to this incident. As long as she could explain to people that Mason was slow to warm up, both parties were happy, and nothing happened.

It's odd how when things are going really well, we tend to take them in stride. We say to ourselves, "Well, that's how he's supposed to act. I'm glad he finally gets it." But when a mistake happens, even if it wasn't our fault, it hurts so deeply that we are ready to throw it all away. My belief is that if we let that sort of thinking rule our response, we never truly accept the dog as he is. You can't change a dog's psyche. You can change his behavior—how he reacts to the world—and equip him with better coping mechanisms so that life is calmer and more enjoyable for both of you.

How you deal with mistakes, whatever their cause, will determine if you should move on. If you have an "incident," there are short-term and long-term steps to take to help both of you recover.

Renew Your Commitment to Your Dog

First, as soon as possible, tend to your dog's needs. In the moment, this may be emotionally challenging for you when your immediate reaction is to be furious that your dog has just muzzle-punched another dog and "betrayed" you or scared the daylights out of you. It's hard to think straight when you're frightened. But here are some tips:

1. Remove your dog from the situation. Emergency Behaviors can help both of you move out of danger.

2. Speak quietly to your dog while gently stroking him. If you feel angry or upset, unleash those emotions later, away from your dog.

3. Take deep breaths to calm yourself. If you visibly relax, your dog will as well.

4. If possible, cue your dog to do a few favorite behaviors and reinforce him accordingly.

5. If your dog has a reactive explosion, know that it can take several days for his brain to return to baseline. He should stay in the house during this time and be kept as calm as possible.

Second, a serious incident (regardless of whose fault it was) can fray the trust your dog has developed in you and erode your relationship. You need to repair it. Remember that your commitment to your dog is to provide the physical, mental, and emotional support that he needs throughout his life. That is going to mean different things to different dogs.

If you give a rambunctious, energetic dog a predictable framework to operate in, he understands what he needs to do to get what he wants. This is a way for both caregiver and canine to work cooperatively. The dog maintains his enthusiasm, but he takes his lead from his caregiver. A win for both! For the fearful dog, it means that you break down behaviors for him in ways that he can understand and protect him from all possible threats. With clarity comes confidence. For the shy dog, it means that you take things slowly and allow him to decide who he wants to meet in his own way. Shy dogs that do things on their own time schedule tend to interact more as their courage grows.

"Potcake Pilgrimage" details the story of a couple who committed to help a pair of puppies that they adopted from Caribbean islands. Puppies George and Jerry suddenly landed in an entirely alien world on the mainland. It was so terrifying that one of the puppies bit a trainer twice. However, the couple persisted and slowly introduced the pups to their new home. Although we can't get inside dogs' heads, this tale offers a glimpse of what some rescue dogs, and their caregivers, go through.

CASE STUDY: Potcake Pilgrimage

Our journey began 15 months ago when a human family rescued us, two brothers, from our impoverished life on the islands of Turks and Caicos through a wonderful adoption shelter, the Potcake Place. The books say that we "potcakes" are "prototypical mixed-breed dogs" that survived off the caked remains from the pots of local people. We're supposed to be extremely smart, loyal, and loving. Determined to keep both of us together, our beloved humans named us George and Jerry.

Since our humans had had many dogs before us, they were confident that they knew just how to care for us. They had recently lost two dogs, wanted desperately to fill their life with the love of canine companions, and diligently found a school for us so we could learn. While our humans thought this was a good idea, it didn't go as expected. I (Jerry) was terrified the moment I entered the loud, crowded class on my first day of school. Would I, or my brother, be killed? Would my humans be maimed? I needed to protect them! The trainer threw George and me out of school after three classes and after I bit the trainer twice in one class. My humans were devastated, frightened, and did not know what to do. Fortunately, the school told our humans to get therapy with Emma Parsons.

Because our humans were a child psychiatrist and child psychologist, they thought they were psychologically sophisticated, but they had no idea of all that they were about to learn. We dogs don't understand mistakes, only learning opportunities.

For George and me, the mainland world was a very scary place, so different from the islands. My humans learned that they had to help us calm our brains because, when we

The Potcake Boys, George and Jerry.

were in "fight-or-flight" mode, we couldn't learn any of the dog cues that humans think are so important. Emma taught our humans to give us a click and a delicious treat whenever we were able to chill out in the face of the many new and frightening sights and sounds all around us. Emma said that only when our brains were calm could we make a choice to "face and embrace" our fears. I remember one time when we both panicked that a basketball in our yard was going to kill us. Emma taught our humans that tossing the ball to us was not only unhelpful, but it frightened us more. Instead, they learned to watch for any signs that we could even glance at the ball for a second and then, of course, give us a click and a wonderful treat. Gradually, after many small steps of looking at the ball, then taking a step toward the ball, and then touching the ball—all steps that were of course rewarded with delectable treats—we began to play with the ball. Our humans slowly developed patience and appreciated that our needs were different from those of all the other "normal" dogs they had loved before us.

Emma also told our humans, "Love is not enough." To love us also meant to work with us and reinforce what we needed to do instead of telling us what we shouldn't do. So many humans say "No! Bad dog!" This, of course, doesn't help us learn. We need to learn what to do instead, like staying calm, paying attention to our humans, and always, no matter what, coming back to them for high praise and rewards. Now our humans know to ignore our quirky behaviors that they don't like and instead reward our many tiny successes throughout the day with praise, clicks, and treats.

One of the best skills our humans taught us is "Go Touch." We both get so incredibly excited when our beloved humans come home from even a 30-minute outing. As Emma told them, to expect us to sit calmly would be like asking a mother not to hug her child after he returns from war. "Go Touch" gives us a way to channel our enthusiasm without knocking over and licking our humans to death.

Emma was on our humans' speed dial. Our humans often worried, felt sad, and cried because we are not "normal dogs." But they've adjusted their expectations and understand us now so that they can safely manage us and give us the rest, play, and structure we need. We adore figuring things out and learning new things, like how to meet strange humans. We love our basket of "destroy toys" that we are free to tear and shred whenever the mood strikes us. Life is good.

Renew your commitment to your dog daily, especially if something bad happens. There is no one else who is going to be as committed to your dog as you are. Your job is to educate your dog and protect him from whatever life throws at both of you.

The Aftermath: Healing Yourself and Moving On

When you think you have your dog's behavior under control, there is nothing that hurts more than realizing that you don't. The reality is that no matter how improved your dog's behavior is, your dog is still the same dog inside. Yes, your dog will make better decisions in the future with your supervision and guidance, but there still will be circumstances that will be difficult for him, whether or not they are your fault.

This fact is incredibly punishing to humans. Why? Because we can't understand why our dogs would revert back to that old behavior when things have been going so well. We, as caregivers, want to believe that the aggression is completely gone.

Here are some tips to help you prepare for life's glitches:

1. Re-evaluate what went wrong during the session or incident. Did something happen that was beyond your control? Did you mismanage your dog's threshold level? Did another person or dog get injured? How badly? Figure out where the breakdown occurred, consider what you could do differently next time, and make changes accordingly.

2. Think seriously about what you will do if the worst-case scenario happens. For example, what if another dog ran up to yours off leash? What would you do? Visualize the plan and teach your dog the necessary skills. (See Emergency Behaviors, p. 63.) What if your dog gets off leash and goes running after a child on a bicycle? An Emergency Recall would be mandatory here.

3. Emotionally, it feels horrible when something goes wrong. It is easy to blame yourself when something bad occurs, regardless of how much your dog has improved. Forgive yourself! Still, you must accept the possibility that something unfortunate can happen at any time.

4. Do not yell at your dog. If you feel resentment toward your dog, get out a notebook and jot down your feelings. In a few days, once you come back to a thinking brain, you can assess what happened and why. Plan a different outcome… and train for it.

5. Decide if your dog's behavioral issue is too much for you to handle. There is nothing shameful about trying everything possible to make a situation work out but not having the strength, knowledge, or finances to see it through.

Carol felt blindsided during an obedience class when her Great Dane Belle dragged her across the floor toward a loose dog zooming around the training room. Upset, she took the time to assess what had happened, why, and how she could prevent a future outburst. She didn't throw the baby out with the bath water.

CASE STUDY: Training Indoors Is a Whole Different Ball Game

Belle was a Great Dane that wasn't fond of other dogs. Her caregiver, Carol, had taught her the Click to Calm methodology, and now Belle could go anywhere that a typical dog could go: to the park, to the town square, and to the beach. At one point, Carol had decided to take an obedience class with Belle at the local YMCA.

Belle did great in the class! She was focused on Carol the entire time, ignoring the dogs that were working around her. One night, as the dogs were practicing off-leash recalls, a springer spaniel got loose and ran around the room. Much to Carol's surprise, Belle started to growl and began to drag her across the room to chase the other dog. Everyone started to panic, since Carol couldn't hold on to her 110-pound dog.

Luckily, the other dog's handler was able to catch her dog and take her out of the room. Shaking, and with the help of the instructor, Carol was able to regain control of Belle. The instructor, frightened by the events, told Carol that she could no longer be part of the class; she would need to take private lessons.

Immediately Carol reprimanded herself for taking Belle to a public class. Belle had been doing so well, but, she realized, all of those successes happened in outside environments. Why did she think she could take Belle to an indoor class for "normal" dogs?

Just as Belle needed time to calm down after an event like this one, owners' and trainers' brains need to calm before future training decisions are made. In coming to terms with this incident, Carol had to renew her commitment to Belle and ensure that, in the future, she would evaluate every training setting. In retrospect, she should never have stood there when the other dog started running around. Instead, she should have heeled Belle to a safe place until the other dog had been caught.

Know that you will always need to support your dog's emotional health regardless of how successful your dog has become. Accepting your dog for who he is throughout his life will help you make smarter decisions and keep you on the lookout for possible limitations. In turn, you have to learn to give yourself the time and space to take a step back when an incident occurs, evaluate what happened objectively, and plan to reduce the possibility of a re-occurrence.

Now that you have the skills to use Click to Calm, better evaluate situations, track your dog's progress, and adjust your training when you encounter setbacks, you may want to move beyond the basic "familiarization" protocol of Click to Calm. I've tailored the next section to show you how to apply the complete Click to Calm program, first to dogs that are uneasy around people and then to dogs that aren't at their best around other dogs. I also address specific problems, such as dogs that react loudly to visitors "invading."

PART V

Tailored Solutions for Troubled Interactions

In Part IV, you learned not only to expect the unexpected, but how to deal with it. Click to Calm training lets your dog feel safe in a stressful situation so that you don't fear an explosion or a meltdown. For a dog that's unsure of people, or that doesn't "know" doggie lingo, or that botches canine social interactions, this chapter provides special tweaks to the Click to Calm program. It also gives you the tools for helping the dog that seems to want to do more than just glance at triggers from a distance.

14

When Your Dog is Uncomfortable Around People

The most common reason that dogs are anxious around humans is because people can be unpredictable. One minute they are holding out their hand for the dog to sniff and the next they are trying to hug the dog. Dogs, like humans, need to know what to expect, especially dogs that have been treated poorly by people in the past. Dogs tend to fear things that they don't understand. Fearful dogs can easily turn into aggressive dogs. The human unpredictability problem is often magnified when children are involved.

Kids and Dogs: A Match Made in Heaven?
Children can pose special challenges to a dog, particularly if it has not been exposed to them. Once children reach the toddler stage, they are often more mobile than the average adult. Kids tend to dart around, their movements are quick, erratic, and unpredictable, and they are prone to making sudden, loud noises. They can't deftly modulate their responses, so they can't slide up and down the arousal scale easily. That means that kids spend more time at the extreme ends of emotion. Moreover, they are just learning the rules of social engagement. They don't readily register or recognize the signals of doggie body language. Crucially, they don't understand proper "social distancing"—between other humans or other species. Some dogs are fine with little kids; they roll with the punches. Others view them as unruly puppies and try to discipline them accordingly. Still others are terrified and want nothing to do with them. The would-be disciplinarian and the fearful dogs are the ones that present potential danger.

There are many situations when you might want your people-sensitive dog to feel more comfortable around family, friends, and strangers. A dog that is at ease would make both of your lives more relaxed and, quite frankly, fun. Consider the following examples:

- Your reactive dog is not sure how to act around strangers. He seems to want to interact with them but scares easily when people reach out toward him. Or he can look as if he wants to meet someone but, once the introduction starts, he reverts to growling, barking, and lunging. In the past when strangers asked if they could pet your dog, you turned and moved away quickly, blurting out some kind of apology. Even if your dog does not want to meet a visitor, can training change these dynamics so you would still have complete control over the situation without having to flee?

• You are having a baby and you have a dog that is uncomfortable with strangers entering his home. Anticipating that family and friends will want to visit after the baby is born, you want to teach your dog that it is okay if people stop by.

• You and your fiancé have moved in together. Your dog, adopted at the age of three, is frightened of new people. Can he learn to accept and even like your fiancé?

When your dog's trigger is other people, your success in making him feel safe and comfortable around them depends not only on following the Click to Calm protocol but on negotiating with the humans involved. If your dog gets testy with your kids, you'll need to get their buy-in and make training a family commitment before you can make reasonable progress. If you have a dog that's shy about guests entering your home, you will have to decide whether to manage or train your dog, in part based on whether you can get the cooperation you need from your visitors. If your dog is conflicted about meeting strangers at the dog park, pick your human triggers carefully to find people who will follow your instructions. Fortunately, humans can talk to each other and plan, and, if you do so judiciously, you and your dog will be successful in overcoming the worst of his "people issues." Especially if your dog is hyper-responsive to human body language, you need to consider not only the actions of family, friends, and strangers, but your own.

If your dog is sensitive to human body movements...

1. Stand up straight in the presence of your dog. Bending over a dog can squash his super-sensitive "bubble." If you need to bend toward your dog for any reason, cue him to jump up onto a higher surface, which will make it easier for you to reach him. I had a tall client who needed to give her medium-sized dog a pill twice a day. Every time she bent toward him to give him a pill-laden meatball, he growled at her. Once I advised her to cue him to jump onto the couch and give him the pill from there, just popping it into his mouth, her problem was solved. If your dog is sensitive to your body movement, instead of leaning down to feed treats to his mouth, toss the treats on the floor.

2. Refrain from approaching your dog in a threatening manner. For example, do not corner your dog for any reason (even if it is for his own good).

3. Use "quiet" body language when you are near your sensitive dog. Dogs can become over-stimulated quickly when your hands are flying and your voice is yelling! For some dogs, these are the cues that a traumatic event is about to take place.

4. Videotape your dog while you and your family are participating in certain activities. For example, what is your dog's body language saying when you are getting ready to leave the house? What about when you are preparing a meal? How about when the children are playing or getting ready to have friends over? Your research will show how your (and your family's) movements impact your dog's emotional state.

Tailor Emergency Behaviors to Your Situation

Before you start exposing your dog to strangers, or if you have a dog that is aggressive to you or another family member, I strongly recommend that you teach your dog Emergency Behaviors (see pp. 63–92) that will enable you to get your dog out of sticky situations with people. These cues let you control your dog's movements better and move him confidently, and they allow a dog to interact safely with a human or an object. You don't need to train every behavior, just the behaviors that you think would benefit you and your dog—see suggestions below. If you are working with a professional trainer, have the trainer review the list with you to see which behaviors might be most suitable for your dog and his issues. Work on them individually at first and, when they are reliable, take them on the road.

The Get Behind cue (see p. 72) allows you to use yourself as a human barrier for your dog if an unexpected trigger appears. You can cue your dog to get behind you if there are people or dogs on the other side of a door, for example.

The Back Up–Sit cue (see p. 82) teaches your dog to spin and come toward you as you back away from him. It can help squelch an impending explosion if your dog starts pulling you toward an oncoming person or dog.

If you have a dog that tries to bite you when you attempt to get him off the couch, the Shifting Location cue (see p. 87) enables you to move your dog from place to place with the sweep of your hand. Your dog simply follows the hand target.

The Walk–Lie Down cue (see p. 68) teaches your dog to switch smoothly between heeling and lying down. You can use it either to halt your dog's aroused approach toward a person or another dog or to jump-start a dog that's balking.

The Go Touch cue (see p. 64) builds on targeting behavior so that you can send your dog away to touch an object. It gives a fearful dog a structure in which to explore his environment, including people he doesn't know.

The Hand-Target Greeting (see p. 66) offers a dog that is uncomfortable around people a framework in which to "Go Say Hi," and it corrals the over-enthusiastic greeter into performing more acceptable behavior.

Teaching a people-sensitive dog to back up from you with your outstretched hand flicking toward him (Back Up cue, see p. 67) enables him to relieve the pressure he feels if people approach him and can keep everyone safer. The back-up behavior also gives you a way of moving a dog that is likely to flee to a safer spot where you can cue a down.

Sometimes you just need your dog to get—and stay—out of the way. Adding an outstretched hand to the Back Up cue (Back Up–Down, see p. 89) cues your dog to move away from some overly friendly stranger he may be afraid of.

The Recall–Back Up cue (see p. 71) is the solution for the over-eager dog that bowls you over when you call him. You combine the recall with the sit–stay and back up cues to provide a braking mechanism to the missile hurtling toward you.

For the dog that can't resist jumping up on you, friends, and family, the Four on the Floor cue (see p. 51) rewards him for keeping all his feet on the floor, no matter how excited his body is. It's a real crowd-pleaser.

If you have to lead your dog somewhere, but he's nervous and you don't want to drag him by the leash or collar, teaching him the Chin Rest (see p. 85), where he rests his chin in your hand, provides reassuring contact with you as you take him where he needs to go.

How Click to Calm Helps Dogs Sensitive to People

This chapter gives you a roadmap for moving forward with your people-sensitive dog by offering you and your dog a predictable structure to work in. The Click to Calm method provides a methodical introduction to the presence of a stranger and then, once the dog decides that he wants to move forward, he can feel free to investigate the person without worrying about reciprocal experimentation. Remember that your dog's fearful, reactive, or aggressive responses are simply behavior, triggered by emotions, and that you can shape those reactions by achieving tiny approximations of "better" behavior. Even if you have a dog that doesn't love everyone, you can still teach your dog to be much more comfortable with the people in your life. This is a way to get there.

To succeed, however, your dog first needs to learn to trust his caregiver to make the best decisions for him. He needs to learn that you will always protect him no matter what the circumstance. That means that you cannot allow strangers to greet your dog without your permission. Every time that you allow another human to greet your dog or interact with him inappropriately, you are further convincing your dog that you do not have his best interests at heart.

Every learner needs to be in an environment that he trusts in order to learn new skills and improve his behavior. If he is anxious or fearful, he cannot learn new behaviors. *Although it is always your decision whether or not to move forward safely, it is ultimately your dog's decision whether or not to participate in this process.* The general rule of thumb is to proceed slowly with your training, always with an eye on your dog's reactions, so that you can keep yourself and others safe and so that you don't overwhelm your dog.

The Click to Calm Process

Whatever your dog's problem with triggers is, the Click to Calm protocol outlined in Part IV can help. If you and your dog have mastered it so that he feels comfortable in the presence of his triggers and can respond to your cues, you can move beyond the basic protocol. Here is a summary of the entire program for a dog that has troubled interactions with people:

Basic Click to Calm		
Phase One: Familiarize	Stage One: Recognize	Your dog earns a click for calmly looking at or listening to a person; he gets reinforcement after he moves away from the person with you.
	Stage Two: Redirect	Your dog earns a click for calmly looking at a person and then turning and focusing on you; he gets reinforcement after he moves away from the person with you.
	Stage Three: Replace	Your dog earns a click for looking at a person calmly and refocusing on you. He moves away from the person for his reward and then performs a cued behavior.
Advanced Click to Calm		
Phase Two: Investigate		Your dog earns a click for approaching and possibly sniffing or otherwise interacting with a person; he gets reinforcement after he moves away from the person with you.
Phase Three: Meet		Your dog earns a click for successive approximations of letting the person pet him; you reinforce him either at the person's side or, after several repetitions, after he moves away from the person.

Preparation and Set-up

Decide where you are going to work with your dog and set up your space: If your dog is sensitive to visitors in your home, work there. If your dog is anxious in outside environments, choose a place where there is no chance that a stranger will come up to you uninvited. If there is no such place, take a friend or family member with you to ward off unwanted strangers or place a leash on your dog that announces that your dog is people-sensitive. Set up a space behind a barrier (for example, a spare room in the house or a fence outside) where you can put your dog's belongings, such as a mat and bowl of water, and rest your dog in between sessions. Use your training equipment. For reactive dogs, that means a leash and a collar (or a harness). For aggressive dogs, use the Two-Leash system outlined on p. 27. Muzzle your dog if you feel it is necessary (as long as your dog is already accustomed to a muzzle).

Session length: Sessions should be short (5–10 clicks are plenty for one exposure). If your dog's behavior deteriorates, end the session immediately.

Decide if you are using a helper or exposing your dog to strangers: If you choose a helper, you can communicate exactly what you want him or her to do. Always work with someone who will follow your instructions, and work with only one person at a time. When you change helpers, go back to the original threshold. If you work alone, follow the guidelines above to keep your dog, yourself, and others safe.

Never tell a stranger that your dog is aggressive: Telling someone that your dog is aggressive will give that person an open invitation to explain to you that he or she is a dog person whom all dogs love! Instead, say that you are obedience training your dog. Most people will understand that explanation, especially if you have a young dog.

Familiarize (Phase One: The Three Stages of Click to Calm)

For a dog to start warming up to strangers (even family members he considers "strangers"), he first has to get used to seeing them and hearing them from a distance—and then closer or with their hands flailing and with their voices growing louder. To help your dog warm up to all kinds of people, you will take your dog through the three stages of Click to Calm described in Chapter 13, "Putting It All Together," p. 127 (Recognize, Redirect, Replace).

You may find it helpful to review the Click to Calm Rate of Reinforcement guidelines, p. 117, and the Secrets to Success for each of the three stages of Click to Calm (p. 130, p. 133, and p. 134). They hold true for these exposures as well. Only when your dog grows familiar and comfortable with the sight and sound of strangers, to the point that he not only readily focuses on you but also can respond to familiar cues, can you decide if he would like to explore people further.

Once everything is prepared, you're ready to start Phase One.

RECOGNIZE (Stage One)

Objective: Your dog earns a click for calmly looking at or listening to a person; with you, he moves away from the person for his treat.

In this stage, you click and feed your dog while he is looking at or hearing people so that he learns to be in the presence of strangers without incident. If you are working with a helper, you can control how much noise or movement he or she makes. If you are working alone, you won't have that control over the human triggers you select, so be particularly sensitive to your dog's threshold distance. Work separately on increasing a stranger's movement or noise level or on getting closer to the stranger. You can ping-pong back and forth between closing the gap to the stranger and making the stranger "livelier," but only work on one criterion at a time. For example, if you ask your helper to wave her arms, start your dog back farther (increase the distance).

How to teach the behavior:

1. Establish your baseline: Start at the invisible line where your dog can look at and hear people without going over threshold, and respect that line.

2. Set up the exposure: If you have a helper, start with the person stationary, sitting in a chair or standing up straight. If you need to work on your own, choose a place where your dog can watch people move from a distance with little chance that they might want to come toward you and visit. A ball field, store, or boardwalk is a suitable site.

3. Ask your helper to shift her weight; click and feed your dog for orienting toward and watching this movement while remaining calm. If you are working alone, start by clicking and feeding your dog for watching people move in your chosen location.

4. After the click, use either the back and forth or the circle movements you taught your dog earlier to move away from the stranger and take pressure off your dog.

5. Give your dog one reinforcement: one treat, one play session (5 seconds), one massage (5 seconds), or one bout of sniffing (about 20 seconds) for watching the person or people.

6. Now ask your helper to move her body a bit more or move closer to the stranger in the ballfield or other site. Click and feed for that as well.

7. Gradually decrease the distance between your dog and the trigger person or expose him to more noise/movement. If at any time your dog reacts, it means that the person is moving too much or is too loud, or you are too close. Go back to an earlier version where your dog was successful and work from there.

Secrets to success:

- Remember that distance is your friend. Any time your dog reacts, the first thing to do is to move away from the trigger.

- It is always easier to decrease your distance slowly and successfully than to station your dog too close to the stranger and then have to increase your distance quickly. For aggressive dogs, moving quickly is even riskier. Respect boundaries!

As your dog becomes familiar with watching and hearing strangers, see if you can move closer to them. Can you walk by them while they are moving? Are you starting to relax when you take your dog for a walk? If you notice that your dog is barely glancing at the stranger and is watching you in anticipation of the treat more than he is watching the person, then it is time to move on to Stage Two.

REDIRECT (Stage Two)

Objective: Your dog earns a click for calmly looking at a person and then turning and focusing on you; with you, he moves away from the person for his treat.

In this stage, you click your dog for turning his attention from the stranger to you, the handler, so that he learns that the presence of the stranger is the cue to turn to look at you for further instruction. It's a brave decision on his part that warrants extra "pay."

How to teach the behavior:

1. Establish your baseline. Until you have completed numerous training sessions, always go back to the original baseline. Start with a still, silent stranger. Warm up with clicking and reinforcing your dog a few times for looking at the stranger (Recognize, Stage One). You want your dog's eyes to be bouncing between the stranger and you.

2. The next time your dog looks at the stranger, wait one to two seconds to see if he offers you voluntary eye contact, expecting his reinforcement.

3. If he does, click, move away, and give your dog five treats individually.

   a. Count the treats out loud to your dog as you give them. If you pair your voice with the reinforcement, the counting becomes both a cue and part of the reinforcement.

   b. If you are using play, interact with your dog for 5 seconds for 3 repetitions.

   c. If you are massaging your dog, touch your dog gently for 5 seconds for 3 repetitions.

   d. If you are releasing your dog to sniff, give him 3 bouts of about 20 seconds each.

4. If your dog does not turn to look at you readily or is only half turning his head toward you, you are too close to the stranger (see "Sticky Head," p. 123). Increase your distance from the stranger. Once your dog's head turns toward you, follow the instructions above. In order to move to Stage Three, you need your dog to give you full eye contact voluntarily.

5. Repeat a few times. You are aiming for ever-quicker head turns from the stranger toward you. You want your dog to become fluent in this behavior.

6. Once your dog turns from the trigger toward you readily, you can start either closing the distance or, separately, making the stranger more distracting (add movement, noise).

Secret to success:

- Be aware of your dog's sensitivity. If he's scared of children's sudden movements but tolerates their noise, for example, work first on getting him closer to a child who is noisy but still (you need a cooperative kid for this one!). Then you can slowly address the movement issue, starting at first from afar.

As your dog continues to give you eye contact calmly and reliably with scarcely a glance at the trigger, think about which behavior you would like to cue. You are ready to replace the inappropriate behavior with a desirable one. Move on to Stage Three.

REPLACE (Stage Three)

Obective: Your dog earns a click for calmly looking at a person, looking back at you, moving away from the person for his treat, and then performing a cued behavior.

When your dog is turning toward you reliably and offering eye contact in the presence of a stranger, you can cue a default foundation behavior so that your dog, instead of lunging and barking, will remain calm and feel secure. He trusts that you will keep him safe in this situation; thus, he can function (respond to cues) with a brain that's not fogged up with fear, arousal, or stress.

How to teach the behavior:

1. Set up your training session as you did in the previous stages.

2. Start by reviewing Stage One. Click and feed your dog for looking at and hearing the trigger.

3. Move on to Stage Two. Wait one to two seconds: did your dog look back at you? If so, click and feed your dog five treats individually (or give him three 5-second bouts of play or massage, or give him three 20-second bouts of sniffing).

4. Repeat this exposure 3–4 more times.

5. If your dog continues to give you eye contact, click and treat him, then pick a reliable behavior and give your dog the cue.

6. Click and reinforce your dog for performing the cue in this challenging environment. If your dog is not able to perform the cue, you will need to shift in and out of Stages One and Two until your dog is comfortable.

7. Repeat this sequence, either asking for different behaviors or increasing the noise, movement, or proximity of the stranger. Remember to work on each aspect of the exposure separately.

Secrets to success:

- Even if you feel that your dog is comfortable being close to loud, active people, continue to start each session by warming up briefly with Stages One and Two—behind the baseline. It is the safer thing to do, especially if your dog is not feeling well that day, for example. Eventually, you can drop this routine but that will not be for a long time.

- As you close the distance between the dog and the trigger person, you can cue any default behavior that your dog can perform reliably, including Sit, Down, or Touch.

- At this stage, assess your dog's comfort constantly. Look primarily for loose body language. At this point you should be able to feel your dog's emotional state when you are working, sense when he starts to relax or tense up, and adjust your training accordingly.

- In addition to your dog's body language, his ability to respond to a cue at all and the speed of his response are barometers of his emotional state and clues to whether you are progressing too fast.

- Once your dog is able to perform the behavior in multiple settings with different strangers, start plugging in default behaviors of your choice when you are out and about. You can use your dog's ability to respond to cues in the presence of people as a direct measure of his comfort level.

Now that your dog is feeling more relaxed around strangers, it is time to decide if you should give him the opportunity to investigate people. If you are unsure if this is a good idea, proceed slowly. There is plenty of time to stop in the middle of the process. Remember that your dog calls the shots!

Investigate (Phase Two)

When your dog is feeling more relaxed around strangers, and if it is safe and he is able, it is time for him to explore humans without any fear of uninvited interaction. Some dogs are content watching people from a distance while others will gravitate toward them naturally, wanting to learn more about them.

INVESTIGATE

Objective: Your dog earns a click for approaching and possibly sniffing or otherwise interacting with a person; with you, he moves away from the person for his treat.

In this exercise, you guide your dog closer to the target person and allow him to sniff or touch the person if he desires. Although you warm up with Stage One of Click to Calm, the object of the exercise isn't for your dog to then check back in with you. Your focus here is on allowing your dog to touch the person freely without the pressure of having to meet the person. Your dog explores the person as an inanimate object; he can interact with the person in any safe way that he chooses.

Set up where you trained Phase One. Make sure that there is a resting place for your dog (some kind of barrier works well). To prepare for this exercise, you may need to place some markers (cones or tape, for example) to measure the oblique path you and your dog will take as you start moving toward the stranger. Using markers makes it easy to measure the distance at which your dog can work happily. Adjust your markers as you proceed. Start by working with the same person you worked with before, either standing or sitting in a chair. If your dog has been aggressive in the past, he should be muzzled. If you need to interrupt a training session, just move your dog away. Be sure that you and your helper have established a cue to end the session if needed, if your helper has to cough, scratch, or move in some way, for example.

I've used treats as the reinforcement for these training steps, but adjust as appropriate if you feel that play, massage, or sniff fests work better for your dog.

How to teach the behavior:

1. Warm up by clicking and feeding your dog for looking at the person, both sitting still and standing up. Remember to move your dog away from the stranger after each click for his treat.

2. If your dog appears relaxed (body is loose), ask the person to sit back in the chair, either with her hands on his knees or in her lap.

3. Start moving your dog toward the person by clicking, moving back, and feeding your dog for looking at the person. Don't approach the person head-on. Instead, walk in a straight line back and forth parallel to the person or make sweeping curves toward him (following your markers). Make sure to move away from the person after each click to reinforce your dog.

4. To test your dog's comfort level as you are moving forward, cue different reliable behaviors, such as a hand target, Go Touch (maybe one of the markers), a sit, or a down. If your dog can't perform these behaviors, that means that he is not thinking clearly, so don't approach as closely.

5. Once you reach the person, allow your dog to explore the person's body. Click your dog if he touches the person's elbow, foot, or knee and then move away immediately to take the pressure off your dog. You can do this by cueing a Back Up–Sit or by tossing a treat away from the person and telling your dog to "Find it."

6. Approach the person about five times. Do not cue your dog to touch the person.

    a. If curious, your dog will touch the person on his own.

    b. If he is not interested, move away slowly and ask for a reliable behavior.

    c. If he moves forward and then his body tenses, toss a treat away from the person, tell the dog to "Find it," and end that session.

7. As your dog progresses, start inserting a verbal cue like, "Say Hi" or "Touch" right before your dog makes contact with the person's body part.

8. At the end of the session, start making your way back to your barrier either by releasing your dog and running back to the barrier happily or by heeling your dog (or practicing other reliable behaviors) as you move closer to your barrier. Party time!

Secrets to success:

- Don't ever pressure your dog to touch a person.

- Always allow your dog to open up distance on his own.

- Spend some time with your dog working reliable behaviors in the presence of the person before actually interacting with the person.

- When your dog starts to touch the person, your initial training sessions should be very short.

- After each touch, move your dog away from the person either by leading him away (as you have in the past) or by tossing a treat to the other side of the room/space.

By the completion of Phase Two, your dog has grown comfortable being in a stranger's presence and has learned to touch a stranger without fear that the person will try to hug, pet, or play with him. In the third and final phase, you determine if your dog wants the human to invite any interaction. Would he feel comfortable allowing the person to greet or even pet him? Note that in Phase Two it is the dog that takes the initiative; in Phase Three it is the stranger who takes the initiative.

Meet (Phase Three)

If your dog has grown comfortable in a stranger's presence and has learned to touch a stranger without fear that the person will try to be his "friend" or throw large gestures at him, this last stage allows you to see if your dog wants the human to reciprocate. Does he want the human to invite limited interaction, like greeting or briefly petting him, always with the option of moving away when he wants to?

MEET

Objective: Your dog earns a click for successive approximations of petting; he gets reinforcement either at the target person's side or, after several repetitions, after he moves away with you.

This final training stage offers your dog a secure process to follow while he considers if he wants a stranger to interact with him. Because of the predictability of this process, your dog always knows that he can end the interaction if needed. He knows that he can move away at a moment's notice and that there will be no pressure if he decides not to make a connection. Thus far, there has been no need to lunge, bark, or bite. The beauty of this process is its predictability; predictability makes your dog feel safe. Until your dog has been through all three phases numerous times, do not deviate from the original pattern.

Before moving on to Phase Three, review Phases One and Two, using the same person as the stranger. Your dog should recognize the person and he should feel confident practicing these behaviors in a familiar situation. The person should be either standing or sitting in a chair with her hands hanging by her side (if sitting or standing) or hands resting comfortably, palms down on her knees (if sitting). Tell your helper that when it comes to touching your dog, she must always use the hand nearest your dog—no reaching over your dog's head, neck, or back—and only make small gestures.

How to teach the behavior:

1. After briefly reviewing the steps in Phases One and Two, bring your dog parallel to one side of the person. Your dog should be facing you, not the person.

2. Cue your dog to sit or assume a position that is comfortable for him.

3. Ask the person to hold the hand nearest your dog parallel to your dog's shoulder for the count of two. Click and feed your dog in place while the person holds her hand there.

   a. If you see your dog tense up, move away, toss treats on the floor, and cue "Find it." Back up to Phase Two.

4. Repeat this behavior several times.

5. When your dog seems ready to move forward, ask the person to touch your dog's shoulder with her index finger gently, using the back of her finger (it's less intimidating and can become a cue to your dog). Click and feed.

6. Is your dog fine if the person touches him for a bit longer? How about a few seconds?

7. With each successive session, ask the person to touch your dog with one finger, then two, then three, and so on.

8. Once your dog accepts that level of touching, see if the person can use one finger and drag that finger an inch on your dog's shoulder. How about two fingers?

9. Will your dog touch the person's hand if it is offered? The person can offer her hand slowly by either raising it to your dog's height or, if her hands are on her knees, she can flip one over at a time. The person is simply providing a clickable opportunity for your dog. She should not bend forward or stare at your dog. If your dog does not want to connect, your helper should slowly drop her hand to its original position.

Secrets to success:

- The key to success is to work on only one criterion (number of fingers, duration of touch, length of movement while touching) at a time for a few repetitions. Then either move away or toss treats and cue "Find it" to release your dog.

- For the highest level of success, practice exercises from Phases One, Two, and Three predictably; follow all of the steps religiously. Over time, your dog will start to trust the pattern of exposure and anyone involved in the experience.

- Just because your dog feels better with your helper does not mean that the helper is your dog's best friend. Continue to proceed slowly, with no physical expressions of affection.

- If your dog continues to warm up to your helper, ask the helper to participate in activities that your dog likes. Playing ball, doing a clicker training session, or going out for a walk are all wonderful ways in which this new person can connect effectively without physically intimidating your dog.

CASE STUDY: From Trixie the Cross to Trixie the Calm

Amelia is a clicker-savvy caregiver who noticed that her young miniature poodle, Trixie, became irate when people came to visit. She barked continuously at the visitor, and, if left unchecked, bit at the person's pant legs. Amelia called me after Trixie bit two people. Though the bites did not break the skin, Amelia was mortified and concerned.

When I arrived, Amelia had put Trixie in a spare bedroom to stop her dog from rehearsing the behavior. I told Amelia that I was going to sit on the couch, pretending to be busy, and instructed her:

1. Put Trixie on her collar and leash. Get out your clicker and great treats.
2. Bring Trixie into the room, and, just as she spots me, click, take her back into the adjoining kitchen, and give her the treats. It's fine if you click too soon.
3. Repeat about five times and then return Trixie to her safe space.

Amelia did as I directed. Sure enough, when Trixie rounded the corner and saw me in the living room, she barked and pulled forward. Amelia had all she could do to hold on to her. Amelia clicked, turned, and brought Trixie into the kitchen for a treat party. I told Amelia to increase the distance from me. She tried again and Trixie showed us a "Sticky Head," (see p. 123) indicating that she was still over threshold. I advised Amelia to take one more step back. For the remaining repetitions, Trixie was able to move in and out of the living room, looking at me, and then, when she heard the click, move back to the kitchen for treat parties.

Ending on this success, I told Amelia to click and feed Trixie for looking at and hearing people talk. When people were visiting Amelia, or she and Trixie were out socially, I wanted Trixie to know that when she saw a stranger she would be reinforced. I made sure that Amelia understood the difference between Click to Calm's Stage One and Stage Two.

When I visited the next week, I saw a different dog. Initially, there were a few moments of barking, but, within a few clicks, Amelia could control Trixie beautifully—even when I got up and moved around. Because Amelia had done her homework, it didn't matter what I did. With every move I made, Trixie looked at me then looked right back at Amelia. Beautiful! She had mastered Stage Two—and Stage Three. Trixie could also respond to cues in my presence.

We moved on to the next challenge (Phase 2) with me sitting motionless in a chair. I gave Amelia the following instructions:

1. Let Trixie touch my hand, thigh, elbow, or foot.
2. When she does, click, back up, and give her the treat, or click and toss a treat away from me and ask her to "Find it."

3. After this one exposure, go back into the kitchen. If I needed Amelia to move away sooner (in case, I had to sneeze, for example), I would say "okay," to cue Amelia to take Trixie away.

Trixie approached cautiously. When she got clicked for touching a part of my body, however, she didn't want to leave. At one point, Amelia almost had to drag her away to prevent her from exploring my face. For safety reasons, I ended the session there. Amelia's homework that week was to do a million Back Up-Sits and to cue Trixie to touch objects that she liked and bounce back to Amelia. To move forward, I needed to know that Amelia could move Trixie away from any distraction safely, including me!

When I saw Amelia and Trixie again a few weeks later, I asked Amelia to click and feed Trixie for relaxing in my presence in the living room, to see if we could move on. Once I saw that Trixie was still fluent in these skills, we practiced the Phase Two behaviors from the previous visit. Trixie had improved! She came over and touched various parts of my body: feet, hands, lap, elbow, and ankle. With each repetition, Amelia was able to move Trixie away easily.

For the next challenge, I sat with my hand hanging loosely by my side. I instructed Amelia to

1. Click and feed Trixie for touching my hand.
2. If Trixie did as she was asked, I would slowly turn over my hand so that my palm was facing up.
3. If Trixie was curious and came forward, click and feed her for touching the palm of my hand.
4. In between each exposure, bring Trixie back to the kitchen where she could relax.
5. On a verbal cue from me, Amelia would allow Trixie to venture forward again.

That day we were able to practice several hand touches, with me extending my hand and Trixie happily coming to touch it. The next visit, we graduated to Trixie sitting by my side, and, although I didn't touch her, I was able to place the back of my hand a few inches above her shoulder (the beginning of Phase 3). I ended up becoming Trixie's friend and hoped that Amelia could work through this process with other cooperative family members. The key to success was not to push Trixie to do something she didn't want to do but to teach her a process so that she could decide how far she wanted to go. Amelia learned to predict accurately how Trixie would react and to understand what Trixie's body language was communicating.

Applying the Lessons of Click to Calm: Phases Two and Three
- Work on the following pieces of criteria in this order:
  - Stationary person (Phase Two)
  - Moving person (Phase Two)
  - Dog touches the person stationary (Phase Two)
  - The person touches the dog stationary (Phase Three)
- With success, add small movements one at a time: dog moving or person moving, not both together.
- You can work with several different people. The only caveats are to treat each person as a single journey and to perform all stages of the process with each person; start at the beginning with each new person. If your dog is fine watching people, then he can jump in on Phases Two or Three, depending on which criteria you want to work on.

You might have a dog that is friendly with people, but when someone visits your home it is a nightmare! At the sound of the doorbell, your dog runs to the front door, barking incessantly. When the visitors come in, your dog either jumps all over them or comes forward to sniff their feet then backs up, barking viciously. Or maybe your dog watches silently from a corner to see if the visitor is going to go near any of his belongings. The next chapter will address some of these special training challenges.

15

Solving Specific Dog–People Issues

Your front door is the passage your dog goes through to get to the outside world, which may be giddily enticing and exciting or intensely intimidating and unsettling. Conversely, it is also the entryway for people, people your dog may view as delightful visitors or as scary intruders. The signal of their presence (the doorbell) is enough to set off many dogs in anticipation or alarm. Since a great deal of obnoxious or even dangerous dog behavior occurs at doorways, with the arrival of delivery people and visitors, the first part of this chapter focuses on accustoming your dog to these events so that they are less traumatic for both of you.

Think back to the case of Colby (p. 9), the two-year-old golden retriever adopted by a family with two children. Colby discovered that he received more attention and had more fun stealing a child's toy and growling and snapping at anyone who tried to take it from him than quietly playing with his purple dinosaur. This is the portrait of a first-class resource-guarder in the making—and a dangerous dog. But there are ways to halt the development of this behavior and cure habitual resource-guarders. Careful management and teaching your dog about touching, holding, and exchanging objects will go a long way toward tackling resource-guarding problems.

Drama at the Door

Do you have a dog that alerts on every delivery truck and lunges and barks at the window as he sees the UPS person coming up the walk? Does your dog "greet" every visitor with frantic barking and jumping? If your dog barks at people when they approach or enter your home, you must stop this reactive cycle before you can teach your dog more appropriate behavior. Your dream is that every time someone comes to your door, the UPS person delivering a package or a friend visiting, your dog will remain quiet, either relaxing in his safe space or accompanying you to the door.

Here are strategies for turning these triggers into cues for calm, quiet behavior. You may find that your dog is more comfortable when he watches people enter the home or you keep him in a room where he cannot see the activity. Use the strategy that your dog prefers. Be observant! You may find that, as your training progresses and your dog becomes calmer at the arrival of visitors, you can use different strategies. For example, if at first your dog needs to be in his safe space when visitors arrive, maybe later in his training you can practice Click to Calm in the doorway for looking at the visitor, or he could greet visitors at the door with a toy in his mouth.

Use your Emergency Relocation Cue (see p. 88): This is a perfect behavior to use when the visitor will be at the door less than five minutes: the UPS delivery person, the mail carrier, or maintenance men checking on a job. If you see the UPS employee coming up the driveway before your dog spots him, grab a favorite treat, calmly call your dog's name, praise him as he comes, and send him to his designated spot where he can enjoy his well-earned chewie. All is quiet as the doorbell rings and you receive your package.

Put your dog in his safe space (see p. 18): If you are not sure if your dog is safe and you are expecting a lengthier visit, put your dog in a secured room that the visitor cannot enter mistakenly. Ask your visitor to text or call before arrival. Exercise your dog prior to the visit and then leave him in his safe space with a noise source (radio or TV) and a mentally stimulating toy.

Change the point of entry: Since we usually reserve the front door for people that we do not know well, change the experience for your dog by asking your visitor to come in through the back door instead. Be aware of what words and tone of voice you use when greeting family or friends and use the same sort of greeting. Keep contextual cues the same. If you greet your visitor with the same carefree, lively tone of voice you use with trusted family members, this can set a friendlier atmosphere from your dog's point of view.

Ask your dog to carry something in his mouth: For dogs that retrieve by nature, keep a favorite toy close by that he only gets when visitors come to the door. Pet and praise your dog as he runs around happily with the toy in his mouth. This is the perfect solution for the overly excitable but harmless dog. Having something in his mouth means that he can't bark; the dog often gets so preoccupied with prancing around that he doesn't jump on your guest.

Ask for a previously reliable behavior: Basic behaviors such as sits or hand touches work well here. Never ask your dog to stay in one position as someone enters the home. Unless you have worked on stay behaviors of long duration under immense stress, it will be impossible for your dog to accomplish this. In turn, you will get frustrated with your dog and feel as if he's not listening to you.

Work the Click to Calm methodology in the doorway (see p. 127): Be sure that your dog is under threshold. Click your dog for watching the visitor come into the house (he should be curious but not reactive). Then take your dog to a neighboring room and feed him a fantastic treat. Repeat this training pattern until your dog quiets down.

Allow your dog off leash: If you know that your shy dog will eventually settle and that he is not dangerous, let him move around off leash. Ask your visitor to ignore your dog as he enters the house and to offer absolutely no eye contact. Click your dog for any interaction that is appropriate, for example, touching the person's shoe or sniffing the floor close to the person. After you click, toss the treat away from the person to relieve the pressure your dog may feel at approaching the person. Repeat this training pattern as long as your dog's body continues to become more relaxed.

Ask your visitor to drop several treats as he moves: If your visitor will follow your instructions, ask him to drop tasty treats as he enters. He should stand upright, ignore your dog, keep his elbows close to his body, and avoid eye contact or bending toward your dog. Your dog will make the association that when visitors arrive, treats happen. Win/win! You can add eye contact with visitors later.

When People Come to Visit

Despite your dog's aggression or reactivity, you still need to socialize. You require social interaction just as much as your dog does. If you are deprived of human companionship, you might start resenting your dog. That means that when family members and friends come to visit, there needs to be a plan.

The hardest challenge in bringing visitors into your home is that, despite your numerous protests, they are going to want to interact with your dog. You could tell them that your dog will bite their heads off, and they will still try to be your dog's friend. I am not sure why. Maybe it is because they feel impolite if they don't acknowledge your dog's existence, or maybe they feel as if they are insulting you if your dog doesn't like them for some reason. Whatever the explanation, even if you tell visitors to ignore your dog, most will not. They will still try to engage him in some way. Those attempts convince your dog even more that humans are not to be trusted. If dogs had the freedom to pick and choose who they wanted to interact with in their homes, dogs would be far more social in this context.

Having a plan allows you to keep both your dog and your visitors safe, as long as everyone follows directions. When people come over, you have two choices: you can either manage your dog or teach your dog. Management involves keeping your dog content (and confined) when new people or known "triggers" come into your home; teaching requires you to have your dog on a collar and leash (and possibly a muzzle) when you are working him with other people present. If time allows, I recommend doing a bit of both.

Keep Your Dog Safe

When people first enter your home, everyone tends to get excited and exuberant. It is best to leave your dog in his safe space during this period. Your dog needs to be content in this space, both when you are home and when you are not. (For more information about acclimating your dog to his safe space, see p. 18.)

It's usually easier on your dog if he can't see the visitors from his space (since that could produce barrier frustration). However, some dogs like being in the middle of all the activity, even if they are crated. Observe your dog's response and choose accordingly. Where is he most comfortable? Here are some general guidelines for using a safe space for your dog.

1. When visitors come, turn on some familiar sounds for your dog, like the TV or some of your favorite music. While you are greeting and entertaining visitors, be sure that he has some kind of mentally stimulating toy that he never gets unless he is in his safe space. (My dogs usually get antlers when my in-laws come to visit.)

2. Make sure that you place a sign on the door of your dog's safe space that states that no one is allowed to enter without supervision. (You don't want a well-meaning visitor walking into that room, especially if your dog is not crated.)

3. Assign one person to feed and exercise your dog at set times while others entertain the guests. If you are there by yourself, let your guests know what you are doing. Tell them how long you will be gone. Give them something to do while you are taking care of your dog. Let them know that they are free to watch you walk or work your dog—through the windows.

4. Set up a route so that your dog can move from his safe space to the yard without having to mingle with the guests. If this is impossible, ask your guests to take a seat while you heel your dog through.

5. Tell your visitors that if your dog escapes and enters the room, they should ignore him.

Reading a Wagging Tail

Too many times the following scenario plays out: You see the UPS person dropping off a package on your doorstep and open your door to get it. Excited to see who is at the door, your dog peeks his head out. The UPS person (an avid dog lover) sees a golden retriever whose tail is wagging. Eager to pet your dog, she sticks out her hand to say hello. CHOMP! She pulls her hand back in horror!

Many people think that a wagging tail is a universal sign that a dog is friendly. If you are about to pet a dog or you are trying to decide if you should let someone pet your dog, it is critical to look at the body language of the whole dog, not just what his tail is doing. Is the dog moving smoothly or is he hardly moving at all? Is he walking slowly, or does he have a spring to his step? Is he staring or looking with soft eyes at you or the other person?

A friendly dog has a soft, "squishy" body, relaxed ears (not pinned back against the sides of the head), his tail wag "wiggles" his whole body, he is smiling (the corners of the mouth are turned up, sometimes with teeth showing in a "grin"), and he is breathing normally. The dog is demonstrating appropriate behavior with the humans involved.

Conversely, if you encounter a dog whose body is stiff with flattened ears and a tail that is barely wagging and either held low (a sign of stress and fear) or held high (a sign of aggression), back off. Recognizing canine signals is the best way to read what your dog, or another, is saying.

Take Advantage of Your Captive Audience

If your guests are visiting for a number of hours, the longer they are there the more likely they will be to forget about your dog. Maybe you have had them over for dinner and they are now tired, or maybe you got together to watch a favorite sports game, and, after a couple of hours, they are less likely to try to interact with your dog. "Later" is a great time to start working with your dog on Phase One of Click to Calm, when he is less likely to encounter unwanted human attention. Here's how to do it.

1. Let the visitors know that for the next 10 minutes you will be training your dog. Again, remind them to ignore you both since you want your dog's attention to be solely on you. Ask visitors to be still and to keep their voices low.

2. Put on your dog's training equipment and take out your clicker and some high-powered treats. Start by clicking your dog the first time that he sees your visitors. After the click, back up and give your dog his treat. Move your dog into a neighboring room if necessary. Repeat numerous times. Be aware that any sudden movement by a guest might trigger your dog's reactivity.

3. As you work through Stage One, withhold your click and see if your dog will reorient to you directly. If so, click, back up, and give your dog five treats! Good boy!

4.   Once your dog grows more comfortable with this training process, take your dog into the room where the visitors are and sit in a chair. Keep your dog close to you and cue him to sit or lie down by your side. If clicking will disturb your guests, simply feed your dog every few seconds for remaining there quietly. Continue clicking and feeding for about two minutes. If at any time your dog appears anxious, leave the room with him.

5.   Practice some of your dog's favorite behaviors in this setting to determine how clearly he is thinking.

6.   When you are finished training, walk your dog outside before returning him to his safe space. Excitement can increase your dog's need to eliminate.

The more you work your dog in the presence of visitors, the more relaxed your dog will become. At some point, you might even be able to click, back away, and feed your dog for interacting with more familiar people (Phase Two training)

Resource-Guarding: Possessions

When a dog steals an object, family members typically become worried, even frantic, about what the dog has swiped, especially if it is an object of great value. The dog delights in this attention! ("Finally, they will play with me!") Often the dog takes the object, runs away, and squeezes into a tight space. A concerned family member may try to get the object back by cornering the dog and reaching to grab it out of the dog's mouth. The dog growls and snaps at the hand. Frightened at the potential outcome, the person retreats and leaves the dog alone with his prize.

Dogs want our attention desperately, especially if they are bored or live a life devoid of mental stimulation. If a dog learns that taking an object makes the family come alive, then he will resort to that behavior frequently. To prevent resource-guarding behavior from developing in your dog, make sure that you challenge your dog mentally each day. Teach him different tricks, take him different places, or take a fun dog-training class with him. Agility, Nose Work, or a Tricks class would work well as long as you make the commitment to teach him each day.

Consider training your dog to interact with objects. For example, say you have a puppy that is cautious around new items, such as backpacks or flags flapping in the wind. You can start by teaching him to touch novel items, like your backpack, on cue. Giving your pup a specific way to interact with the object changes his emotions about it. He comes to perceive it not as something scary or concerning, but as offering the potential for rewards. Next, work on the flag. In the future, when he is "meeting" objects firsthand, your puppy will no longer fear them and, eventually, will feel comfortable exploring new objects on his own.

If you have a dog that gets possessive when he gets a bully stick, try treating the bully stick as a target object and teach your dog to touch it. Teaching the dog to touch the bully stick makes him view the item in a different way; the bully stick now provides an opportunity to earn treats. Dogs that learn to touch and hold objects (especially with the caregiver holding the other end) are less likely to become possessive of their, or others', things. If you are holding the other end of an item that your dog has in his mouth, the context has changed from your dog's point of view; he no longer feels in control. One of the first lessons that I teach my puppies is how to chew on a bone or bully stick while my hand holds the other end. I immediately create the construct where my presence is part of the fun. As my dogs grow older, they often bring a toy or bone to where I am reading and play quietly by my side.

No Testing!

When people acquire a dog or a puppy, one of the first things they often do is see if they can take things away from him like food, toys, or other possessions. Traditionally, this is used as a test to see who is more "dominant." The logic is that a "submissive" puppy would allow you to take anything from him, so he'd be "safe" with the kids. This is the perfect set-up for, inadvertently, teaching a dog to guard his food and possessions. A dog catches on to the cues right away. He is chewing on something, a person approaches, makes eye contact, and crouches down. Why wouldn't he think that this is another test? In this way we start reinforcing potentially dangerous behaviors unintentionally, behaviors that are dangerous for ourselves and for our dogs.

Train Your Dog to Share

Object exchanges lie at the heart of training a dog to release potentially dangerous or coveted objects he may have in his mouth. Before you begin this training, as a safety precaution, first teach your dog to touch objects. Getting him comfortable with these sorts of interactions with more neutral objects can help diffuse any possessive tendencies he may have and will make training the release of objects less stressful for both of you (if you have a dog that has displayed possessiveness or aggression over objects). I start this kind of training with my puppies.

TOUCH GAME

Obejective: On cue, your dog will touch a named object with his nose.

Teaching your dog to touch an object with you holding the other end is a fun game that will get your dog used to you being around his toys or other items that he likes. Dogs that grow comfortable with this game rarely show possessive or aggressive tendencies, so it's perfect for puppies! To make the game more challenging, eventually you can send your dog to an object in a foreign location or practice object discrimination.

How to teach the behavior:

1. Pick a "fun" object like a toy or bright exercise disc.

2. Hold out the object in front of your dog's nose.

3. As he leans forward to touch the toy, click, put the toy behind your back, and give your dog a really yummy treat.

4. Present the item again, and repeat Steps 2 and 3 about five times.

5. When you are sure that your dog will touch the item, give it a name. Say the object's name right before your dog touches the object.

6. Continue to practice Steps 2 and 3.

7. Change the location of the object, by putting it on a chair or on the floor, for example. Give the cue for your dog to touch the object.

8. When he does, click, pick up the item, and toss your dog the treats.

9. Practice these steps with another item. When your dog is solid on touching the second named object on cue, put down both items and cue one of them to see if your dog can discriminate between the two. Make it a game. Have fun with it!

Secrets to success:

- Use an item that your dog likes but is not possessive about.

- When you present the item, be sure that your dog is reaching toward it with his nose. That is the nanosecond you want to click, not after he's started moving away from the object. Do not help him by putting the item on his nose.

- Practice this exercise with different objects that your dog likes.

- Do not allow your dog to take the object himself. Pick it up. Your dog will learn that when you pick up a toy, he gets tons of treats. This game is a way for you to be around his stuff with him getting big bucks!

- If at any time your dog begins to act threateningly, stop the training with that particular object.

- If your dog acts threateningly with an object, be sure that he views the reinforcement you are offering as more valuable than the item itself.

Once your dog is comfortable touching objects, you can proceed with training Formal Object Exchanges as outlined on p. 55. Basic Object Exchanges (p. 55) can save you if you are not far enough along in your training to simply cue your dog to drop or give you something he has in his mouth. If you have a known resource-guarder, a few further tips will help keep you and your dog safe:

- Never grab or chase your dog if he has stolen an item, especially as he slides under a piece of furniture

- If there are only a few items that your dog guards, change your dog's associations with those objects by teaching him to touch and retrieve these items on cue.

- Keep a long line on your dog while you are practicing these exercises so that you can maintain control if he becomes aggressive. You can hold him away from your body, stabilize him so that he cannot chase anyone, or escort him to his safe space.

- If you fear approaching your dog, don't. If you turn your back on him and leave, at least he hasn't precipitated an exciting game of chase.

- Work on one item to exchange at a time. It may take four or five sessions for your dog to become reliable in giving up that item. Only then can you move on to an item of greater value.

CASE STUDY: Impossible is possible!

At one point I had a client whose dog Sherry was growling at her teenage son whenever he came near her as she chewed on a bone. Here was the protocol I recommended:

1. Pick up all bones.

2. First practice nose targeting on "boring" things like a hand target and a spatula.

3. Only give Sherry bones when the son is absent. (The dog is fine then.)

4. Each day have your son present a part of a bone to Sherry and ask her to touch the bone with her nose. Start with the least meaty part of a bone.

5. When Sherry touches the bone with her nose, click and give her a piece of meat.

6. Continue in this fashion until Sherry can touch every part of the bone with her nose.

7. When she touches the bone, allow her to lick the bone a few times, click, remove the bone, and give her a wonderful piece of meat.

8. Slowly extend the time that Sherry has access to the bone. Only give her full access to the bone for a few seconds after you have the ability to hand it to her and take it back.

After repeating these behaviors for several months, Sherry no longer had a problem with the client's son being around her when she was chewing on bones. I was amazed that my client, an excellent trainer, later taught Sherry to retrieve the bone to give it to her or to her son on a verbal cue!

Resource-Guarding: Food

Your dog needs to feel confident that no one is going to try to steal or take his food (or food he views as his) from him. Unfortunately, we sometimes test this confidence without first teaching the dog what we want him to do. For example, say you adopt a shelter dog, bring him home, and lovingly give him a bowl of food. When you lean over to pet him as he's eating, he growls at you. Or, when your two-year-old drops a cracker on the floor and you approach to pick up the cracker, the dog that you have raised from puppyhood snaps at you.

Once they get a snap or a growl over food, people often feel that they have to test the dog even more. Some caregivers cannot believe that their dog has actually threatened to bite them. "My dog can't possibly do this again!" they think. So, at the next meal, they start to pet the dog again. Again, the dog growls or snaps. They move away in silent horror! Now they are building a pattern of behavior where they are definitely reinforcing the growling and snapping.

If you have a dog that has severely bitten over a bowl or a piece of food, seek the help of a veterinary behaviorist. If your dog has snarled or snapped over food, the steps below can help you manage his behavior and train him to become more comfortable with people around his food.

Take Basic Safety Precautions
Management aims to stop the behavior from occurring.

1. Stop testing! Every time that you go near your dog while he is eating and he growls, you are teaching him to growl at you near the food bowl (or wherever else this behavior is happening).

2. Feed your dog in a separate, quiet space, and pick up the bowl after he has finished eating.

3. If your dog has snatched a piece of food, let him eat it.

Train Your Dog to Relax around Food

Imagine the following scenarios, where you have trained your dog to view people around his food as normal and nonthreatening. You have visitors and, unknowingly, they walk by your dog as he is eating. He's confident that they won't bother him and keeps chewing. Or, at a party, one of your friends' children drops a chocolate brownie on the ground. Afraid that your dog might get sick, her mother hurries to clean it up, but your dog has already started to eat the yummy morsels. He remains unperturbed by the dustpan and brush and yields ground.

To prevent food-stealing and food-guarding, practice the exercises below.

RELAXED EATING

Objective: Your dog feels comfortable with humans around him when he is eating.

Dogs should never fear that their caregivers are going to snatch their food away. If you were eating your favorite food and a family member or friend pulled away your plate mid-bite, how would you react?

Variation 1: Feed by hand: Your dog's aggression around his food bowl decreases when he starts associating your hand in the bowl with lots of food.

If your dog absolutely cannot bear for you to be near the food bowl because of aggression issues, feed your dog by hand so that he learns to associate your presence with good things.

How to teach the behavior:

1. Ask your dog to demonstrate a well-known behavior, something easy like a hand touch, sit, or down.

2. When your dog responds, click and feed your dog several pieces of his meal. See if you can put his food bowl at a distance on the counter and feed the pieces of food by hand. If your dog is afraid of the clicker, do not use it.

3. Slowly allow your dog to see the food bowl. If he reacts to the sight of it, put it away. Continue to feed by hand.

Variation 2: Feed with Praise: Receiving praise while he eats makes your dog relax.

This method of teaching your dog to relax in your presence around food requires no overt training.

How to teach the behavior:

1. While you give your dog pieces of food, simply tell him how great he is.

2. Finish his entire meal in this fashion.

3. Continue feeding him his meals with praise until he feels more comfortable. If you notice that your dog starts to get pushy, by barking or nudging you, start to train him, asking for easy behaviors that he enjoys doing before giving him the next morsel.

Variation 3: Drive-by Bounty: Your dog learns that people approaching his food bowl means manna will fall from heaven.

A person moving toward your dog's food bowl often triggers a reaction. This exercise associates human approaches with very good things.

How to teach the behavior:

1. As your dog is eating, click as you approach and drop a huge chunk of meat (assuming your dog loves meat) near the bowl as you walk by. Don't stop to see where it lands or if your dog is going to react.

2. Continue to move past your dog until you are far beyond his threshold (the distance at which he starts to feel threatened that you will take his food).

3. If your dog stays relaxed, then repeat this pattern a few times during each meal.

4. Eventually, your dog will welcome your presence.

Secrets to Success:

*   Stop testing!

*   Just because your dog will allow you to be near him when he eats does not mean that you can touch him. This is not an open invitation. See below for training your dog to accept petting while he is eating.

*   If a piece of food falls to the ground, cue your dog to "Find it!"

*   If you need to be able to cue your dog to leave dropped food, work on the "Leave It" exercise separately (Emergency Behaviors, p. 80).

PETTING WHILE EATING

Objective: Your dog remains calm while eating, even when someone is petting him.

Although I never suggest that caregivers pet their dogs while they are eating, some want to do so. Personally, I feel that when a dog eats, he should not feel anxious or bothered. It is his time to enjoy his food, in peace and by himself, especially in a multi-dog household. But if you want to pet your dog to show him how pleased you are that he is eating again after being sick, for example, this is the way to train him so that he'll feel confident that you won't disturb his meal.

How to teach the behavior:

1. Have your dog's filled bowl in your lap.

2. Touch your dog once on the chest or under the chin.

3. Feed him a few pieces of kibble with something else that is appetizing.

4. Touch your dog in another spot and feed him some more.

5. Continue until you have touched your dog all over his body. If your dog objects to being touched in a certain area, back up and work on that area separately.

6. Extend the duration of the touch until it turns into a light stroke.

7. When your dog is comfortable with a light stroke, start to lower the bowl to the floor from your lap. Place the bowl in your lap, pet your dog once, and then put the bowl on the floor with something fun and a few pieces of kibble in it. Allow him to eat while you praise lightly, always using the same word. These words will become a relaxing cue. Pick up the bowl when your dog is done and start again.

8. Your dog will soon start to see this pattern: my caregiver pets me and then I get food. Your dog stays relaxed. Awesome!

9. Next, you can try putting down the food bowl with a small amount of kibble, petting your dog once while he eats and then, when his head comes up, giving him a piece of something amazing like a piece of meat or cheese.

10. Eventually you will be able to pet him while he is eating his regular meal on the floor.

Secrets to Success:

- Start with a touch, not a pet.
- Try not to lean over your dog.
- Touch your dog on all parts of his body first before petting.
- If there is an area of your dog's body that is more sensitive, increase the quality and rate of reinforcement.
- Slowly extend the length of the stroke only with previous success.

- Don't use the clicker during this exercise because the click can cause a startle reflex. You want your dog to relax into your touch. If you want to use a marker signal, use a verbal one.

- You can train this behavior on your dog's mat or bed, assuming it is safe to do so.

- This exercise also works well for training husbandry behaviors.

16

When Your Dog is Uncomfortable Around Other Dogs

Living with a dog that isn't good with other dogs can be difficult. Dogs that are fearful and stressed present a different set of problems than reactive and aggressive dogs. Even the over-exuberant teenage dog can be a physical handful. There are many reasons why a dog might not be comfortable around other dogs: he might fear what another dog might do, he might not understand how to read canine body signals, or he might have learned that when another dog passes by, his caregiver pulls hard on his leash, and that hurts his neck. It can be hard for a caregiver to accept that she may be the cause of her dog's reactivity, as the following example shows:

The Origins of Reactivity

For many caregivers, a dog's reactivity is something that creeps up on them until one day it results in a full-blown explosion. They never see it coming, but if you know what to look for, there are clues, as in the following case. One day I was sitting with my husband at the park eating ice cream, watching a man and a woman, each with a dog, eating ice cream. The man's Shih-Tzu simply watched the world go by, but the woman's Bernese Mountain Dog puppy, about six months old, was not so blasé. Every time a person with a dog walked by, the puppy lunged excitedly at the end of his leash, and every time, the woman yanked him back and told him "No!" The correction didn't work. Remember, giving a behavior even negative attention can be reinforcing. I told my husband, "That's how reactivity is born!" The woman was rehearsing the behavior chain regardless of how her puppy felt about strange dogs (a dog passed by, the puppy lunged, the woman reinforced the lunging by yelling at her dog). I wondered what was going on in that puppy's brain. It helps to be aware of which behavior you're reinforcing, even when you're not formally "training."

If the woman had had just a few treats, she could have turned her puppy away from the distraction or offered him treats every time he saw another dog. Most concerning was that over time the reactivity would grow as the dog got bigger and stronger. Soon the woman would not be able to handle the dog that she had inadvertently reinforced for lunging. I hoped she would seek help from an experienced positive reinforcement trainer instead of giving up on the dog.

Imagine trying to deal with following situations:

- You are raising your bouncy, exuberant puppy to be a competition dog, and you want to be the most reinforcing element in any environment that you walk into. Can you teach your puppy that when anything changes in the environment, he should check in with you?

- You want to be able to walk your dog in your neighborhood without him lunging and barking at the end of his leash every time he sees another dog. Can you train him so that the sight of other dogs is a cue to relax and look at you?

- You would like to show your dog in agility, but he feels stressed in the queue and loses concentration. Can you teach your dog that the dog running before him is the cue to focus on you?

- Your neighbor's dog always barks and lunges at your dog behind his invisible fence. Can you train your dog to ignore this rude challenge and calmly heel by?

- After training your reactive dog so he feels comfortable around other dogs, how can you assess whether he would like to engage further with them, taking a walk side by side, for example?

The challenge is not only dealing with your dog but dealing with people's attitudes toward him. People who have dogs typically hang out together. It can be awkward if you keep getting invited to canine social activities, but you need to leave your dog at home. Publicly, you often feel an element of shame. People who see your dog explode may automatically assume that he is aggressive, not only with other dogs but also with people. In reality, that could be far from the truth. Some yell at you to "Train your dog!" while others warn that if your dog bites them, they will demand that you "put your dog to sleep!" The difficulty is that your dog isn't aggressive or reactive most of the time. Those of us with challenging dogs wish that the world could see them as they are at home: quiet, calm, and loving.

When I work with clients whose dogs have reactivity or aggression issues with other dogs, their main goal is to have a dog that can accompany them in a public setting. I don't remember the last time that I had a client who said, "I want my dog to have doggy friends." Some clients may want their dog to get along with their mom's dog over the Christmas holidays or with their fiancée's dogs, but most are happy with a dog that is calm and happy staying by their side.

Although I have had a few clients over the years whose dogs I helped get used to other dogs, this book focuses on the most common dog-to-dog issues, such as teaching dogs to accept other dogs in their environments, training dogs to focus on the handler in the most challenging times, and acclimating dogs to special circumstances where they are surrounded by loud, fast-moving, and boisterous dogs. This chapter outlines how to move forward with a dog that gets over-excited, stressed, or explosive when he sees other dogs. As with dogs that are sensitive to people, you need to teach your dog a pattern of behavior so that he knows exactly what to expect in the circumstances. The more predictable the outcome, the easier it is for you to guide your dog to be calm in social settings with other dogs.

Tailor Emergency Behaviors to Your Situation

If you have a dog that has issues with other dogs, and you cannot control your dog, an environment with other dogs is one of the most difficult and potentially dangerous situations you will encounter. Before you expose your dog to other dogs, you and your dog must have some reliable Emergency Behaviors to fall back on if the situation looks as if it may get out of hand. You need to be able to remove your dog from the setting instantly or hide him from the trigger. Even if you have taught your dog many different behaviors, they won't do you any good if you get too flustered to cue those behaviors or if your aroused dog is unable to respond to cues in the presence of other dogs.

As part of your training plan, I recommend working on the following behaviors separately from actual exposures. You can work on your Click to Calm exposures at the same time. Knowing that you can exit a sticky situation quickly will give you confidence to work your dog in a variety of settings.

The Get Behind cue (see p. 72) lets you use yourself as a human barrier to keep your dog safe from unwanted encounters with other dogs, for example, when you are walking into a building or when you stop to talk with your neighbor who has his dog in tow.

The "Let's Go!" cue (see p. 77) teaches your dog to turn and trot by your side as you move away from another dog that he might charge at otherwise.

The Back Up–Sit cue (see p. 82) offers yet another way to quickly change direction with your dog to exit a risky situation. It teaches your dog that, as you take a few steps backward, he needs to whip around to you, give you his full attention, and move into you so that you can increase distance from the trigger.

Finally, the "Come, Quick!" cue (see p. 78) allows you and your dog to move forward past another dog before your dog has a chance to react to the trigger.

How Click to Calm Helps Dogs Sensitive to Other Dogs

When you have a dog that is anxious about being around other dogs, the first thing that you want to teach your dog is that the environment is okay (Stage One of Click to Calm). Nothing bad is going to happen to him so he no longer has to feel fearful or stressed in these circum-stances. You will make sure of it! Other dogs can be around as long as you are protecting him. This is an exercise in trust. Only *after* your dog starts to acclimate to other dogs being present can he think about doing something else (like looking at you and demonstrating previously learned behaviors) and dare to follow through.

Success in Stage One presents many handlers with a dilemma: they love that their dog is calmly looking at other dogs without reacting so much that they don't move on to Stage Two. Stage Two teaches your dog the critical building block of turning the trigger into the cue to focus on you, the handler. If you spend too much time rehearsing Stage One, you get what you pay for: a dog that stares at other dogs, as I found out early on with Ben. One time in obedience class while we were standing in line waiting to practice our recall cue, Ben looked up at me and started to look at the dog seated beside us. I chose to ignore this behavior since we were in class, and he seemed to be in control. Much to my horror, Ben started to nose poke the shoulder of the neighboring dog. I froze! Afraid of what might happen, I clicked and fed him for the head turn only.

I can always spot a dog that was only taught Stage One. He constantly scans the environment for other dogs so that his handler can see that he is looking and reward him. He only gives his handler a second of eye contact because he has learned the pattern: if I look at the other dog, then I get a treat, so he repeats this pattern. Training only Stage One produces a dog that stares and tries to engage another dog, not because he will enjoy the company but because he wants reinforcement. This is dangerous territory, especially for an aggressive dog! To move on from reactivity, you need that second step (Stage Two), as Amy's and Chadwick's story illustrates.

CASE STUDY: The Perils of Getting Stuck in Stage One

A client, Amy, who took several reactive dog classes with me, lived in Boston. On aver-age, her dog, Chadwick, saw 30 to 40 dogs each day. She told me, "I like what you say about preventing rehearsals but, in all honesty, that is impossible for me to do." I told her to do the best that she could. Amy started teaching her dog Click to Calm. Although Chadwick was getting much better in class looking at other dogs, he still wasn't giving her much eye contact. I asked if she had started teaching Stage Two yet. She said, "Oh yeah, he is looking at me sometimes."

I didn't think much of it until she showed me a video of Chadwick on a walk. All he did was look at other dogs, sometimes to the point of staring. Amy didn't seem bothered by it—until she started taking sport classes where she knew that she needed her dog's attention. Then she asked me, "Why doesn't my dog look up at me like your dog Austyn looks up at you?" I asked whether she had started working on Stage Two yet. She told me, "I was so happy that I could walk my dog in the city without any lunging and barking at dogs that I didn't care about much else!" But now eye contact mattered to her. For her homework, I told Amy to stop clicking and feeding for Stage One. Instead, she should wait until Chadwick's head snapped back to hers, as it had done occasionally in the past. Only click for eye contact and feed him tons of treats while he was still focused on her. In one week, Chadwick came back a different dog! Instead of feeding five treats when Chadwick turned back to her and offered eye contact, she fed him ten after every click!

You will know when it's time to move on to Stage Two when your dog looks at the other dog but then looks at you directly. His body stays relaxed, and he gives you full attention. Now you can start clicking him for focusing on you instead of staring at the other dog. The first time it happens is a feeling that you will never forget!

The Click to Calm Process

This chapter customizes the Click to Calm protocol outlined in Chapter 12 for a dog-reactive dog and shows you how to move beyond it if your dog seems interested in more than just observing other dogs. Here's the full program:

Basic Click to Calm		
Phase One: Familiarize	Stage One: Recognize	Your dog earns a click for looking at or listening to a trigger dog calmly; he gets reinforcement after he moves away from the trigger with you.
	Stage Two: Redirect	Your dog earns a click for looking at a trigger dog calmly and then turning and focusing on you; he gets reinforcement after he moves away from the trigger with you.
	Stage Three: Replace	Your dog earns a click for looking at a trigger dog calmly and refocusing on you. He moves away from the trigger for his reward, and performs a cued behavior.
Advanced Click to Calm		
Phase Two: Investigate		Your dog earns a click for approaching and possibly sniffing or otherwise interacting with a trigger dog; he gets reinforcement after he moves away from the trigger with you.
Phase Three: Meet		Your dog earns a click for successive approximations of letting the trigger dog approach or interact with him; he gets reinforcement either at the trigger's side or, after several repetitions, after he moves away from the trigger with you.

Preparation and Set-up

Decide where you are going to work your dog and set up your space: Find a place where your dog can see the trigger dog at a distance but where the trigger dog cannot come up to him uninvited (the moment this happens, he will lose trust in your ability to keep him safe). If you do not have a trigger dog to work with, find places like obedience classes or pet store parking lots where you can click and feed your dog for seeing other dogs at a distance. Always set up a space behind a barrier where you can put your dog's belongings and rest him in between sessions. Allow your dog to relax in between sessions by tossing treats on the ground and asking your dog to "Find it." Taking a break behind a barrier and playing Find It tend to be calming as well as reinforcing activities. You can also cue other enjoyable behaviors, give your dog his favorite massage, or let him work on a frozen, stuffed Kong. For reactive dogs, use a leash and a collar (or a harness). For aggressive dogs, use the Two-Leash system outlined on p. 27. Muzzle your dog if necessary (if he is already accustomed to the muzzle).

Session length: Keep your exposure sessions short (5–10 clicks are plenty). Start with just one to four exposures. If your dog tenses or reacts, stop immediately.

Be careful how you use helpers and helper dogs: To choose your helper dog (and handler), look for the following:

1. Make sure that the dog that you choose is stable and non-reactive. You need a dog that is essentially "bomb-proof," which means that it would take a huge distraction to scare or intimidate him.

2. Be sure that the handler can position her dog in different ways. For example, in the beginning of an exposure, you will want to ask your helper to position her dog so that your dog sees her dog's back. If the handler does not have this kind of control, there will be no predictability to the exposures, which could be unproductive or even dangerous.

3. Although many helpers have lots of ideas about how a training session should proceed, choose someone who will listen to your instructions and follow them (whether or not she agrees).

4. Make sure that your helper is willing to reinforce her dog throughout the session, especially if your dog has a reaction of some kind.

5. Work with only one person-dog team at a time. If you change the helper team, go back to your original threshold.

EXPOSURES OUT IN THE WILD

If you, like me when I was training Ben, do not have the option of working with a dog-handler team, you can still improve your dog's reactivity dramatically. Start by going to places where you know there will be other dogs and their handlers: pet stores, obedience classes, public on-leash walking places. Work your dog beyond where the action is. Make sure that you have enough space to increase distance if you need to. Have your vehicle nearby so that you can use it as a barrier.

When Ben's behavior started to improve, I used to go out and "stalk" people with dogs in our nearby on-leash park. I scanned the area and spotted a woman walking her dog. I took Ben out of my van, and, with clicker and treats ready, I started walking toward them. When I got close, I pretended I was working on Ben's heeling. I purposely looked up and smiled as we passed the woman and her dog on the walkway. Ben got tons of treats for passing her dog successfully.

Keep in mind that if you decide to work through Phases Two and Three, you must be able to do so with a dog-handler team that is reliably solid. Otherwise, the situation would be too unpredictable to guarantee the safety of everyone involved. You could also seriously erode the trust you've built with your dog if something goes wrong. Even though I could not move on to Phases Two and Three until years later, Ben's behavior improved tremendously. I could take him to any social setting, and you would never have known about his original reactivity issue.

Familiarize (Phase One: The Three Stages of Click to Calm)

If you want a dog to warm up to the presence of other dogs in the environment, he first has to get used to seeing them and hearing them. He needs to learn to watch them from a safe distance in a more controlled setting and, gradually, learn to tolerate dogs that are closer, more active, and louder, even racing around and barking. Only after he's comfortable in the presence of other dogs (Stage One of Click to Calm) will he dare to turn and look at you, and, eventually, be able to follow your cues (Stages Two and Three).

Before you start, review the Click to Calm Rate of Reinforcement guidelines, p. 117, and the Secrets to Success for each of the stages (p. 130, p. 133, and p. 134). Once your dog relaxes at the sight and sound of other dogs and can turn to you and respond to cues, you can determine if he would like to interact with other canines.

RECOGNIZE (Stage One)

Objective: Your dog earns a click for looking at or listening to another dog calmly; he receives his treat or his sniffing session after he moves away from the other dog with you.

In this stage, you click and feed your dog while he is looking at or hearing another dog so that he learns to be calm in the presence of dogs. As you progress, work on moving your dog closer to the trigger dog or allow your dog to watch the trigger dog move more. Do not work on both criteria at the same time. Make sure that the trigger dog gets lots of treats for working with the reactive dog. If there is ever an explosion, the trigger dog should get a huge jackpot!

How to teach the behavior:

1. Establish your baseline: Mark (mentally or physically) the invisible line where your dog can look at and hear the other dog without going over threshold and set up your dog behind it.

2. Ask the handler to position the trigger dog beyond that line. The trigger dog should start stationary and turned away from the working dog.

3. Allow your dog to look at the other dog. Take a breath while he does so.

4. Click, move away, and give your dog one reinforcement: one treat, one play session (5 seconds), a massage session (5 seconds), or one sniffing session (about 20 seconds).

5. Repeat Steps 2–4 a few times and note your dog's emotional response. If all is well, have the handler move the trigger dog ever so slightly, for example, by cueing a down from a sit or by walking slowly with him a few steps, parallel to you and your dog. Continue as above.

6. You can only work on one piece of criteria at a time. For example, you do not want the trigger dog to become more active and decrease your distance from the trigger dog at the same time. You can either ask the handler to cue the trigger dog to jump around while you increase your distance, or you can close the distance from the trigger dog while his body stays quiet.

7. Gradually decrease the distance between your dog and the trigger dog. If at any time your dog reacts, it means that you are too close. Go back to the previous step and work from there.

8. Eventually, your dog will be able to look at the other dog without incident, no matter how close or "exciting" he is.

Secrets to success:

• Respect your dog's threshold! It's much less stressful and more successful to start far back from the trigger dog and slowly approach him than to station your dog too close to the trigger dog and then have to back away quickly. For aggressive dogs, having to back away quickly is far riskier!

- If you have difficulty moving your dog away from the trigger dog, work on the Back Up–Sit or "Let's Go!" exercises on pp. 82 and 77 before attempting more exposures.

- When you are moving toward the trigger dog, do so in a slight curve or approach from the side. Never move forward head-to-head.

- Remember that any time your dog reacts, the first thing to do is to move away from the trigger. Use distance to your advantage.

- Giving your dog an opportunity to sniff is an excellent choice of reinforcement for this exercise because it's a calming activity. Just be sure that you can cue a beginning and an end to this behavior so that you can resume training.

As your dog becomes familiar with watching and hearing another dog, his body should become looser. Watch for signs that he's getting more comfortable around other dogs. Are you and your dog both starting to relax during these exposures? Can you walk your dog by the trigger dog as the other dog's handler is walking him? If your dog barely glances at the other dog and instead watches you, waiting for his treat, then move on to Stage Two.

REDIRECT (Stage Two)

Objective: Your dog earns a click for looking at the trigger dog calmly and then turning and focusing on you; he receives his treat or his sniffing session after he moves away from the other dog with you.

In this stage, you click and reinforce your dog handsomely for turning away from the trigger dog and focusing on you, the handler. He is learning that the presence of the other dog is the cue to turn to look at you for further instruction. Remember that this step takes courage: your dog is telling you that he feels relaxed enough, and, more importantly, feels safe enough to turn his head away from a trigger to look at you. It is a triumph of his trust in you and deserves generous reinforcement.

How to teach the behavior:

1. Set up your dog behind the original baseline, at whatever distance from the trigger dog that works.

2. Warm up by clicking and reinforcing your dog a few times for looking at the trigger dog (Recognize, Stage One).

3. The next time your dog looks at the other dog, wait one to two seconds: Did your dog look back at you as if to say, "Hey, I'm looking at you! Aren't you going to click and give me cookies for looking at that other dog?" If so, click, move away and give your dog five treats individually.

   a. Count them out loud to your dog as you give them.

   b. If you are using play or massage, interact with your dog for 5 seconds for 3 repetitions.

   c. If you are rewarding with a sniff fest, allow your dog to do so for three rounds of about 20 seconds each.

4. If your dog does not turn to look at you easily or only turns halfway toward you, then increase your distance away from the other dog (see "Sticky Head," p. 123). Once your dog's head turns toward you, follow the instructions above.

5. Repeat Steps 1–4, closing the distance between the two dogs and, separately, asking your helper to make her dog livelier and louder. Take your time.

6. Eventually, your dog will be able to look at the other dog without incident, no matter how close or "exciting" he is, and readily turn his focus to you.

Secret to success:

- Start with a quiet, stationary trigger dog and have your helper gradually increase her dog's movement and noise level. Have the handler move the trigger dog ever so slightly, for example, by cueing a down from a sit or by walking slowly with him a few steps, parallel to you and your dog.

When your dog is able to give you eye contact calmly and reliably with scarcely a glance at the trigger, you are ready to replace the formerly inappropriate behavior with a desired one by cueing a default behavior. Move on to Stage Three.

REPLACE (Stage Three)

Objective: Your dog earns a click for looking at the trigger dog calmly, looking back at you, moving away from the other dog for his treat, and then performing a cued behavior.

When your dog is turning toward you in the presence of the other dog reliably, you can cue a default behavior. Instead of reacting, your dog can function in a calm manner. He trusts that you will keep him safe; therefore, he can respond to cues with a clear and confident brain.

How to teach the behavior:

1. Set up your training session as before.

2. Start by reviewing Stage One. Click and reinforce your dog for looking at and hearing the trigger dog.

3. Move on to Stage Two. Wait one to two seconds and if your dog looks back at you, click and feed your dog five treats individually (or give him three 5-second bouts of play or massage or 20 seconds of sniffing).

4. Repeat the Stage Two exposure 3–4 more times.

5. If your dog continues to give you eye contact, click and reinforce him, and then cue a reliable behavior.

6. If your dog performs the behavior, click and feed him. If your dog is unable to perform the behavior, you will need to shift in and out of Stages One and Two until your dog is comfortable.

7. Repeat this sequence, either asking for different behaviors or increasing the noise, movement, or proximity of the trigger dog. Remember to work on each aspect of the exposure separately.

Secrets to success:

- Even if you feel that your dog has made a lot of progress being around other dogs, continue to start each session by warming up briefly with Stages One and Two, behind the baseline. Expect that it will be a while before you can drop this routine.

- As you get closer to the trigger dog, vary which default behaviors you cue as long as your dog can perform them reliably. His reliable performance is an indication of his comfort level.

- Watch your dog for any signs of discomfort, especially tension. At this point, you should feel confident that you can sense when your dog starts to relax or tense up. Adjust your training accordingly.

- Once your dog is able to perform the behavior in multiple settings with different dogs, you can start cueing default behaviors of your choice in different situations. Remember that your dog's ability to respond to cues in the presence of other dogs is a direct measure of his comfort level. Read the signs and act accordingly.

CASE STUDY: A Walk in the Park: A Client's Perspective

Since puppyhood, Bodhi has been "dog selective." He becomes over-aroused easily and reacts inappropriately to other dogs, so we have always managed and trained him carefully to help him become more tolerant. Emma's Click to Calm sequences have built a protective bubble around Bodhi and me. We have been able to return to the beautiful wild places we love most and to successfully navigate the increasingly inevitable collisions we have with off-leash, overly forward, and under-trained dogs.

Even so, walks in our favorite woods were becoming a nightmare of trying to fend off loose dogs that were relentless in trying to engage, jump on, and interfere with Bodhi, my other dog, and/or us. In several cases, Bodhi encountered dogs pushing their muzzles into his open panting mouth while their owners were out of sight or otherwise incapable of retrieving their dogs. The place where we found the most peace now had become the site of so much tension and required hyper-vigilance to maneuver through.

Thankfully, the simple, predictable patterns of Click to Calm increased clarity, connection, protection, and actual fun even while off-leash dogs were jumping on, harassing, and threatening Bodhi. It made all our lives so much easier that sometimes I could even do a little training with the friendlier loose dogs until their owners were able to collect them. Win/win!

Despite being vigilant, last year we were blindsided in the woods by a much larger and more powerful loose dog. Bodhi suffered a repeated and sustained attack as he tried to get away from the dog and back to me. We were incredibly lucky that we escaped with only minor physical injuries, but we were badly shaken after such a protracted and terrifying event.

Thanks to our Click to Calm games, we (Bodhi more than me!) started to bounce back much faster than I would have dreamed possible. Even as we race-walked to the car (thinking an emergency room visit was our next stop), I could see the terror draining from Bodhi's body as the joy of those patterns kicked in. We were able to channel all that adrenaline into one of our more animated Click to Calm sessions. We have both become so much calmer because we recognize when we need to implement Click to Calm measures: we do so early, so we can avoid issues and enjoy ourselves.

These experiences have taught me what a difference Click to Calm has made for Bodhi, and how easy it was for me to practice the Click to Calm games—even and *especially* when I was scared, anticipating another dangerous experience, and simply in reactive rather than thinking mode. As a result, I now incorporate these games into my new dog-training clients' repertoires. Whatever the trigger, having the muscle memory of these patterns means that we can become calmer and more capable of proactively preventing problems and peacefully co-existing with whatever triggers cross our path.

—Mary Ann Callahan

Investigate (Phase Two)

If you think that your dog might be ready to meet other dogs safely, you can set up an exposure for him to investigate a solid, stable dog. You can never be sure, so proceed slowly. Your dog should always have the choice to participate. Respect his choice. You can always stop. Safety is paramount! Always use a helper with a trusted dog. These are not exercises that you can do safely with your dog at the dog park or along the bike path with anyone you run into.

This technique is not for all dogs! This process is primarily for dogs that are shy or that have not had a lot of social interaction with other dogs. Proceed with these activities slowly so that a fearful or an inexperienced dog has plenty of time to acclimate to the movements and sounds of the other dog. Dogs that are severely aggressive toward other dogs are not candidates for this training.

Although I have worked this technique successfully with a handful of students, I don't recommend it to the amateur trainer. First, it is really hard to find another dog that will remain calm and collected as your dog explores him. Second, you and whoever is helping you must take the utmost care to ensure a safe encounter for both dogs. Put a safety protocol in place beforehand. If you are unsure if your dog will benefit from a program like this, start by muzzling your dog. Do not allow direct contact with the other dog.

INVESTIGATE

Objective: Your dog earns a click for approaching and possibly sniffing or otherwise interacting with another dog; he receives his treat or his sniffing session after he moves away from the other dog with you.

This exercise gives your dog the structure for approaching the trigger dog and allows him to sniff or touch the dog if he desires, in any way that is safe for both dogs. Safety is the first concern. Setting up a barrier of some kind between the dogs ensures that you never risk one dog injuring the other. For example, look for a workspace where there is a fence and a grassy area all around. Make sure that there is also a resting place for your dog. If you can, use the same trigger dog that you have worked with in the past.

As it was when you were allowing a shy dog to explore a person, the emphasis is on your dog taking the initiative. Warm up with some reps of Stage One, but then let your dog investigate. You're not looking for your dog to check back in with you after he's walked up to or sniffed the other dog. Just let your dog explore the other dog as an object and interact as he chooses. If at any time your dog becomes aggressive or fearful of the other dog, stop the session immediately. After more Click to Calm work with your dog, you may be ready to repeat this exercise at a later date.

How to teach the behavior:

1. To start, have your helper place her dog on one side of, and a bit away from, the fence. Your dog remains on the other side of the fence.

2. Warm up by clicking and feeding your dog for looking at the trigger dog, both sitting still and walking slowly. Remember to move your dog away from the other dog after each click to give him his treat or other reinforcement or let him sniff.

3. If your dog appears relaxed (body is loose), ask the handler to bring the trigger dog closer to the fence, moving in a horizontal direction.

4. Once the other dog is in place, start moving your dog toward him by clicking, moving back, and feeding your dog for looking at the other dog. Don't approach the trigger dog head on. Instead, walk in a straight line back and forth parallel to the other dog or make sweeping curves toward him. Make sure to move away from the other dog after each click to reinforce your dog.

5. To test your dog's comfort level as you are moving forward, cue different reliable behaviors, such as a hand target, a sit, or a down. If he can't respond to your cues, back off; his brain is foggy.

6. Once you reach the other dog, allow your dog to explore this "object." Click your dog if he sniffs the other dog's shoulder, foot, or flank, then move away (at this point, your dog will probably move away on his own) to take the pressure off your dog immediately. Allow your dog to either eat a treat or sniff the grass after each click. Your dog needs this distance and "time off." Respect it!

7. Approach the trigger dog about five times, but don't cue your dog to move forward or interact with the other dog.

    a. If he is curious, your dog will approach on his own. Keep your leash loose.

    b. If he is not interested, move away slowly and ask for a reliable behavior.

    c. If he moves forward and then his body tenses, toss a treat away from the other dog, tell your dog to "Find it," and end that session.

8. As your dog gains confidence, you can insert a verbal cue like "Say Hi" right before your dog touches the other dog's body. Ideally, you want your dog to sniff or touch the hind end of the other dog.

9. At the end of the session, release your dog (still on leash) back to your barrier. You can run back happily with him or heel him as you move closer to your barrier. Party time!

Secrets to success:

- Before interacting with the other dog, practice cueing reliable behaviors in the presence of the other dog.

- Don't ever pressure your dog to touch or even notice another dog.

- Let your dog open up distance from the other dog as he wishes.

- When your dog starts to make contact with the other dog, keep your initial training sessions very short.

- After each touch, move your dog away from the other dog either by leading him away or by tossing a treat away from the fence. Allowing your dog to sniff is the reinforcement of choice in these sessions.

Meet (Phase Three)

Once your dog has had the experience of sniffing another dog calmly without fear that the other dog will jump on him or chase him, you may move on to the next phase to see if your dog tolerates the other dog approaching and sniffing him. This time, it is the other dog taking the initiative.

MEET

Objective: Your dog earns a click for successive approximations of allowing the trigger dog to look at him up close or sniff him through the fence. He receives his treat or his sniffing session after he moves away from the other dog with you.

This final training stage offers your dog a predictable process to test whether he wants to interact with another dog and, if so, what sort of interactions he would like. Your dog has learned that there's no pressure in this situation. He can stop and walk away at any moment, and that makes him feel safe. Until your dog has been through all three phases multiple times, do not deviate from the original pattern. Before moving on to Phase Three, review Phases One and Two first, using the same trigger dog. Your dog should feel confident practicing these behaviors in a familiar situation with a familiar dog.

How to teach the behavior:

1. Start with the trigger dog either standing or lying down on the other side of the fence.

2. After briefly reviewing the steps in Phases One and Two, bring your dog parallel to one side of the fence. Make sure that there is some distance between your dog and the fence (wherever he feels comfortable). Your dog should be facing you, not the other dog.

3. Cue your dog to sit or assume a position that is comfortable for him.

4. Ask your helper to bring her dog closer to the fence. Click and feed your dog in place while the handler keeps her dog at that distance.

   a. If you see your dog tense up, move away, toss treats away from the fence, and cue "Find it." Back up to Phase Two and, after a few repetitions, stop for the day.

5. As long as your dog remains calm, repeat this behavior several times, with the helper dog getting closer and closer to the fence.

6. When your dog seems interested in the other dog, allow the dogs to sniff each other through the fence. You are looking for a slow approach and gentle, calm investigation from both sides of the fence.

7. Click and toss a treat away or allow your dog a sniff fest.

8. If your dog comes back to the fence calmly, allow the other dog to sniff him again.

9. This time allow the mutual sniffing to go on a bit longer, assuming your dog is comfortable.

10. Click for all successful approximations. Remember to toss the treat away from the fence at the end of each exposure.

Secrets to success:

• The key to success is to train a few repetitions, working on only one criterion at a time (get a little closer, sniff for one second, then two). Then click and release your dog to "Find it" or allow him a sniff fest.

• If you practice the steps from Phases One, Two, and Three faithfully, over time your dog will learn to trust the pattern of exposure and the dogs involved in the experience. These precautions lead to the most success.

• Just because your dog is acclimating nicely to the trigger dog does not mean that he is ready to meet many dogs.

• As your dog starts to enjoy the presence of the trigger dog, gradually remove the fence so that there is no barrier between the dogs. Watch carefully to see if your dog's body remains relaxed without that physical boundary. Muzzle your dog if you are unsure of what your dog will do.

• If your dog continues to feel comfortable with the trigger dog, see if you can go on a Parallel Walk (see p. 195) or set up some Team Training exercises (see p. 214). You can include the "new" dog in the environment where your dog is playing, as long as you can keep both dogs safe.

Applying the Lessons of Click to Calm: Phases Two and Three
- Work on the following pieces of criteria in this order:
  - Stationary trigger dog (Phase Two)
  - Moving trigger dog (Phase Two)
  - Your dog touches and/or sniffs the other dog (Phase Two)
  - The two dogs sniff each other, with your dog stationary (Phase Three)
- With success, add small movements—only one at a time and with only one dog moving, not both at the same time.
- Work with several different dogs. Treat each dog as a brand-new trigger and start at the beginning with each new dog. You must perform all stages of the process with each dog. If your dog is fine in the presence of other dogs, he can jump to Phases Two or Three, depending on the criteria you want to work on.

CASE STUDY: Detente

Years ago when I decided to introduce a new puppy into my home, I knew that it would be difficult for my golden retriever Kayden to adapt. When Austyn first arrived, Kayden, never a fan of other dogs, couldn't even bear to look at him. He would run up to the baby gate that separated the two dogs, pause momentarily, and then run to the back of the house. To start, the baby-gate holes were really small so that Kayden could not have hurt Austyn if he were so inclined.

I put the Click to Calm protocol into practice! As Kayden started to move closer to the baby gate, I clicked and fed him for watching the puppy, tossing the treats away from the gate to decrease the pressure. At times, I also worked on Team Training. I asked Kayden to sit and, when he did, clicked and fed him, and then gave Austyn a treat for watching. Next, I helped Austyn with his baby sit, clicked and fed him, and then gave Kayden a treat for watching. Soon a relationship started to develop. (See Team Training, p. 214.)

Slowly, and with more exposure, I graduated to a baby gate with larger holes. When I played Kayden's favorite tennis-ball games, Austyn was either in his X-pen or tucked under my arm. Austyn got tons of treats for being Kayden's "play" partner.

I knew that I was getting close to making introductions when I saw Kayden push a ball to Austyn underneath the baby gate. Kayden left his front feet there on the other side.

Every once in a while, Kayden would "bat" the ball to Austyn with his front feet. Austyn responded in kind. They were building their own bond!

As time went on, I continued to integrate the two dogs. I taught Austyn to station when Kayden was close by. Because of his possession/aggression issues, Kayden had a really strong cue to back up. In the beginning, I allowed Kayden and Austyn loose in the house for very short periods of time and only while they were both doing something constructive like training, playing, or stationing. It took about five months for Kayden to feel totally comfortable around Austyn, but eventually they could be left alone in the house together without constant supervision. Though they played together for short periods of time and slept together on the couch, my golden Lizzie remained Kayden's favorite!

17
Solving Specific Dog–Dog Issues

Now that your dog feels calmer around other dogs in social settings, where do you go from here? If you decide not to move to Phases Two and Three (interacting with other dogs), there is still more your dog can learn to make him more confident in canine company. For example, after I taught Ben to feel more comfortable around other dogs, I knew that I wanted to meet a friend with a dog and go for a walk like a "normal" person. I asked my friend Leland to meet me with his dog Tsunami, a Shiba Inu, at an enormous field.

I asked Leland to start walking his dog and told him that I would follow and slowly catch up to them. I clicked and fed Ben each time he looked at Tsunami and then looked at me. Before long, Leland and I were walking almost side-by-side with Leland and me next to each other and our dogs on the outside. Parallel walking worked nicely to introduce Ben to "dog-to-dog" activity! From there, I asked a variety of friends to meet us at different places to expand Ben's experience. The best part? I felt like a normal canine caregiver!

Careful training beyond the basic Click to Calm protocol can broaden your, and your dog's, horizons. With each success, you and your dog will feel more comfortable and confident in new settings.

Here are suggestions and solutions for dealing with scenarios that you and your reactive dog may encounter.

Walking with Other Dogs
Finding out that you can walk your dog with certain other dogs is a huge step in breaking through the isolation felt by many caregivers with reactive or aggressive dogs. Let's start there.

PARALLEL WALKING

Objective: Your dog learns to relax walking in the same direction as another dog and handler, first following and then walking side-by-side with the other dog-handler team.

This exercise is a wonderful way to introduce your dog to walking with another dog, preferably on neutral territory. You and your dog follow another dog-handler team at a distance while your dog is relaxed looking at the other dog and volunteering to look at you. Over time, you close the gap until you are walking side-by-side with the other dog-handler team, first in a "sandwich" formation, where the handlers are the bologna and the dogs are the bread. Later, you can alternate in a dog–handler–dog–handler pattern. Click and feed your reactive dog for anything and everything he does that is appropriate in that context. For example, if he looks at the other dog, he gets a click and treat. If he looks at you, he gets a click and treat. If the other dog barks at him and he doesn't respond, he gets a click and treat. Capture as much successful behavior as you can. If at any time the dogs get too close, simply increase the distance between them.

Parallel walking can introduce a semblance of "normalcy" into the life of a reactive dog by teaching him to relax while walking with another dog. What starts off as a Stage Two Click to Calm exercise, with the dog following the trigger dog and his handler (left), turns into walking side by side as the reactive dog slowly closes the gap between him and the trigger (right).

How to teach the behavior:

1. Ask a friend and her dog to meet you in a place where there will not be any off-leash dogs.

2. Ask her to start walking her dog.

3. Get your dog out of your car, bringing your clicker and lots of great treats with you.

4. Start by following your friend at a distance.

5. Click and feed your dog every time he looks at her dog.

6. Continue to move in their direction.

7. If you notice your dog getting tense, open up the distance from the other dog.

8. Find the threshold where your dog is walking and looking at your friend's dog comfortably.

9. Stay at that distance until your dog relaxes.

10. Then close the gap between the dogs just slightly. Always monitor your dog's body language.

11. Walk with that dog and handler on several occasions until you can walk the dogs side-by-side.

12. Practice these steps with a variety of dog-handler teams, always one team at a time.

Secrets to success:

• Make a plan with your friend ahead of time.

• Make sure to tell her that you will only go as far as your dog will allow in any particular session.

• Make sure that there are no off-leash dogs where you are walking.

• Capture as much successful behavior as you can.

• For safety, consider using the Two-Leash system (see p. 27).

• Once you and your dog have "mastered" a dog-handler team, see if there is another friend with a dog that you can walk with.

When People with Dogs Come to Visit

When you ask family members to leave their dogs at home when they visit, they may not listen. This disrespect can make visits hard even for dogs that usually get along with other dogs. Consider the following example: Your parents are coming to visit and they have an older dog. Katie is an eleven-year-old Maltese. You have two dogs: a German short-haired pointer (Max) about five years old and a Labrador retriever (Jake), aged two. Max can hang out beautifully with the Maltese, but Jake thinks she is a remote-controlled toy! Poor Katie can't even walk down the hallway without your Lab trying to pounce on her head.

Not only is this situation dangerous for the smaller dog, but it teaches Jake that he can have his way with any dog he chooses. This is not what you want an adolescent dog to learn. Not only could Jake injure Katie, but, at some other point, he might pounce on a dog that is more willing and able to retaliate.

In situations like these, you have two choices: manage your dog for safety or teach your dog new behaviors to replace over-excited behavior. Management, clicker training, and Click to Calm guidelines can help you with all of the dogs in the example scenario and in other circumstances.

Manage People, Dogs, and the Environment:

Keep the dogs separated: No matter how big your house is, it may feel very small when several dogs are roaming around in it. Make sure to keep your dog separated from the others, especially at mealtimes and if the other dogs start to play with each other. (In my house, all play happens outside.) Inside a house, lots of canine activity can quickly start to feel confining to some participants; a fight can break out in a second.

Pick up toys and bones: Before your visitors arrive, make sure to pick up all of your dog's toys and bones. The last thing that you need is for another dog to come into your living room, pick up your dog's favorite toy, and trot off with it to another room with your dog in hot pursuit!

Create a plan: Depending on how long your visitors stay, you and other household members who live with you should have a plan to ensure that your reactive dog is, and feels, safe and is not forgotten amid the festivities. You must feed your dog, keep him in his safe space at risky times, and give him physical exercise even when someone is visiting. Consider assigning tasks to certain household members.

Be consistent: Family members can be convincing when they try to talk you into something that you know you shouldn't do. If you feel that your dog needs to be confined while people visit with their dogs, do not let family members talk you into allowing your dog to play with the others—period.

Capitalize on Visiting Dogs to Train Your Own

As long as you can control the visitors and their dogs, their presence may offer a valuable training opportunity. Ask your guests if they would be willing to put their dogs on leash for a bit so that you can work on some clicker training exercises with your dog.

1. Put on your dog's training equipment and take out your clicker and some high-powered treats. Start by clicking and feeding your dog for looking at the other dogs. If the visiting dogs are being feisty, make sure that you increase your distance accordingly. If you are working in the house, after you click go into a neighboring room and feed your dog.

2. As you work through Stage One, withhold your click and see if your dog will reorient to you directly. If so, click, go to a neighboring room, and give your dog five treats! Good boy!

3. If the visiting dogs are in the same room, see if you can cue your dog to sit–stay or down–stay by your chair. Reinforce your dog heavily for staying in position. Be sure that your dog knows the cued behavior reliably before attempting it.

4. Take a parallel walk with one of the visiting dogs following the instructions for Parallel Walking (see p. 195).

5. Make sure to work your dog for only a short period (10 minutes at the most) and then let him rest in his safe space.

The more you work your dog in the presence of the visiting dogs, the more relaxed your dog will become.

Tolerating Rude Dog Behavior

If you have ever watched two well-socialized dogs introduce themselves to each other, it is a dance. Their bodies come together smoothly, curving around each other, so that each can sniff the other dog's hind end, since this is where all of the important information can be found. Anal sacs secrete chemicals that can convey an individual dog's gender, reproductive status, health, diet, and even his emotional state.

Some dogs do not know how to interact with others naturally. Instead of being soft and gentle, they get over-excited and rush up into the face of another dog. Many times, this is the fault of a caregiver who has little control over her dog. Her dog drags her over to other dogs, regardless of their willingness to participate, and she usually considers any dog who reacts to her dog to be at fault. No matter how many times you ask her to keep her friendly but "rude" dog on leash, she may disregard your simple request. You may get the retort, "Your dog shouldn't be out in public if he can't deal with another dog sniffing him," as if all kinds of sniffing were the same for all dogs. Some of these dogs assault other dogs physically. Meeting such a forward, aroused dog is a nightmare for a sensitive dog!

I am conflicted as I write this section. My brain tells me that no dog should have to tolerate the rude behavior of any other animal. All dogs should have the freedom to walk, run, and play in a safe environment. That's why so many cities and towns have leash laws. It's fine if caregivers want to give their dogs off-leash time, but some dogs' freedom should not come at the expense of other dogs that find the environment more challenging. Dogs should be able to walk, run, and play in places with rules that everyone follows so that everyone can enjoy the beauty of the interaction and the setting. However, this ideal often is not the reality.

Once your dog feels comfortable in the presence of other dogs, start teaching him to tolerate the "rude" behavior of more inquisitive dogs. When another dog stares at your dog or brashly sniffs his hindquarters, that can make even the friendliest of dogs testy. Through clicker training, you can teach your dog that these events are all opportunities for reinforcement—and you can change his perspective on such boorishness.

The key to desensitizing your dog to potentially volatile situations is to turn them into "clickable" events by clicking and feeding your dog each time they happen. He will learn that the occurrence of a stressful event means that he should look to you immediately instead of barking, lunging at, or attacking the other dog. Dogs that do not have reactivity issues can usually handle situations like these easily, but a sensitive dog can overreact and become aggressive.

To prepare for rude canine encounters, begin by listing in your training journal all the canine behaviors you have witnessed that seemed to set off your dog. Set up training sessions with a dog that your dog likes, clicking and feeding him as the "obnoxious" behaviors that you set up with your helper occur.

These behaviors can include the following, but search your memory for more:

- Another dog being pushy about sniffing your dog's hindquarters.
- Another dog walking toward your dog head-on.
- Another dog unintentionally slamming into your dog in tight spaces.

Remember that when other dogs exhibit rude behaviors, they're not necessarily being aggressive; what makes the behavior a problem is if your dog perceives it as threatening.

Capture the Moment

If your dog has issues like these, take your clicker and treats out with you in the real world. Be ready to capture the moment that another dog interacts with your dog in a seemingly rude way and mark (click and feed) when your dog tolerates it nicely. This is especially important for puppies and young dogs. If we teach tolerance early, other dogs' rude behavior will never become a problem.

If you are working on these behaviors with a helper and her dog, the basic set-up is the same as for training the Click to Calm protocol:

1.   Work with a handler and dog that your dog likes.

2.   Work in a secure area where no other unleashed dogs will interrupt the training session.

3.   Keep both dogs on leashes and with their handlers.

PASSING THE SNIFF TEST

Objective: The act of another dog sniffing your dog's hindquarters cues your dog to look at you.

This common "getting-to-know-you" canine signal can make some dogs nervous. You can teach your dog to accept this interaction nicely, as a clickable moment.

Your dog will be able to tolerate rude doggy behavior if you teach him that a dog sniffing him is, in the Click to Calm rubric, a cue to look at you. If you take it slow, working with a reliable helper and a stable dog to approach in a series of exposures, you'll be successful.

How to teach the behavior:

1. Be seated with your dog's head near your lap.

2. Ask the helper to walk her dog back and forth, horizontally, in a straight line behind your dog.

3. Click and feed your dog for feeling that pressure. Allow your dog to turn to see who is behind him if necessary. Click him for the head turn in the other dog's direction.

4. If all goes well, ask the handler to decrease her distance slowly, keeping the line she is walking straight.

5. Click and feed your dog for all approaches the other dog makes.

6. At one point, ask the helper to stop and allow her dog to sniff your dog's hindquarters for a second or two.

7. The instant her dog gets close, click and feed your dog five treats individually.

8. After the initial sniff, ask the handler to move away with her dog.

9. After reinforcing both dogs, end the session and begin again.

10. This time work the behavior session with you standing up.

11. Work this behavior with a variety of dogs that your dog already knows. Start practicing with a wider range of dogs only after your dog begins giving you eye contact when the sniffing starts.

12. In the future, work on this behavior with unfamiliar dogs.

13. When out in public, click and feed your dog spontaneously if any other dog sniffs his hindquarters or any other part of his body.

Secrets to success:

• Work with one dog at a time.

• If your dog reacts at any time, stop the session. Make a note about where the breakdown occurred. In your next session, review the behavior before this point and see if you can move through it.

• Always remember that your dog calls the shots. He must offer to work voluntarily.

ACCEPTING DIRECT ADVANCES

Objectives: When a dog approaches your dog head-on, he remains relaxed and checks in with you.

When an incident like this occurs, you can teach your dog to take it in stride. Instead of creating panic, your dog will react by making immediate eye contact with you.

How to teach the behavior:

1. Ask your dog to sit on your left.

2. Ask the other handler to slowly walk her dog up to your dog head-on (in a straight line).

3. Click and feed your dog for each step the other dog takes as he approaches.

4. When you are about 10 feet apart, start to walk your dog forward as well, making sure that the dogs don't bump into each other. Click and feed your dog for the slow heel.

5. Have the handler continue to walk, passing you quietly. Make sure to continue clicking and feeding your dog when the approaching dog is closest. Stop reinforcing as the other dog is moving away.

6. Repeat the previous steps with familiar dogs.

7. As your dog gains more experience, increase the speed at which the other dog approaches.

8. As you continue to work this process, your dog will see the approaching dog and look up at you in anticipation of the click and treat. Once you have reinforced your dog, release him, and allow him to look at the other dog again.

Secrets to success:

• When you are working with a new dog, start at the first step.

• During this exercise, the dogs do not actually meet each other but just walk past each other.

• Click and feed your dog for silence and calm anytime another dog walks up to him head-on. Feel free to click and feed your dog, give your release word, and move to a more secure area.

TOLERATING BODY BUMPS

Objective: If a dog accidentally jostles your dog, your dog turns to you calmly and gets reinforced.

It's bound to happen. Sometimes dogs just bump into each other. If this happens when handlers are moving their dogs and not paying attention to their surroundings or when dogs are playing off-leash, you can desensitize your dog to this incidental contact with other dogs. Whatever the cause, your dog learns that a bump is a cue to look to you.

How to teach the behavior:

1. Practice in short sessions, five minutes at the most.

2. Maintain a high rate of reinforcement.

3. Have your dog either in a sit–stay or stand–stay.

4. Have the other handler walk by you with her dog, in the same direction as you and your dog are facing (just as with parallel walking). Click and feed your dog as they pass by.

5. Practice this exercise again, this time with the other handler moving her dog closer to your dog. Click and feed your dog when the two dogs are closest.

6. Next, have the other handler walk her dog so close to yours that her dog gently brushes up against yours. Go only as close as you can comfortably with both dogs. Click and feed your dog right at the moment of contact. Toss the treat away from the other dog.

7. Repeat the steps above until your dog is completely calm. Click and treat your dog for offering you eye contact as well.

8. Now that your dog is comfortable with this dog touching him, move through the steps at a quicker pace with other well-socialized dogs.

9. As your dog's behavior becomes increasingly reliable, start working with an unfamiliar dog. With an unfamiliar dog, start back at step 1.

Secrets to success:

• Capture the behavior and reinforce it by clicking and feeding your dog anytime another dog touches him, moves toward him, and so on.

• Expose your dog to nearby dogs for short amounts of time.

• Remember that you must be able to control the environment at all times. Do not take your dog to a place where dogs are running off-leash until your dog is ready for this kind of exposure.

Succeeding in a Classroom Situation

If your dog has been reactive in the past and you want to take a public class, practice the following:

1. Let the instructor know your dog's history and assure him/her that you do not have a dog that bites.

2. Before you take a public class, take private lessons with the instructor so that you will already be familiar with the terminology, the exercises, and the site.

3. Enter the building where the classes are being held 15 minutes after everyone has entered the class. This eliminates the chance that you will need to squeeze into tight spaces, like through the doorway, or get jammed against a ring gate.

4. Do not stay in the ring the entire time, especially if there are off-leash exercises. Jump in and out of the class based on what you think your dog can do best. For example,

when I took an obedience class with my rescued dog Kayden, I worked the Click to Calm methodology outside the ring and then jumped into the class to practice heeling and stays.

5.   Leave the class about 10 minutes early for the same reason that you came in late, to avoid classroom traffic.

As the weeks go by, you will be able to stay in the class for longer and longer periods.

Succeeding in the Sports Arena

Competition dogs need the right amount of pizazz and focus to do whatever sport they do best. Unfortunately, sometimes reactivity comes with this stellar package. If reactivity is part of your "package," ask yourself: Is my dog so excited that he overreacts to other dogs in the environment (in which case, you may be able to temper his exhilaration)? Or is he a dog that wants to do bodily harm to another dog? If your answer to the second question is yes, it does not matter how talented your dog is at his given sport. No other dog should be put at risk because you want to show your dog. Doing so would be selfish and irresponsible.

This section is for handlers who have dogs that are easily excited by other dogs during competitions. This is the obedience dog that watches another dog play tug with his handler outside the ring and gets so aroused that he can't control himself. Or this is the agility dog that gets so fired up watching the dog before him run that he cannot focus once he gets into the ring.

Set Up for Success

Make sure that you are calm when you are going to a competition: The night before, pack what you will need. Make sure that you know how to get to the competition site and what time the competition begins. If you do not plan beforehand, your dog can interpret your rushed body movements as stress and anxiety.

During the competition, keep your dog where he is comfortable: Some dogs feel better in their crates while others feel more comfortable in the car. In either case, make sure that your dog is in a spot where he can rest, a portable safe space. For example, if you crate your dog in a building, cover the crate so that other dogs do not pester your dog by looking in his crate. You don't want your dog to spend his time lunging at each dog that walks by. Remember that any behavior that your dog practices becomes a habit (see "Curing the Crate Crazies" below).

Protect your dog from all rude dog behavior: Practice common-sense behaviors like asking your dog to get behind you as you open the door to enter the building, body block your dog from competition handlers who are not watching their dogs, or, if you are in a queue, let the person behind you know that your dog needs space.

Bring treats with you as you make your way to the ring: Treat your dog for walking with you and ignoring all of the distractions present at a show site. Use a treat that your dog never gets unless he is doing this type of work.

Teach your dog a predictable pattern before going into the ring: Dogs (like humans) rely on patterns. Before you go into the ring, make sure that your dog has a predictable pattern to practice. For example, before I show Austyn in agility, I cue him to get into heel position and then I work on some positional changes, feeding him for each one. Next, I ask him to sit beside me and, with my left hand, I massage his head. This gesture keeps us both connected until it is our time to run. Have a predictable pattern coming out of the ring as well so that you can channel all that energy and excitement from the ring without having it spill over in unpredictable ways.

Train Your Dog for the Competition Environment

Here are some exercises to work on with your competition dog.

1. Teach your dog to Get Behind (see p. 72) you so that you can protect him from other dogs charging into his face. This is especially important when you are going through doors and cannot see what's on the other side. You can also use yourself as a human barrier if there is an especially rambunctious dog that you think your dog will have a problem with.

2. Teach your dog the Click to Calm methodology (see p. 127) so that your dog will watch you every time an overwhelming distraction (trigger) is present in the environment. For example, you can teach your dog that the dog running before you is a cue to focus on you, not the trigger—no matter how loud and speedy that agility dog is.

3. If your dog becomes over-excited and it is hard for him to calm down, work on Leslie McDevitt's "Off Switch" game *(Control Unleashed)*. Play with your dog for about 10–15 seconds, then ask your dog for a reliable behavior, like a sit or a down. As soon as he responds, start up the play again. You are building your dog's ability to respond to cues even when he's aroused.

If you have a dog that can be crate-reactive, you are not ready to compete. Having a crated dog that reacts every time another dog barks or a dog walks past his crate will fray your nerves, make your dog anxious and frustrated, and possibly ruin your run. Before you even think about competing, work on the following exercise.

CURING THE CRATE CRAZIES

Objective: Your dog learns that life is better when he remains calm in his crate, no matter what dogs and handlers are doing outside it.

A competition dog must be able to remain in his crate quietly during a dog show. If your dog is nervous in his crate, then he is wasting all of that energy on his anxiety rather than preserving it for a later performance. Every time your dog rushes to the front of his crate (and barks) as another dog walks by, he's rehearsing, so he'll likely continue to engage in this behavior. (Not to mention the stress it causes to those dogs who innocently walk past.)

Your dog should feel secure in his crate. Teach him that being there keeps him safe from other dogs, no matter what behavior occurs in and around it.

How to teach the behavior:

1. Put your dog in a crate and sit or stand by his crate. Make sure that there is an opening so that you can toss treats in.

2. Ask a friend to walk her dog by your dog's crate at a distance that your dog can handle. Make sure that she does not walk her dog directly up to the crate; there should be no eye contact!

3. Click and feed your dog generously for calmly accepting each of the following elements:

   a. Proximity: How close can the dog be? Begin to close the space so that, eventually, the other dog can walk right next to the crate.

   b. Direction: At first, your friend and her dog should walk past your dog's crate without any opportunity for eye contact between the two dogs. Then have them walk past the crate and allow eye contact. Click and feed your dog as he looks at the other dog. Gradually work up to having the other dog and handler walk all the way around your dog's crate, eventually doing laps. Finally have the other dog walk right up to the crate head-on.

   c. Speed: Start slowly and gradually increase the speed.

   d. Duration: Gradually increase the amount of time the other dog is ambling about the crate.

4. If at any time your dog explodes, you went too far, too fast. Back up to an earlier successful stage.

5. Once this behavior is solid, start going out "into the wild," and click and feed your dog for remaining calm during any activity around his crate.

Secrets to success:

- No matter where you are, click and feed your dog anytime he does not react when another dog walks by his crate.

- At a dog show, place your crate in a quiet section where you have full access to your dog. Bring a blanket to cover him up if necessary.

- Stay away from doors or other high-traffic areas.

- If you are training without a helper, take your dog's crate to your class and put him inside. Sit beside the crate, clicking and feeding him for not reacting to other dogs.

- Never leave your dog in his crate when you are training him to be calm in his crate. If you cannot manage him, put him in the car. (You do not want him to rehearse reactive behavior, especially in public areas.)

- Work on each piece of criteria separately. How close can another dog get to the crate? How long can your dog tolerate another dog being around his crate? How fast can another dog walk by?

Especially for dogs that will compete, part of the challenge is the competition setting itself. Dogs form relationships with beings or things that they spend lots of time with, even if that "thing" is the outside environment. I have counseled more than one client who wants her dog to have tremendous freedom outdoors (that is why she bought that fenced, five-acre yard with the doggy door), but she gets frustrated when she takes her dog to an outside agility trial and all he wants to do is run and chase squirrels or rabbits. "It's almost like I don't even exist!" she complains.

Just like people, dogs are influenced by environmental factors. If they run free 70% of the time, then good luck trying to get their attention, especially in the action-packed, exciting atmosphere of an agility trial. If you want your dog to focus on you in high-distraction environments like an agility trial, then you must work hard to expose him to those settings. You can start by cueing recalls from the dog park or on walks or by asking for a Sit–Stay on a crowded urban sidewalk. Many dog-sports competitors bring their young dogs to trials not to compete, but to get them used to the sights, sounds, and distractions of a trial and to practice basic behaviors on site. Use your imagination. "We are what we practice."

CASE STUDY: Curing an Agility Dog's Motion Sensitivity

Patricia found Sam on Petfinder: a lovely Australian shepherd maybe five years old whose owner had died. The owner's adult children confirmed that Sam was good with their dogs when they came to visit during the holidays. Sam settled in well. He seemed to understand "Heel" and was gentle when Patricia introduced him to a few of her neighbors. Everyone loved him! Patricia, who had competed in agility with her last dog, decided to take Sam to an agility class. He excelled. He loved to run with Patricia, and, before long, they had moved up to the competition class. Soon Patricia took Sam to his first trial.

She got there early so that she could acclimate Sam to the show environment. She crated him in her car as she went to check in. Before her run, she cued him over the practice jump, and he didn't miss a beat. The crowds of people and dogs didn't seem to affect him. Everything was fine until Patricia got Sam into the queue. Sam could not take his eyes off the speeding Border Collie that was running before him. He started to lunge forward and bark, nearly knocking Patricia off of her feet. When it was their turn to go, she couldn't control him. Although the dog before them had left, Sam's eyes were still searching the exit area for him. Patricia couldn't get Sam to sit, so she cued him to jump as she started to run, but Sam made a beeline for the exit gate looking for the border collie; a quick bystander caught him. Humiliated, Patricia drove Sam home and emailed me.

I advised Patricia to bring her clicker and treats to agility class so that she could start practicing the three stages of Click to Calm. I told her to click and feed Sam for watching other dogs run as close to the ring gate as he could handle without going over threshold. There was no need to click and feed Sam for the presence of all dogs; the running dogs were the trigger! Within a few weeks, Patricia was able to reinforce Sam for looking at a running dog and then looking at her. Once she had Sam's attention, she could cue him to do a few favorite tricks before it was their turn to run. The goal was for Patricia to develop a routine with Sam so that she could repeat it in the agility competition queue while they were waiting their turn.

When the routine was going well in the agility class, we had to transfer the skills over to the show ring. I asked Patricia to switch to a verbal marker instead of the click so that she could give Sam information ringside without distracting any of the other competitors. I accompanied Patricia and Sam to the next show. About an hour before Patricia went in, I asked her to bring Sam to the ring area. I wanted to be sure that Sam understood her marker word. I coached Patricia on the timing for marking the behavior and on feeding Sam for watching the speeding dogs. Although Patricia was nervous, Sam did great!

When it was their turn to compete, Patricia entered the queue and started cueing Sam to perform the pattern they had rehearsed, and he kept his focus on her. When they were next to go in, Sam's eye caught the dog running before him. He watched for a moment and then looked up at Patricia. Patricia was so happy she could have cried! Although they did not qualify during that agility run, Patricia was ecstatic that Sam never took his eyes off of her, even when he was momentarily distracted glancing at the dog that ran before him. Now that Patricia had Sam's attention at competitions, she was free to start honing their competition skills!

I hope I have been able to touch on some of the individual situations that may confront you as you maneuver the world with a reactive or otherwise challenging dog. But what if you have several dogs at home and one of them is sensitive or reactive? How do you navigate that world? We will explore that situation in the next section.

PART VI

Managing a Multi-Dog Household

In Part V, you learned how to help your dog move beyond simply tolerating the presence of his triggers to explore whether he might want to interact with them—his choice. But what if he lives with other dogs in your household? What precautions do you need to take and what training should you pursue to make your home a peaceable kingdom?

18
Group Foundation Behaviors

Being the caregiver for several dogs can be quite the challenge, especially if one dog does not get along well with the others. But you can take precautions to ensure that all of your dogs stay healthy and safe. Regardless of the number of dogs in the household, each dog must be respected as an individual. Every dog needs to be physically and mentally stimulated every day.

As the caregiver, you must be willing to make different decisions for different dogs. Some dogs are quite robust, while other dogs are more sensitive. Although it can take more time and planning, you'll need to handle the sensitive dogs differently than the rabble-rousers! This often involves separating dogs and walking (and playing) with them separately. In some families, this is hard to do. Family members sympathize with the pup that has to stay at home while the other dogs get to go to doggy daycare. Or they feel sorry for the dog that has to be kept in a crate while the family (and the other dogs) walk freely in the kitchen.

Dogs need to take their cues from their human caregivers, especially in situations where multiple dogs are involved. No matter how inconvenient it may be, the health and safety of all members of the household depend on these cues.

Your relationship with each of your dogs has to be more powerful and influential than the bonds that exist between the dogs. These relationships can be especially tough to establish when you are raising two puppies at the same time. As the caregiver, you should be able to cue the dogs individually and as a group. No matter how many dogs you have, follow the Home Management principles discussed in Part I (p. 15). Be sure to work with your dogs both individually and in a group.

The training plans included in this section will help you work on home management behaviors such as name recognition, stationing (important at feeding times), and traffic control in the home. For dogs that race to the door barking, refer to the Emergency Relocation Cue presented in the Emergency Behavior section (p. 88).

Team Training

Team Training is a wonderful exercise that teaches dogs that do not get along how to work together to achieve a desired end. An increasing number of animal studies suggest that a variety of animals, even animals of different species, can develop cooperation with each other to reach a common goal (reinforcement, for example). The best example I saw of this was years ago when I attended an Animal Behavior Management Alliance (ABMA) conference that offered four days of amazing lectures, field trips, and video presentations, all about the science of learning. The presenters have taught a myriad of species, and everything is documented in real time.

At the conference, a marine mammal trainer described work with a female walrus and an aggressive female sea otter. Each time the staff tried to combine these two animals in the same enclosure, the sea otter would attack the walrus. After much thought, the trainers decided that they needed to teach both animals a "spectator-friendly" behavior. The behavior that they chose was for the sea otter to climb up on the walrus and balance herself there while the walrus barrel-rolled.

First, they separated the animals for six months. Separately, they taught each animal the behavioral element that it would need to know to complete the final behavior. They taught the sea otter to balance herself on an ice floe and trained the walrus to barrel-roll in the water at a certain speed. Then the trainers started to re-integrate the two animals. When the trainers exposed the animals to each other and the animals looked at each other calmly, the trainers gave each a marker signal and a favorite treat. Slowly, the animals started working together.

The presenters had documented the pieces of the training process beautifully. Inexplicable "miracles" occurred! For example, when the sea otter tried to balance herself on top of the walrus, the walrus tried to slow down her barrel-roll speed accordingly. If the sea otter fell off, the walrus extended a fin to help her climb back up. The biggest miracle of all: as long as the training continued, both animals lived together peacefully in their enclosure! Amazing! What was really happening here?

My guess is that both animals discovered that, in order to receive reinforcement, each had a role that included the other. If one animal didn't perform her behavior, then neither animal received reinforcement. It took cooperation to obtain the largest amount of reinforcement.

After the conference and this revelation, I understood why when I was trying to teach Ben to hold his dumbbell with all of my other dogs present, they seemed to get along much better. They all waited expectantly to see if Ben would earn a click. Most of the time he did, and I reinforced all of the other dogs for watching this process. Every once in a while, I gave Ben the cue to take his dumbbell and he looked away. I did not reinforce that! All of the other dogs shifted restlessly and sighed. I had to laugh when I saw my American Eskimo, Corey, get up from his sit, walk around the room while shaking his head, and then come back to resume his original location. He looked like a little old man swearing to himself as he returned to his front-row seat!

TEAM TRAINING

Objective: When the dog you're working with performs a behavior successfully, all the dogs on the "team" get reinforced.

This exercise teaches all of your dogs to be on the same team. This strategy works beautifully for dogs that don't get along, but it is also useful for maintaining order and a modicum of calmness in a house with lots of dog bodies milling about, especially when they're excited. If the assigned dog completes the behavior, then all of the other dogs receive reinforcement. If the assigned dog does not complete the behavior, then none of the dogs receive reinforcement.

This exercise is also a godsend in a pinch when you need to keep all of your dogs safe. Consider these examples. Usually, you keep two of your dogs separated but now, because of a family emergency, you need to travel with both of them. Because of the Team Training work you've done, you can cue each dog individually and reliably. You can cue one to wait in a stay while you escort the other to his crate. In another example, you have a new roommate and, although your dog does not typically get along with other dogs, after some Team Training exercises, he acclimates to your roommate's dog much faster.

How to teach the behavior:

1. Start with two dogs spaced at a distance that is comfortable for both. To begin, they should be facing away from each other. For safety, you can have a friend hold one of the dogs on a leash or you can set up a barrier between them.

2. Start with Dog A. Say Dog A's name and cue Dog A to do a favorite behavior.

3. When Dog A does the behavior, click and feed Dog A. Turn and give Dog B reinforcement for watching quietly.

    a. If Dog A does not perform the behavior, neither dog gets reinforcement.

    b. Try again and use a behavior that is more reliable.

4. Now turn to Dog B. Ask Dog B to do a favorite behavior, and follow the same steps as you did with Dog A.

5. Keep these sessions short and successful.

6. If you are training more than two dogs, follow the same instructions. The only difference is that after the chosen dog does the behavior, you feed all of the dogs.

Secrets to success:

• Be sure that the dogs are stationed at a safe distance so that they can concentrate on the task.

• Ask the dogs to demonstrate a favorite, reliable behavior. The key here is to cue a behavior that they are familiar with and comfortable doing. It might be a different behavior for each dog.

• If you are using a baby gate as a barrier, decide how big the holes should be. You don't want dogs staring at each other through the holes.

• As the dogs begin to understand this concept, start cueing more challenging behaviors like asking one of the dogs to stay while the other heels around him.

• If you are Team Training a group of dogs, call on the dogs in the same order each time until all of the dogs seem comfortable. Then you can change the order.

Dogs That Do Not Get Along

If you have dogs in your household that do not get along, it is even more important for you to be able to communicate with each individually as well as in a group. Set up training situations where some dogs move while others do not. For example, you may send one dog to his crate while the other dogs play with their toys.

Make a list of all of the activities that the dogs love to do together and, under your thoughtful supervision, allow them to continue. The more they can enjoy each other's company and practice calm behavior, the less reactive they will be. These activities might include going for walks, going for car rides, or sleeping in bed together.

If there have been aggressive episodes between certain dogs, make a list of those as well. Evaluate each situation and determine the cause if you can. See if you can change the logistics of the situation to discourage the aggressive behavior from happening. For example, it could be that your dogs get along fine until they know that they are going outside to play with their tennis balls. In excited anticipation, they all try to squeeze through the door at the same time and a spat erupts. Instead, teach your dogs to wait at the door until you release them one-by-one into the yard.

Observe your dogs and interrupt any interactions that appear threatening. Don't wait until a fight breaks out before stepping in. If a dog in your household shows threatening behavior to another dog, separate both immediately. You can either put the aggressor in a crate or bring him to a separate room. Before combining the two dogs again, be sure that you know what caused the original behavior. What was the context? Does it only happen in a certain situation? Analyze the circumstances so that these dogs don't repeat this behavior. Having dogs that pose a threat to each other is an extremely dangerous situation in a household, especially if it involves a small dog with a large dog and/or if there are small children in the room.

If there is a real possibility that there could be a dog fight, you may need to think about rehoming a particular dog. If you are unsure, have items like deterrent spray within reach. (You must be able to stop a fight immediately.) Consider that it can take at least 3 to 7 days for a dog's brain to return to baseline after a traumatic incident. This is important information to know before re-combining both dogs.

Stopping Dog Fights

If a fight breaks out, separate the dogs as safely and quickly as possible. It is usually best to grab dogs that are fighting by the hind legs or tails and attempt to pull them apart. You might also try throwing cold water on the dogs or, if you are outside, spraying them with a hose. Loud noises like an air horn can also interrupt a fight.

As tempting as it is, do not reach in with your bare hands to tear the dogs apart. Don't grab their collars and stay away from their heads and necks. If you reach in to grab a collar, it is not uncommon for a dog, in his frenzy, to whip his head around and sink his teeth into your hand, by accident or not. You can be injured as well as worsen the damage that the two dogs may suffer.

Once the dogs are separated, put them into their respective safe spaces. Make sure both dogs are calm before you slowly re-expose them to each other. If this is not possible, seek the help of a qualified veterinary behaviorist.

19

Foundation Behaviors for Multiple Dogs

As descendants of wolves, dogs are pack animals, used to living in social groups. Just as with humans, brawls can erupt over space (crowding), resources (food, toys), or the general emotional tenor (excitement, arousal). Some of the most common multi-dog problems include: all dogs coming at once and jamming themselves into a tight space (especially through doorways and on stairways), one dog getting overstimulated by the excitement of another, and major mishaps around food.

Teaching your dogs to perform the following behaviors reliably will almost guarantee that your dogs can live together peacefully and that the arousal of one dog will be less likely to trigger the others. Work these exercises with dogs individually or with the dogs as a group.

NAME RECOGNITION IN A CROWD

Objective: On cue, each dog in your household responds to his name only and to none of the others.

If you have multiple dogs, you need to be able to call one out of the group without the others responding. This exercise helps in mundane situations if you need to call dogs, one-by-one, out into the play yard as well as in more charged situations. Think about what you would do if you needed to keep your reactive dog in a stay as the others move forward over a boundary. Or if you were handing out new toys to dogs that have had possession issues in the past. It would ease tensions all the way around if each dog responded individually to take his toy and go into his safe space.

How to teach the behavior:

1. Gather all of your dogs together in a larger general area like the living room or kitchen. If you have an aggressive or reactive dog, keep him separate. Behind a baby gate works well. That way, you can see him, and he is still included.

2. Say one of the dogs' names. In the beginning (the next three months or so), use the same order. As you continue to work this exercise, change up the order.

3. When that particular dog orients to you, give him a treat.

4. Ignore the others!

5. Go off and do something else for about 5 to 10 minutes.

6. Return and repeat the steps above.

7. Continue until each dog has received a treat for orienting to you when you say his name.

Secrets to success:

- As difficult as it is, ignore the dogs that you did not signal. Remember: each dog will get his turn.

- When you feed the dog that you signaled, do so close to your body.

- For this exercise, refrain from using the clicker, which could get the other dogs more excited. Try to play this game as nonchalantly as possible.

- If the dogs get overexcited, it is better to use a lower-value food item.

SIMULTANEOUS STAYS

Objective: On a single cue, all of your dogs will stay simultaneously.

It is both a convenience and a matter of safety to be able to cue all of your dogs to stay at the same time. Imagine a situation where you are driving on the highway and see smoke billowing from the hood of your car. Concerned that your car might catch fire, you pull over into a rest area and get your dogs out of the car. You can cue them to sit and stay while you get all of their leashes on. Simultaneous stays can serve you equally well at home. Say you drop a glass in the kitchen, sending splinters everywhere, and the dogs come running. In a loud voice, you can cue all of them to stay while you clean up the shards.

How to teach the behavior:

1. Gather all of your dogs in the same room.

2. Click and feed them as they remain in one spot. In the beginning, it doesn't matter which body position they are in. You're not cueing the stay; you are simply catching the behavior happening, as if you were clicking whatever position they "froze" in. Plan for a set period of time. (Use a timer for accuracy.)

3. If one or two dogs get up, ignore them, clicking and feeding those that have remained in position. Be ready to reinforce the ones that keep roaming around when they return to position. Soon all dogs will be ready and watching.

4. After about 15–20 seconds, release all of the dogs with a single cue.

5. After you have had success with this game, you can assign a different body position to each of your dogs if you like and follow the instructions above to cue the group as a whole to stay. Be sure that each dog knows the position you've chosen for him.

There are both convenience and emergency situations when you need to be able to cue your entire pack to stay. Train for those situations by clicking and treating the behavior you want; the dogs that aren't staying will catch on quickly.

6. If your dogs already know how to stay individually, you can give them that cue as well.

Secrets to success:

- Initially, it works best to use the down position.

- Use the appropriate value of treat that will give you the best results.

- Record data! How long can the dogs stay before one gets bored or distracted or stressed? You need to know this value in order to extend the duration of the stay.

FEEDING TIME

Objective: At mealtime, each dog goes to his assigned mat and waits quietly until you release him to go to his safe space to eat his meal.

Feeding time can be a nightmare, especially if you have an unpredictable dog and you feed all of your dogs at the same time. You can avoid a feeding frenzy by teaching all of your dogs (even the food-aggressive one) to stay on their mats while you make their meals and then to go to their safe spaces to eat. With this routine you won't have to just hope that everything will remain harmonious and serene after you distribute the food bowls. You'll have an actual solution: your dogs will learn that you will assemble them, make their meals, and give the meals to the dogs one-by-one as they wait calmly.

First you need to teach each dog (separately) to station on a mat (see p. 52) and to go to his safe space (see p. 18). Then teach each dog to go to his mat while you are preparing the meals. Once the bowls are ready, you release each dog to go to his safe space to eat.

How to teach the behavior:

1. Assign a mat to each dog. The mat can be anything: a bathmat, towel, or blanket. Make sure that there is ample space between the mats.

2. Cue one of your dogs to go to the mat, saying his name and ignoring the others.

3. Click and feed that dog for standing or lying down on the mat. Feed all of the other dogs for watching quietly.

4. Cue the next dog following the instructions above. At first, all of the dogs do not have to stay on their mats, but over time you will shape their behavior by only reinforcing them for staying on their mats. Teaching the mat behavior separately will make this step much easier.

5. Once your dogs are all in place, you can either release them all together to their designated areas if it is safe to do so, or you can cue each of them individually to go to his safe space.

Secrets to success:

- If the dogs get excited, it is your cue to be calm. Never move as fast as they want you to.

- Practice the mat work in an area that is separate from where you feed the dogs.

- The minute you start making the meals, the distraction level goes through the roof! Recognize that fact and adjust your behavioral expectations accordingly.

- If you have a food-aggressive dog, separate him at a distance where he will feel comfortable.

DOORWAY MANNERS

Objective: At doorways, each of your dogs knows to wait until you call his name before he goes across the threshold.

The most sensitive places for dogs in the home are the boundaries. Thresholds, the boundaries between rooms, can be zones of contention, in part because they are narrow. Caregivers of multiple dogs need to have control over these zones. Many bites, of both dogs and humans, happen in doorways! What is the typical scenario at your house when you put the dogs out in your fenced-in yard to play a much-anticipated game with tennis balls? Do all of your excited dogs try to squeeze through the door at the same time? Maybe because of heightened arousal, your dog-sensitive dog may even go after one of the others. If you don't want that to happen again, this is the exercise for you and your pack.

How to teach the behavior:

1. Assemble all of your dogs in the doorway.

2. Call one dog by name. If others step forward, quietly cue those dogs to go back to their original positions.

3. Click and feed the dog you called for moving through the doorway and release him to another activity.

4. Reinforce all of the other dogs for remaining in position. Because it is harder for your remaining dogs to wait in position (especially if the other dog is now playing in the yard), use higher-value treats to reinforce the dogs

Doorways are doggie traffic hazards just as stairs are. The same rules apply to an orderly passage through a doorway: one dog at a time.

for holding position than for rewarding the dog that you called through the doorway.

5. Cue the next dog by name.

6. Proceed as above.

7. Continue until all of the dogs are released outside.

Secrets to success:

- Cue the most excitable dog to come through first. That will help the others be successful.

- Close the door in between each of the trials.

- You can also set up the game so that the click causes the door to open instead of using a treat. After all, for most of your dogs, being released outside is probably a higher-value reinforcer than a treat.

STAIR MANNERS

Objective: When going up or down stairs, your pack knows that you will call each dog individually from the top or bottom of the stairwell and will not tolerate an en masse rush of dogs.

Dogs should not run down the stairs all at one time. Not only is it hazardous for a dog-sensitive dog, but it is dangerous, especially if the dogs are different sizes. Dogs can be injured physically or get into spats on stairs as they jostle for position. For example, from your second-floor apartment, imagine that you are taking all of your dogs for a ride in the car. The minute they see the leashes coming out, the dogs start bouncing around. Left to their own devices, they'd career down the stairs all together, but you can train self-control for a safer, more orderly descent. One by one, you can call each dog down and put him into his crate in the car. Teaching each dog to wait his turn to be called upstairs or downstairs is safer for all and makes for calmer comings and goings.

As daunting as it may seem, you can train your pack to go up and down stairs individually. Just stick to the rules, working one dog at a time (left). If the dogs left at the top of the stairs "creep," send them back to the top and make them wait their turn (right).

How to teach the behavior:

1. Gather all of your dogs at the top of the stairs and ask them to stay.

2. Walk down about three steps. Make sure that you can stand safely on the stairs without falling backward!

3. Call the name of one dog.

   a. If all of them rush down together, simply put them back, and call the one dog down the first couple of steps.

   b. Click and feed that dog.

   c. Go back up and feed the rest of the dogs who are waiting for their turn.

   d. Go down another couple of steps.

   e. Proceed as above until the first dog is all the way down the stairs.

4. Click and feed that dog for the completed behavior. Release him to go and play.

5. Go back upstairs and reinforce the rest of the dogs for waiting their turn.

6. Ask the remaining dogs to stay. Walk down about three steps as before.

7. Cue the next dog. Proceed as before until he's down the stairs and out the door.

8. Continue until all of the dogs are downstairs.

9. Practice the same training routine going back upstairs.

Secrets to success:

- To keep everyone safe, start this behavior on a stoop with just a few steps, on the porch stairs leading to your yard, for example.

- If the dogs break position, calmly cue them to return to their original spot.

- If the click of the clicker gets the dogs too excited, use a verbal marker.

- Cue the most excitable dog (more than likely the youngster) to come down first. That will help the others be successful.

A Final Word

Canine aggression and reactivity are difficult issues to live with. So are over-the-top exuberance and lack of socialization. These behavior traits may be fleeting, depending on the circumstances, or they may plague a dog for the rest of his life.

Your goal is to teach your dog all that he needs to know to make better decisions for himself and the human family he lives with. Although your challenging dog may never be perfect, most dogs can live a happy life as long as you—the caregiver—manage your dog well and teach him the behaviors that will make your lives together safer and easier.

As with my first book, *The New Click to Calm* is a work in progress. My hope is that as people start to use the Click to Calm protocol with their dogs, they discover that it works really well in entirely new sets of circumstances, with their bouncy Jack Russell terrier puppy or their motion-obsessed Border collie, for example. It's sometimes hard to appreciate how difficult it is for dogs to adjust to human society. By establishing a partnership based on mutual respect, I hope you gain insight into the challenges your dog might face in adapting to our lives. By communicating clearly and teaching your dog a set of basic and emergency behaviors, you build a framework for tackling the harder issues.

Only you know your dog! The Click to Calm protocol allows you to treat your dog's reactivity, aggression, shyness, or other unwanted behaviors as you would any other behavior—without the emotional entanglements that can inhibit your dog's progress. Over time, that strategy reduces your stress so that you can think more clearly, show more patience, and, ultimately, be a better teacher for your dog.

As Karen Pryor once told me, "Remember, it's only behavior!" I hope that through these pages I have helped you see that you have the power to change that behavior.

Resources

Learning Theory

Don't Shoot the Dog by Karen Pryor

Reaching the Animal Mind by Karen Pryor

Handbook of Applied Dog Training and Behavior, Volumes One–Three, by Steven Lindsay

Animal Training: Successful Animal Management Through Positive Reinforcement by Ken Ramirez

First Course in Applied Behavior Analysis by Paul Chance

General Positive Learning

Control Unleashed, Creating a Focused and Confident Dog by Leslie McDevitt

Dealing with Fear and Reactivity

TACT: A Training Program for Dogs That Are Fearful or Reactive Toward People DVD by Julie Robitaille and Emma Parsons

Recommended Websites

www.behaviorworks.org

Dr. Susan Friedman, a psychology professor at Utah State University, has pioneered the application of Applied Behavior Analysis (ABA) to captive and companion animals. She teaches the professional course: Living and Learning with Animals: the Fundamental Principles and Procedures of Teaching and Learning.

www.kenramireztraining.com

Ken Ramirez, the Executive Vice President and Chief Training Officer of Karen Pryor Clicker Training, is an internationally known trainer, who focuses, he says, "on training people so that people can focus on training animals."

www.learningaboutdogs.com

Kay Laurence, a professional trainer for more than 35 years, develops innovative and creative training techniques that blend passion, joy, and enthusiasm in fostering connection between dogs and people.

www.theclickercenter.com

Alexandra Kurland is an expert in training loops.

www.clickertraining.com

Training info, clickers, and more!

www.clickerexpo.com

Premier clicker training conferences

www.karenpryoracademy.com

Animal training courses designed for animal enthusiasts at every experience level

www.iaabc.org

International Association of Animal Behavior Consultants

www.theabma.org

The Animal Behavior Management Alliance

www.avsab.org

The American Veterinary Society of Animal Behavior

www.kongcompany.com

Kongs and other toys for dogs and cats

www.chewy.com

Pet foods, products, and supplies

www.nina-ottosson.com

Puzzle games

Acknowledgements

I want to thank my editor, Nini Bloch. Without her tireless effort, this book would never have been completed! To Aaron Clayton and Julie Gordon, thank you for believing that the principles of the Click to Calm method are valuable and its training methods should be shared.

I owe a great debt to the many people who helped me explore, refine, and expand the techniques of Click to Calm, as well as to people who made their own independent contributions to this field and often shared their time so that I could learn from them. These generous trainers include Ken Ramirez, who can both bridge science and technique like no one else and separate the underlying science at work in various procedures, and Dr. Susan Friedman, whose teachings on emotions and behavioral science are brilliant. I'm grateful to Dr. Jesús Rosales-Ruiz for the clarity in his statements, including "It's all operant," and for his own substantive work on dog aggression.

I thank all of my students throughout the years who have trusted me to counsel them and their dogs. The wealth of information and experience that you have provided gives me so much more to share with others.

Thank you to my golden retriever Lizzie-Taylor: Although your life ended before this book was published, I want you to know that you were my rock. You taught me what it was like to have a dog that could compete at the highest level of agility and still play happily with other dogs and people. You didn't flinch when 30 children surrounded you after an obedience demonstration at a friend's middle school, and you were a wonderful demo dog when we were working with reactive dog clients. Whether you were lying quietly under my desk or sitting beside me on the couch, your strength inspired me every day. Rest peacefully, my baby girl.

Thank you to Kayden-Blue whose life ended shortly after Lizzie's. Kayden, you were the puppy that was abandoned on the side of the road. Greg and I adopted you at the tender age of eight weeks. Along with the trauma came food and possession aggression and a natural dislike of other dogs. You, like Ben, inspired me to step out of my comfort zone to explore new behavioral issues. What do I miss about you most? Your head cuddled underneath my chin, on the recliner, while we watched a movie together. I will miss your presence forever, Puppy-K.

Thank you to my coaches—Christie McNamara, Terri Arnold, Kay Laurence, Beth Szczygiel, and, of course, Karen Pryor: I will always carry your lessons with me.

Thank you to my husband, Gregory Parsons, who is my constant support. I don't know what I would do without you. I can't forget Mary Ann Callahan, who continually lifts my spirits by reminding me about the good my teaching is doing in the world, even if it doesn't seem visible to me. How blessed I am that you are my friend.

To my mother, Irene Spinelli, who I am sure watches me from above, and to the most precious of all:

The Lord God who made us all.

Emma Parsons

March 2021

About the Author

Emma Parsons, author of the revolutionary books *Click to Calm: Healing the Aggressive Dog* and *Teaching the Reactive Dog Class: Leading the Journey from Reactivity to Reliability*, has been training dogs for more than 20 years. She specializes in managing and rehabilitating reactive and aggressive dogs, teaching and giving seminars on this subject around the world. Emma owns her own dog training business (Emma Parsons, LLC), is a Canine Behavior Consultant for Surefire Dogs in Westborough, Massachusetts, and is a faculty member of Karen Pryor Academy for Animal Training & Behavior and the Karen Pryor Clicker Training ClickerExpo conferences. She is a member of the Association of Pet Dog Trainers (APDT) and a Certified Dog Behavior Consultant of the International Association of Animal Behavior Consultants (IAABC). Emma holds a BA degree from the University of Massachusetts, Lowell, and shares her life with her husband, Greg, and their three clicker trained dogs—a golden, Austyn-Roque, a Papillon, Wylie-Rae, and a border collie, Joshua-Hunt.

Printed in Great Britain
by Amazon

32472507R00132